Merriam-Webster's
STUDENT ATLAS

Merriam-Webster, Incorporated
Springfield, Massachusetts

GLOBE TURNER

ISBN: 978-0-87779-729-6
1st printing Quad Graphics Sussex, WI July 2021

Material on the inside covers and on pages 113–132
© Merriam-Webster, Incorporated.

Merriam-Webster's Geographical Dictionary, 2007 was used as a source of information throughout.

The Merriam-Webster logo and *Merriam-Webster's Collegiate* are registered trademarks of Merriam-Webster, Incorporated.

Acknowledgments:
"How to use this Atlas" written by Elspeth Leacock, updated by Ian Turner.

Photograph on page 13 (Rosetta)
Copyright © 2021 ESA/Rosetta/NAVCAM

Photograph on page 13 (Hayabusa)
Copyright © 2021 JAXA

Base map, diagram, and photograph on pages 18-19 Copyright © 2021 Shutterstock.

Diagrams on pages 20-21 Copyright © 2021 Shutterstock.

Photographs on pages 24–25 Copyright © 2021 Corel Corp. Except "Arid" World Landmarks and Travel/Getty Images and "Tropical Wet" World Commerce and Travel/Getty Images.

Photographs on pages 26–27 Copyright © 2021 Corel Corp. Except "Midlatitude grassland" US Landmarks and Travel/Getty Images; "Coniferous forest," "Subtropical broadleaf evergreen forest" US Landmarks and Travel 2/Getty Images and "Mixed forest," "Tropical rain forest" Nature, Wildlife and the Environment/Getty Images.

Photographs on page 29 Copyright © 2021 The National Snow and Ice Data Center, Glacier Photograph Collection.

Photograph on page 42 Library of Congress, LC-W861-35.

Photographs on page 46 Copyright © 2021 Shutterstock.

Photographs on pages 58–59 Copyright © 2021 Shutterstock.

Photographs on pages 60–61 US Landmarks and Travel/Getty Images. Except "Tropical Wet" US Landmarks and Travel 2/Getty Images and "Mediterranean," "Tundra" Copyright © 2021 Corel Corp.

Photographs on pages 62–63 Copyright © 2021 Corel Corp. Except "Coniferous forest" Copyright © 2021 FreeStockPhotos; "Midlatitude scrubland" US Landmarks and Travel/Getty Images and "Mixed forest" Nature, Wildlife and the Environment/Getty Images.

Photograph on pages 68–69 © Royalty-Free/Corbis.

Photographs on page 80 Copyright © 2021 Shutterstock.

Photographs on page 86 Copyright © 2021 Shutterstock.

Photographs on page 92 Copyright © 2021 Shutterstock.

Photographs on page 98 Copyright © 2021 Shutterstock.

Photographs on page 104 Copyright © 2021 Shutterstock.

Sources for statistical information in International Data section:
CIA World Factbook, (www.cia.gov/library), updated May 20, 2021, and Flags of the World (www.fotw.net)

WORLD FACTS AND FIGURES . Inside front and back covers

AN ATLAS is a collection of

maps that can be used to find information about your world. The very latest data has been collected to make these maps. Hundreds of satellite images were used to map the dramatic shrinking of Earth's forests. The latest census data from each and every country was used to build a picture of Earth's current population. The most recent scientific research was used to create thematic maps of continental drift, the ocean floor, the environment, and our natural resources. Look closely and you will see that the information for the maps comes from many different sources such as NASA, the U.S. Department of the Interior, or the World Bank. You can use these maps to explore your world, discover connections between places, and see relationships between places and peoples.

But this atlas is more than just a wealth of information. It is fun to look at too. You will find that these maps and photographs can evoke images of far away places. They invite you to pause and to dream. With a map you can journey the world without ever getting wet, cold, tired, or hungry. You can imagine great adventures and not leave the comfort of your favorite chair!

To get the most out of this atlas you need to know how to read maps. Just as you learned to read words like the ones on this page, you can learn how to read the language of maps. The map skills you need to know are:
1. locating places
2. measuring distance
3. finding direction
4. reading map symbols.

Locating Places
To find places in this atlas, you can begin with the index. To find Dallas follow these steps.

1. Look up Dallas in the index at the end of this book.
2. The index tells you that Dallas is a city in Texas and that it can be found on page 50. You will also learn that Dallas is located at 32°47'N (32 degrees 47 minutes north) and 96°48'W (96 degrees 48 minutes west.)
3. Go to page 50 and find the line of latitude nearest to the number 32°N and the line of longitude nearest to the number 96°W. You will find Dallas close to where those two lines meet. You can learn more about latitude and longitude on pages 8–9.

Measuring Distance
To measure distance most maps have a distance scale. You can learn more about measuring distance on page 7.

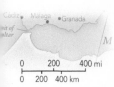

Finding Direction
To find directions use the map's compass rose. You can also use lines of latitude and longitude to find direction. Every line of longitude points north and south. Every line of latitude points east and west. You can learn more about latitude and longitude on pages 8–9.

Reading Map Symbols
Every map symbol shows the location of something. It could be something as large as a continent or as small as a birdhouse. A dot shows the location of a city. A blue line shows the course of a river. But map symbols are not the same on all maps. One map might show a city with a square. Map legends or keys help explain the symbols used on a map. You can find out more about legends and the map symbols used in this atlas on page 6.

Special Features of this Atlas

This atlas has been designed and organized to be easy for you to use. Here is a "road map" to your atlas.

The Blue Tab Bar
Somewhere along the top blue tab bar of each spread you will see a darker blue tab. It tells you

the subject of the map or maps you are looking at. The light blue tabs tell you the subjects of the surrounding map spreads. If, for example, you are looking at the World Climate map and would like to compare it to the World Vegetation map, you can use the tabs to find that map quickly and easily.

Map Skills
Look at the blue tab bar above and you will see that you are in the map skills section. This section should be called "Read Me First" because it is here that you will find all sorts of helpful information about maps and how to read them. Even if you are a practiced map reader, read this section!

The World
In this section you will find a world political map, a world physical map, and 32 world thematic maps. The world political map shows the most up-to-date national boundaries. On the world physical map you can see huge deserts,

great mountain ranges, and even the sea ice that covers much of the Arctic. The thematic maps include the most up-to-date information on everything from world population growth rates and internet access to life expectancy, religion and literacy. If you want to see the ocean floor, or to find where in the world volcanoes form, this is the section to look in.

Continents

The continent units are designed to all have the same kinds of maps. This will enable you to compare and contrast one continent with another with ease and accuracy. There is a political map, a physical map, and a total of six thematic maps per continent.

Used individually each map can provide answers to many questions. But all together, each set of maps can be used to tell a story.

Imagine a journey crossing a continent. You can see the regions visited, the mountains climbed, or the deserts crossed. You can tell if many people are passed along the way or few. You can describe the activities of the people. Will you see miners or ranchers or farmers? And you can tell about the different climates experienced along the way. All of this information and more is on the maps for every continent but Antarctica.

Environmental Issues

This atlas begins to tackle some of the most important environmental issues facing the Earth in the 21st century. On page 29 you can see one of the effects of climate change by viewing time-lapsed photographs showing glacial retreat in Alaska and Iceland. Each continent series explores the effect that pollution alone factors in national death rates.

The United States

In the section on the United States you will find a political map with two pages of political facts, a physical map with two pages of physical facts, and seven thematic map spreads.

Canada and Mexico

Canada and Mexico both have their own spreads that include a political and physical map.

Geographic Features

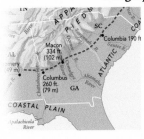

There are two special "Geographic Features" included in this atlas. To find out how the continents, Earth's greatest land features, have been drifting around the globe, turn to pages 22–23. To take an in-depth look at fall lines, divides, and faults turn to the United States Geographic Features spread on pages 58–59.

Charts and Graphs

This atlas is filled with charts, graphs, and diagrams. They are used to give more information about subjects shown on the maps. To make these charts and graphs, long lists of the most up-to-date data was gathered. Then all those numbers were organized into graphic displays that can be read simply and accurately.

Line graphs are used to show change in amounts over time.

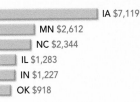

Bar graphs are used to compare amounts.

Pie charts show percentages of a total.

Glossary

There are many geographic terms found on maps such as *fjord, isthmus,* or *plateau.* You can find the meaning of these and other terms in the geographic glossary located on pages 129–132.

Did You Know?

Scattered throughout the atlas you will find trivia facts relating to the information shown on that page.

Legend

The following symbols are used here for general reference maps. Maps with special subjects (thematic maps) have their own unique legends.

General Reference Maps

- ⊛ National capital
- ★ Other capital
- • Other city
- International boundary (political map)
- International boundary in dispute/undefined (political map)
- State or provincial boundary
- International boundary (physical map)
- International boundary in dispute (physical map)

- Nonsubject area
- ▲ Mountain peak
- ▽ Lowest point
- � Perennial lake
- Intermittent lake
- Perennial river
- Falls

Physical Maps Legend

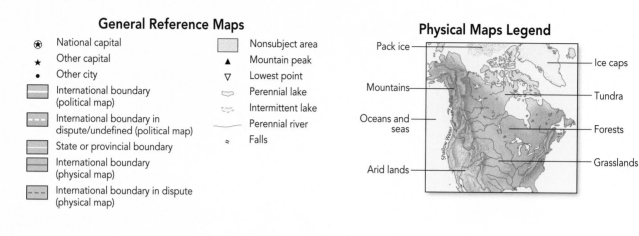

Pack ice — Mountains — Oceans and seas — Arid lands — Shallow Water — Ice caps — Tundra — Forests — Grasslands

Projections

A globe is the most accurate picture of the Earth. Only a globe can show distance, direction, and the true shape and area of land and sea. Mapmakers struggle with how to show the round world on a flat map.

Imagine the Earth as a large balloon.

Cut it apart, and flatten it to make a map.

Mercator Projection

Gerardus Mercator, a Dutch mapmaker, wanted a map projection that showed direction and shape accurately. The problems with distortions are more obvious on this projection. You can see that the land areas are very distorted the closer to the poles that you get. So, this projection ended up greatly distorting distance and size.

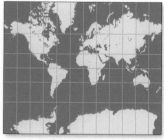

To show the round Earth on flat paper, mapmakers used different **projections**, or ways of showing a round shape on a flat surface.

With every projection the shapes of places are changed somewhat. This is called distortion. To find distortion, you can compare the latitude and longitude lines of a map to those same lines on a globe.

This diagram shows how a Mercator projection distorts the sizes of places. Compare Greenland on the map and the globe.

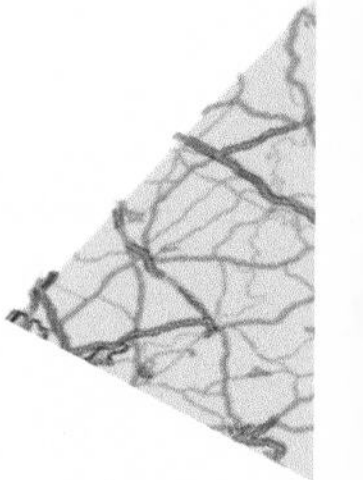

Projections – Making the Round World Flat

Robinson Projection

Arthur Robinson, an American mapmaker, wanted to develop a map projection that "looked" right. This projection uses many distortions but none are significant. You can see this by comparing one of the large scale World maps in this atlas to a globe.

Azimuthal Projection

This is a projection used to show Antarctica and the Arctic. Azimuthal maps show direction and distance accurately, if measured from the center of the map. But, other distances, shape and size are distorted.

Map Scale

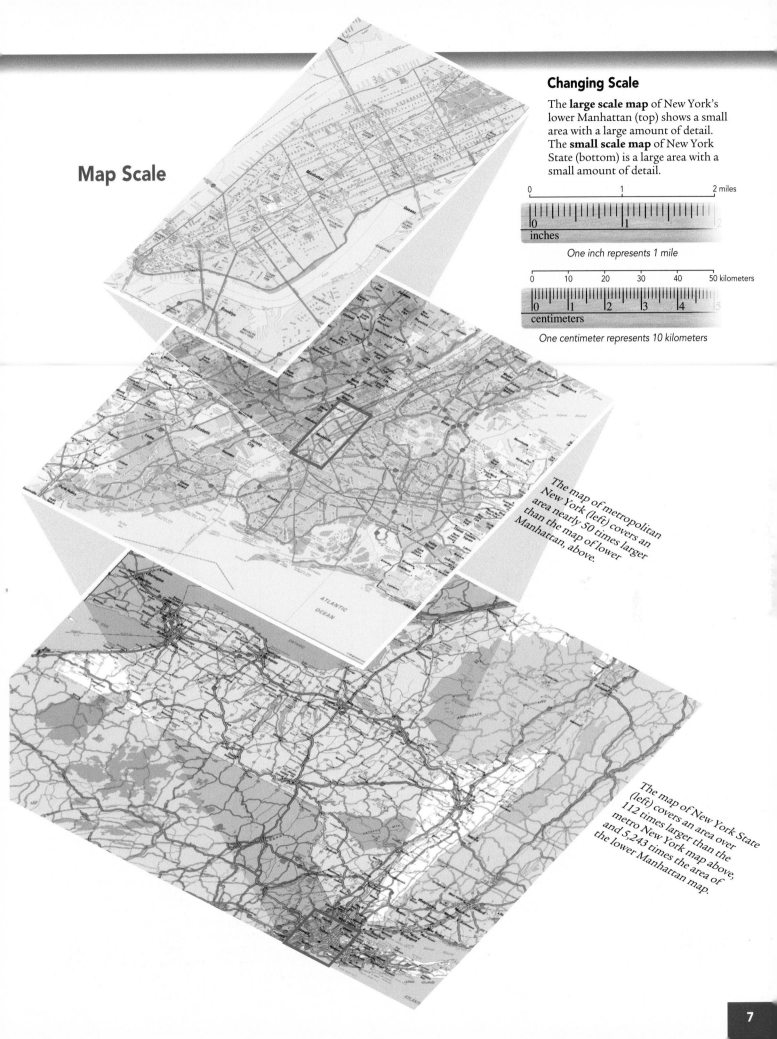

Changing Scale

The **large scale map** of New York's lower Manhattan (top) shows a small area with a large amount of detail. The **small scale map** of New York State (bottom) is a large area with a small amount of detail.

One inch represents 1 mile

One centimeter represents 10 kilometers

The map of metropolitan New York (left) covers an area nearly 50 times larger than the map of lower Manhattan, above.

The map of New York State (left) covers an area over 112 times larger than the metro New York map above, and 5,243 times the area of the lower Manhattan map.

Latitude and Longitude

Since ancient times, mapmakers, geographers, and navigators have worked to develop a system for accurately locating places on the Earth. On a sphere, such as the Earth, there are no corners or sides, no beginning or end. But since the Earth rotates on an axis, there are two fixed points: the North Pole and the South Pole. These points make a good starting place for a system of imaginary lines.

These imaginary lines form a grid over the Earth, allowing us to pinpoint the exact location of any spot on the Earth. This spherical grid is called the **graticule**. It is formed by lines called **latitude** and **longitude**.

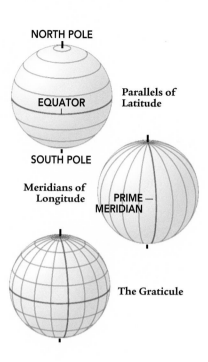

Parallels of Latitude

Meridians of Longitude — PRIME MERIDIAN

The Graticule

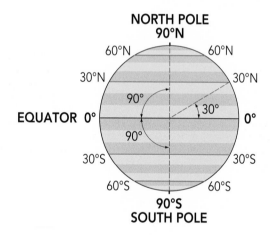

Latitude

Halfway between the poles the Equator circles the globe in an east-west direction. Latitude is measured in degrees north or south of the Equator, which is 0 degrees (°). Lines of latitude are called **parallels** because they circle the globe parallel to the Equator. Parallels are numbered from 0° at the Equator to 90°N at the North Pole and 90°S at the South Pole.

Longitude

Running from pole to pole, lines of longitude—called **meridians**—circle the globe in a north-south direction. As in any circle or sphere, there are 360 degrees (°) of longitude. The meridians are numbered from the Prime Meridian which is labeled 0°. Meridians east or west of the Prime Meridian are labeled E or W up to 180°. The International Date Line generally follows the 180° meridian, making a few jogs to avoid cutting through land areas.

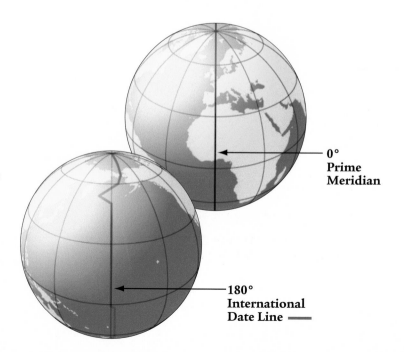

0° Prime Meridian

180° International Date Line ——

Parallels and Meridians—The Facts

Parallels
- are lines of latitude used to measure location north or south of the Equator
- are always the same distance apart (about 70 miles)
- differ in length
- The Equator, the longest parallel, is almost 25,000 miles long

Meridians
- are lines of longitude used to measure location east or west of the Prime Meridian
- meet at the poles
- are all the same length

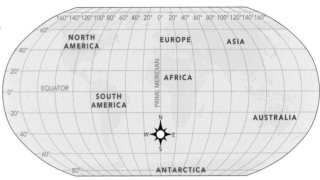

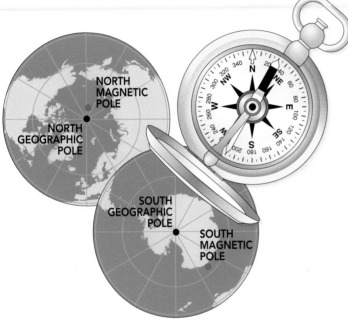

Which way north...

The geographic North and South Poles are fixed points located at each end of the Earth's axis. The Earth's magnetic fields cause the needle of a compass to point toward magnetic north, not geographic north. The north magnetic pole has been moving from northern Canada towards Siberian Russia since its discovery in 1831. The south magnetic pole has been drifting more slowly near the coast of Antarctica since its determination about a century later. Not only do the magnetic poles move, the Earth's magnetic field can strengthen, weaken, and change polarity.

Degrees, Minutes, Seconds

A degree (°) of latitude or longitude can be divided into 60 parts called minutes ('). Each minute can be divided into 60 seconds ("). The diagram at right is an example of a place located to the nearest second.

It is written as:
42° 21′ 30″ N   71° 03′ 37″ W

● This place is city center, Boston, Massachusetts.

The index at the back of this Atlas uses degrees and minutes of latitude and longitude to help you find places.

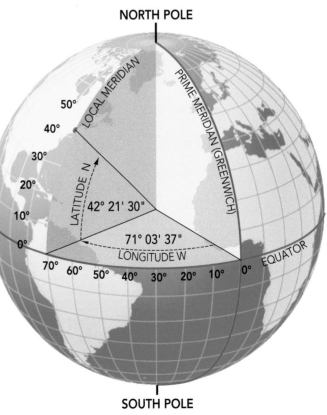

Different Kinds of Maps

Maps are special pictures of places on Earth.

All maps are alike in these important ways:
- All maps are a view from above.
- All maps show selected information using symbols.
- All maps are smaller than the real place on Earth that they show.

Because people want to show many different things on Earth, they create many different kinds of maps.

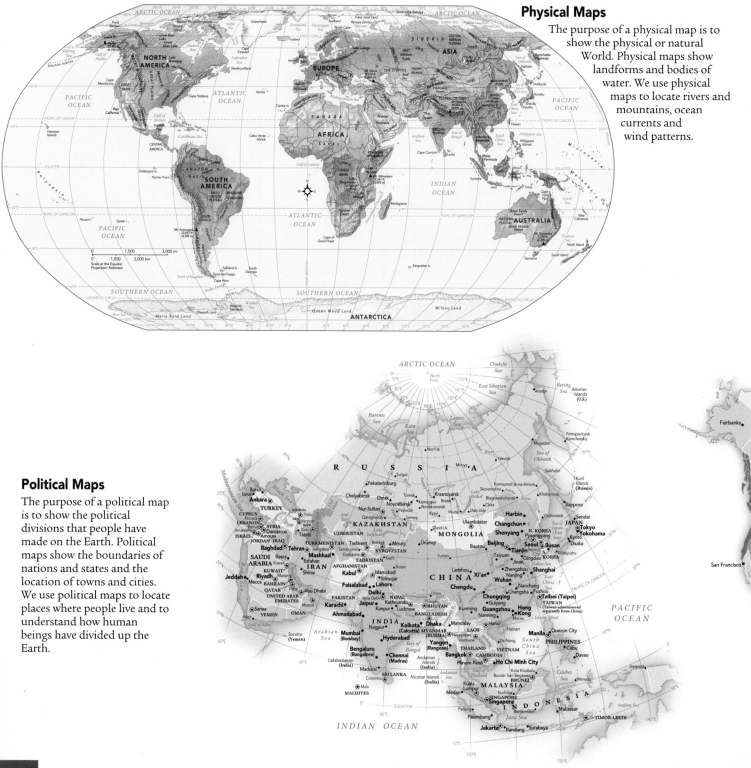

Physical Maps

The purpose of a physical map is to show the physical or natural World. Physical maps show landforms and bodies of water. We use physical maps to locate rivers and mountains, ocean currents and wind patterns.

Political Maps

The purpose of a political map is to show the political divisions that people have made on the Earth. Political maps show the boundaries of nations and states and the location of towns and cities. We use political maps to locate places where people live and to understand how human beings have divided up the Earth.

Thematic, or Special Purpose Maps

These maps show a specific subject (theme) or very limited number of subjects (such as vegetation, climate, or historical topics). They can be used to show distributions and relationships among map features.

This page contains examples of the many types of maps to be found throughout the *Student Atlas of the World*.

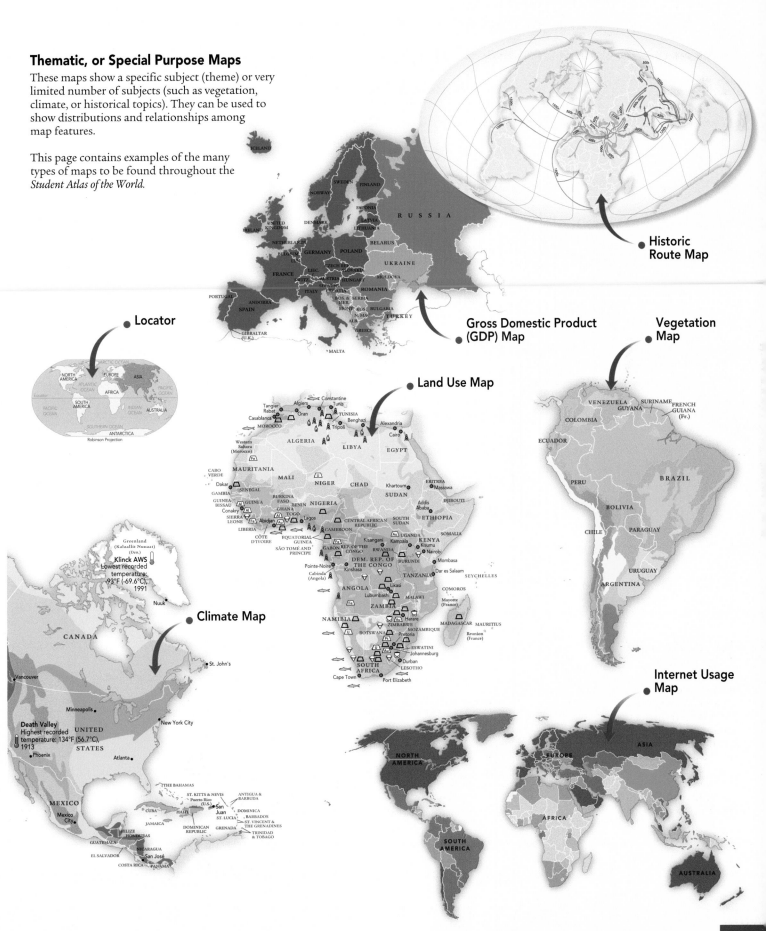

Historic Route Map

Locator

Gross Domestic Product (GDP) Map

Vegetation Map

Land Use Map

Climate Map

Internet Usage Map

Mercury

Venus

Earth

Mars

Jupiter

	Sun	Mercury	Venus	Earth
Time to orbit the Sun (approximate, in Earth years)	—	0.2 (88 days)	0.6 (225 days)	1
Average surface temperature	9,941°F (5,505°C)	333°F (167°C)	867°F (464°C)	59°F (15°C)
Diameter	865,000 mi (1,392,000 km)	3,023 mi (4,879 km)	7,521 mi (12,104 km)	7,926 mi (12,756 km)
Mean distance from Sun (in astronomical units)	—	0.390 AU	0.723 AU	1 AU

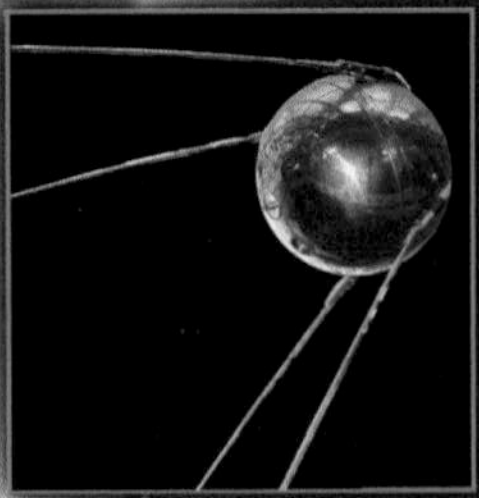

1957
First satellite: Sputnik (USSR)

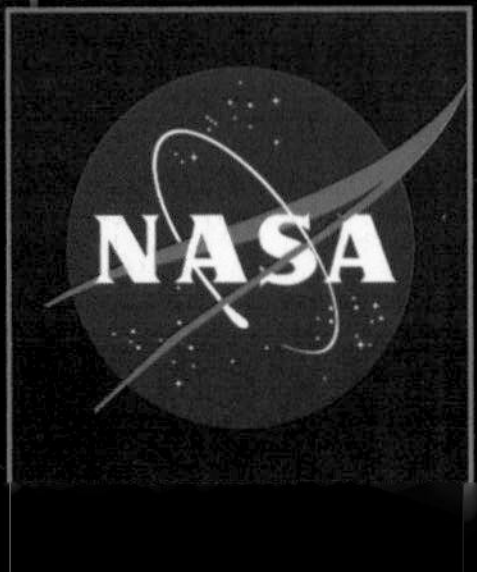

1961
First human in space: Yuri Gagarin (USSR)

1969
First humans on Moon: Apollo 11 (USA)

1977
Voyager 1&2 are launched (USA)

1958
NASA program established (USA)

1966
First probe on Moon: Luna 9 (USSR)

1970
First probe on Venus: Venera 7 (USSR)

1981
First reusable space shuttle (USA)

NASA

Uranus

Neptune

Saturn

Mars	Jupiter	Saturn	Uranus	Neptune	Pluto (dwarf plan
1.9	12	29.5	84	165	248
−81°F (−63°C)	−162°F (−108°C)	−218°F (−139°C)	−323°F (−197°C)	−330°F (−201°C)	−387°F (−233°C)
4,212 mi (6,779 km)	86,882 mi (139,823 km)	72,368 mi (116,465 km)	31,518 mi (50,723 km)	30,602 mi (49,249 km)	1,485 mi (2,390 km)
1.524 AU	5.203 AU	9.539 AU	19.18 AU	30.06 AU	39.48 AU

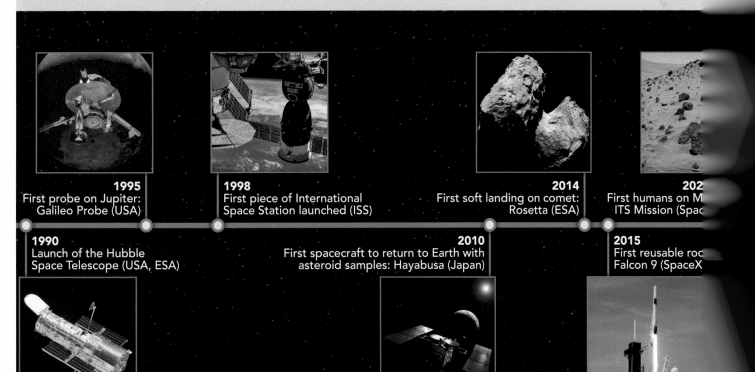

1995
First probe on Jupiter: Galileo Probe (USA)

1998
First piece of International Space Station launched (ISS)

2014
First soft landing on comet: Rosetta (ESA)

202
First humans on M ITS Mission (Spac

1990
Launch of the Hubble Space Telescope (USA, ESA)

2010
First spacecraft to return to Earth with asteroid samples: Hayabusa (Japan)

2015
First reusable roc Falcon 9 (SpaceX

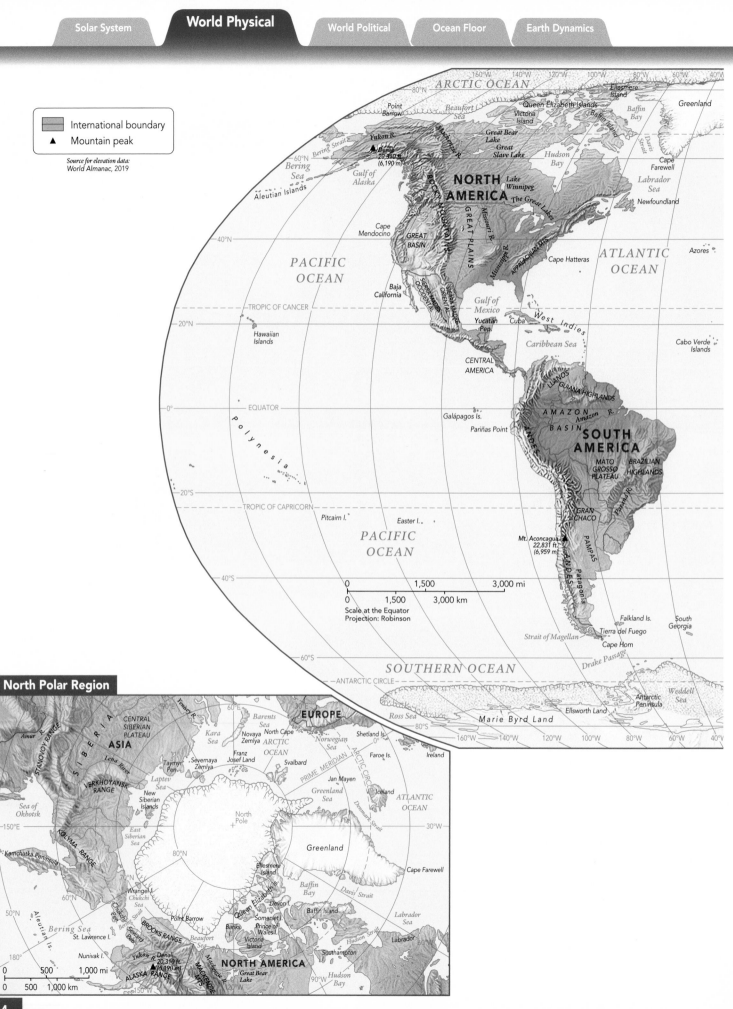

Legend:
- International boundary
- ▲ Mountain peak

Source for elevation data:
World Almanac, 2019

ARCTIC OCEAN

Point Barrow
Beaufort Sea
Queen Elizabeth Islands
Victoria Island
Baffin Island
Baffin Bay
Ellesmere Island
Greenland

Bering Strait
Yukon R.
Denali 20,310 ft. (6,190 m)
Mackenzie R.
Great Bear Lake
Great Slave Lake
Hudson Bay
Davis Strait
Cape Farewell

Bering Sea
Gulf of Alaska
NORTH AMERICA
Lake Winnipeg
The Great Lakes
Labrador Sea
Newfoundland

Aleutian Islands
ROCKY MOUNTAINS
GREAT PLAINS
Missouri R.
APPALACHIAN Mts.

Cape Mendocino
GREAT BASIN
Mississippi R.
Cape Hatteras
ATLANTIC OCEAN
Azores

PACIFIC OCEAN

Baja California
SIERRA MADRE OCCIDENTAL
SIERRA MADRE ORIENTAL
Gulf of Mexico
Cuba
West Indies

TROPIC OF CANCER

Hawaiian Islands
Yucatán Pen.
Caribbean Sea
Cabo Verde Islands

CENTRAL AMERICA
LLANOS
GUIANA HIGHLANDS

EQUATOR
Galápagos Is.
AMAZON BASIN
Amazon R.

P o l y n e s i a
Pariñas Point
ANDES
SOUTH AMERICA
MATO GROSSO PLATEAU
BRAZILIAN HIGHLANDS

GRAN CHACO
Paraná R.

TROPIC OF CAPRICORN
Pitcairn I.
Easter I.
PAMPAS

PACIFIC OCEAN
Mt. Aconcagua 22,831 ft. (6,959 m)
ANDES
Patagonia

0   1,500   3,000 mi
0   1,500   3,000 km
Scale at the Equator
Projection: Robinson

Falkland Is.
South Georgia
Strait of Magellan
Tierra del Fuego
Cape Horn
Drake Passage

SOUTHERN OCEAN
ANTARCTIC CIRCLE
Antarctic Peninsula
Weddell Sea

Ross Sea
Marie Byrd Land
Ellsworth Land

EUROPE
North Cape
Shetland Is.
Faroe Is.
Ireland
Jan Mayen
Iceland

North Polar Region

CENTRAL SIBERIAN PLATEAU
ASIA
Amur
STANOVOY RANGE
S I B E R I A
Lena River
Yenisey R.
Barents Sea
Novaya Zemlya
Kara Sea
ARCTIC OCEAN
Norwegian Sea
Franz Josef Land
Svalbard

VERKHOYANSK RANGE
Taymyr Pen.
Severnaya Zemlya
Laptev Sea
New Siberian Islands
Greenland Sea
Denmark Strait
ATLANTIC OCEAN

Sea of Okhotsk
KOLYMA RANGE
East Siberian Sea
North Pole
Greenland
Iceland

Kamchatka Peninsula
Wrangel I.
Chukchi Sea
80°N
Ellesmere Island
Cape Farewell

Aleutian Is.
Bering Sea
St. Lawrence I.
Chukchi Pen.
Bering Strait
Seward Pen.
Queen Elizabeth Is.
Devon I.
Baffin Bay
Davis Strait
Labrador Sea

Nunivak I.
BROOKS RANGE
Point Barrow
Banks
Somerset I.
Prince of Wales I.
Baffin Island

Yukon R.
Denali 20,310 ft. (6,190 m)
ALASKA RANGE
MACKENZIE MTS.
Victoria Island
Southampton
Hudson Strait
Labrador

NORTH AMERICA
Great Bear Lake
Hudson Bay

0   500   1,000 mi
0   500   1,000 km

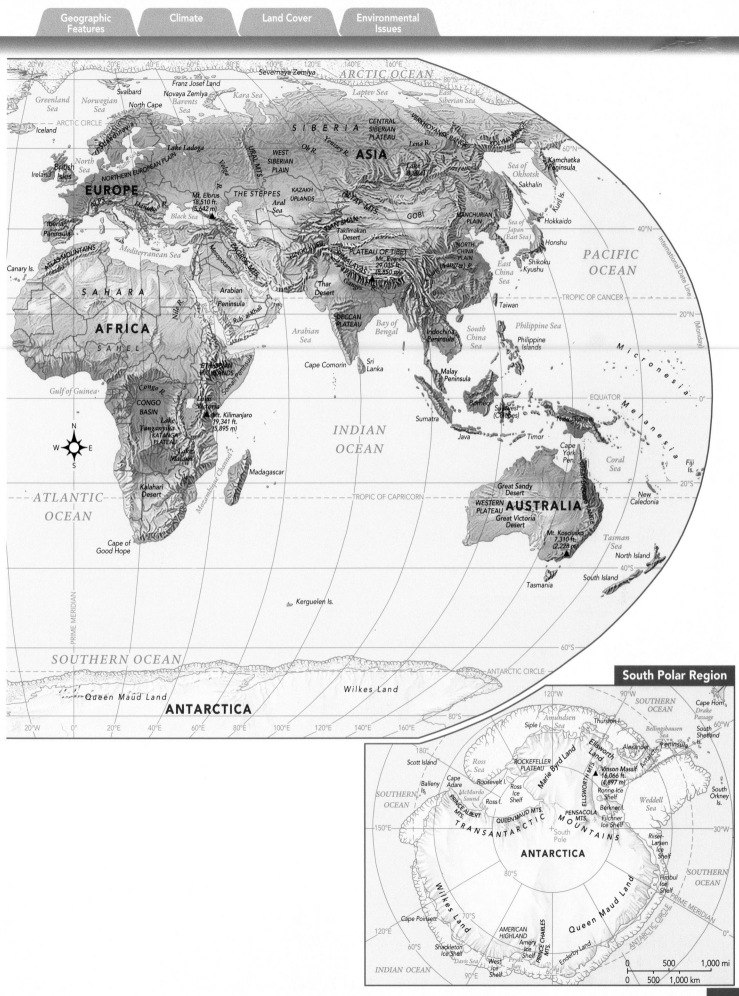

20°W 0° 20°E 40°E 60°E 80°E 100°E 120°E 140°E 160°E

ARCTIC OCEAN 80°N

Greenland Sea — *Svalbard* — *Franz Josef Land* — *Severnaya Zemlya* — *Laptev Sea* — *East Siberian Sea*

Norwegian Sea — *North Cape* — *Novaya Zemlya* — *Kara Sea* — *Barents Sea*

Iceland — ARCTIC CIRCLE

British Isles — *North Sea* — SIBERIA — CENTRAL SIBERIAN PLATEAU — VERKHOYANSK RANGE — KOLYMA RANGE — 60°N

Ireland — Lake Ladoga — *Ob R.* — *Yenisey R.* — ASIA — *Lena R.* — *Kamchatka Peninsula*

EUROPE — Volga R. — URAL MTS. — WEST SIBERIAN PLAIN — *Sea of Okhotsk* — *Sakhalin*

ALPS — Mt. Elbrus 18,510 ft. (5,642 m) — THE STEPPES — *Aral Sea* — KAZAKH UPLANDS — ALTAY MTS. — GOBI — MANCHURIAN PLAIN — *Sea of Japan (East Sea)* — *Hokkaido* — 40°N

Iberian Peninsula — Danube R. — *Black Sea* — *Caspian Sea* — TIAN SHAN — Taklimakan Desert — NORTH CHINA PLAIN — *Kuril Is.* — *Honshu* — PACIFIC OCEAN

ZAGROS MTS. — HINDU KUSH — PLATEAU OF TIBET — Mt. Everest 29,035 ft. (8,850 m) — HIMALAYAS — *Shikoku* — *Kyushu*

Canary Is. — ATLAS MOUNTAINS — *Mediterranean Sea* — Mesopotamia — *Persian Gulf* — *Yangtze (Yangtze) R.* — *East China Sea*

SAHARA — Arabian Peninsula — Thar Desert — Ganges — *Taiwan* — TROPIC OF CANCER

AFRICA — *Nile R.* — *Red Sea* — Rub' al Khali — DECCAN PLATEAU — *Bay of Bengal* — Indochina Peninsula — *South China Sea* — *Philippine Sea* — 20°N

SAHEL — Somali Peninsula — *Arabian Sea* — Cape Comorin — *Sri Lanka* — Philippine Islands

ETHIOPIAN HIGHLANDS — Malay Peninsula — *Micronesia*

Gulf of Guinea — *Congo R.* — Lake Victoria — Mt. Kilimanjaro 19,341 ft. (5,895 m) — INDIAN OCEAN — *Borneo* — *Sulawesi (Celebes)* — *New Guinea* — *Melanesia* — EQUATOR — 0°

CONGO BASIN — Lake Tanganyika — KATANGA PLATEAU — *Sumatra* — *Java* — *Timor* — *Coral Sea* — *Fiji Is.*

Lake Malawi — *Cape York Pen.* — *New Caledonia*

N W E S — *Madagascar* — *Mozambique Channel* — Great Sandy Desert — AUSTRALIA — 20°S

ATLANTIC OCEAN — Kalahari Desert — TROPIC OF CAPRICORN — WESTERN PLATEAU — Great Victoria Desert — GREAT DIVIDING RANGE — *Tasman Sea*

Mt. Kosciusko 7,310 ft. (2,228 m) — *North Island*

Cape of Good Hope — 40°S

Tasmania — *South Island*

Kerguelen Is.

PRIME MERIDIAN — 60°S

SOUTHERN OCEAN — ANTARCTIC CIRCLE

Queen Maud Land — *Wilkes Land* — 80°S

ANTARCTICA

20°W 0° 20°E 40°E 60°E 80°E 100°E 120°E 140°E 160°E

International Date Line — (Monday)

South Polar Region

120°W — 90°W — SOUTHERN OCEAN — *Cape Horn* — *Drake Passage* — 60°W

Amundsen Sea — *Thurston I.* — *Bellingshausen Sea* — *South Shetland Is.*

Scott Island — *Siple I.* — ROCKEFELLER PLATEAU — Ellsworth Land — *Alexander I.* — Antarctic Peninsula

180° — *Ross Sea* — Marie Byrd Land — Vinson Massif 16,066 ft. (4,897 m) — ELLSWORTH MTS.

Balleny Is. — *Cape Adare* — *Roosevelt I.* — *Ross Ice Shelf* — Ronne Ice Shelf — *South Orkney Is.*

SOUTHERN OCEAN — McMurdo Sound — *Ross I.* — PENSACOLA MTS. — Berkner I. — *Weddell Sea*

PRINCE ALBERT MTS. — QUEEN MAUD MTS. — South Pole — Filchner Ice Shelf

150°E — TRANSANTARCTIC MOUNTAINS — 30°W

80°S — *Riiser-Larsen Ice Shelf*

ANTARCTICA — *Fimbul Ice Shelf* — SOUTHERN OCEAN

Cape Poinsett — *Wilkes Land* — Queen Maud Land — PRIME MERIDIAN

120°E — AMERICAN HIGHLAND — PRINCE CHARLES MTS. — Enderby Land — ANTARCTIC CIRCLE

60°S — *Shackleton Ice Shelf* — Amery Ice Shelf

Davis Sea — West Ice Shelf — *Prydz Bay* — 60°

INDIAN OCEAN — 90°E

0   500   1,000 mi
0   500   1,000 km

15

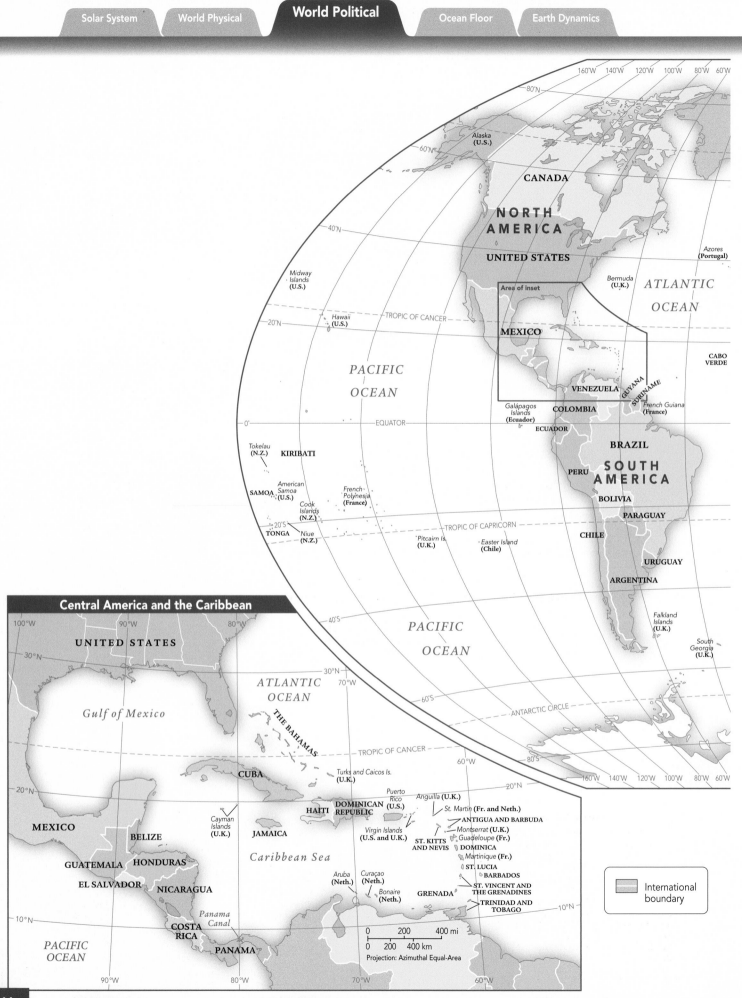

160°W 140°W 120°W 100°W 80°W 60°W

80°N

60°N

Alaska
(U.S.)

CANADA

NORTH
AMERICA

40°N

UNITED STATES

Azores
(Portugal)

Midway
Islands
(U.S.)

Bermuda
(U.K.)

ATLANTIC
OCEAN

Area of inset

TROPIC OF CANCER

20°N

Hawaii
(U.S.)

MEXICO

CABO
VERDE

PACIFIC
OCEAN

VENEZUELA   GUYANA
SURINAME

French Guiana
(France)

Galápagos
Islands
(Ecuador)

COLOMBIA

0°   EQUATOR

ECUADOR

BRAZIL

Tokelau
(N.Z.)

KIRIBATI

SOUTH
AMERICA

PERU

American
Samoa
(U.S.)

French
Polynesia
(France)

BOLIVIA

SAMOA

Cook
Islands
(N.Z.)

PARAGUAY

20°S

CHILE

TONGA   Niue
(N.Z.)

TROPIC OF CAPRICORN

Pitcairn Is.
(U.K.)

Easter Island
(Chile)

URUGUAY

ARGENTINA

Falkland
Islands
(U.K.)

40°S

PACIFIC

South
Georgia
(U.K.)

OCEAN

60°S

ANTARCTIC CIRCLE

80°S

160°W 140°W 120°W 100°W 80°W 60°W

Central America and the Caribbean

100°W   90°W   80°W

UNITED STATES

30°N

ATLANTIC
OCEAN

70°W

Gulf of Mexico

THE BAHAMAS

TROPIC OF CANCER

20°N

CUBA

Turks and Caicos Is.
(U.K.)

60°W

20°N

Cayman
Islands
(U.K.)

JAMAICA

HAITI

Puerto
Rico
(U.S.)

Anguilla (U.K.)

St. Martin (Fr. and Neth.)

MEXICO

DOMINICAN
REPUBLIC

ANTIGUA AND BARBUDA

BELIZE

Virgin Islands
(U.S. and U.K.)

Montserrat (U.K.)

Caribbean Sea

ST. KITTS
AND NEVIS

Guadeloupe (Fr.)

GUATEMALA   HONDURAS

DOMINICA

Martinique (Fr.)

EL SALVADOR

NICARAGUA

Aruba
(Neth.)

Curaçao
(Neth.)

ST. LUCIA

BARBADOS

ST. VINCENT AND
THE GRENADINES

Bonaire
(Neth.)

GRENADA

TRINIDAD AND
TOBAGO

10°N

10°N

Panama
Canal

COSTA
RICA

PACIFIC
OCEAN

PANAMA

0   200   400 mi

0   200   400 km

Projection: Azimuthal Equal-Area

90°W   80°W   70°W   60°W

International
boundary

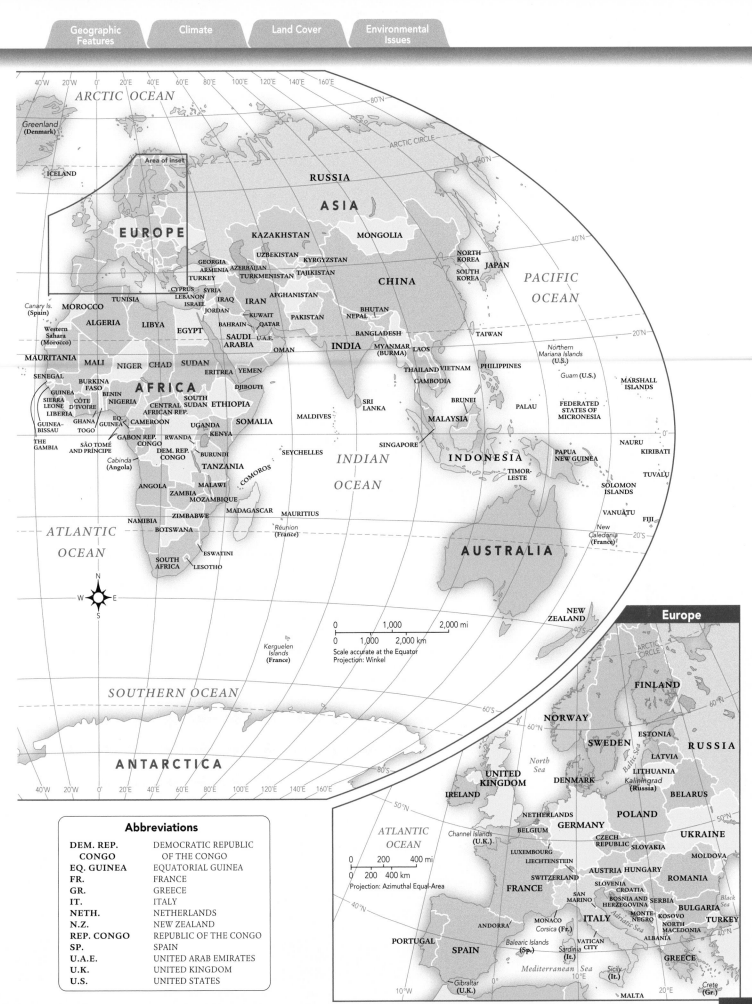

ARCTIC OCEAN

Greenland (Denmark)

ICELAND

Area of inset

RUSSIA

ASIA

EUROPE

KAZAKHSTAN

MONGOLIA

NORTH KOREA

JAPAN

PACIFIC OCEAN

GEORGIA
ARMENIA AZERBAIJAN KYRGYZSTAN
TURKEY TURKMENISTAN TAJIKISTAN
CYPRUS SYRIA
LEBANON IRAQ IRAN AFGHANISTAN
ISRAEL JORDAN KUWAIT PAKISTAN
TUNISIA

UZBEKISTAN

CHINA

SOUTH KOREA

Canary Is. (Spain) MOROCCO

Western Sahara (Morocco)

ALGERIA LIBYA EGYPT

BAHRAIN QATAR
SAUDI ARABIA U.A.E.
OMAN

BHUTAN
NEPAL

BANGLADESH

TAIWAN

INDIA MYANMAR (BURMA) LAOS

Northern Mariana Islands (U.S.)

Guam (U.S.)

MARSHALL ISLANDS

MAURITANIA MALI NIGER CHAD SUDAN ERITREA YEMEN

THAILAND VIETNAM PHILIPPINES

SENEGAL BURKINA FASO DJIBOUTI
GUINEA BENIN
SIERRA LEONE CÔTE D'IVOIRE NIGERIA CENTRAL AFRICAN REP. SOUTH SUDAN ETHIOPIA
LIBERIA GHANA EQ. GUINEA CAMEROON UGANDA SOMALIA
GUINEA-BISSAU TOGO
AFRICA

CAMBODIA

SRI LANKA

MALDIVES

BRUNEI

MALAYSIA

PALAU

FEDERATED STATES OF MICRONESIA

THE GAMBIA SÃO TOMÉ AND PRÍNCIPE GABON REP. CONGO RWANDA
Cabinda (Angola) DEM. REP. CONGO BURUNDI KENYA

SEYCHELLES

SINGAPORE

INDONESIA

PAPUA NEW GUINEA

NAURU

KIRIBATI

TANZANIA

ANGOLA MALAWI
ZAMBIA MOZAMBIQUE
ZIMBABWE
NAMIBIA BOTSWANA

COMOROS

MADAGASCAR MAURITIUS

Réunion (France)

INDIAN OCEAN

TIMOR-LESTE

SOLOMON ISLANDS

VANUATU

TUVALU

FIJI

New Caledonia (France)

AUSTRALIA

ATLANTIC OCEAN

SOUTH AFRICA ESWATINI
LESOTHO

N
W E
S

Kerguelen Islands (France)

0 1,000 2,000 mi
0 1,000 2,000 km
Scale accurate at the Equator
Projection: Winkel

NEW ZEALAND

SOUTHERN OCEAN

ANTARCTICA

Abbreviations

DEM. REP. CONGO	DEMOCRATIC REPUBLIC OF THE CONGO
EQ. GUINEA	EQUATORIAL GUINEA
FR.	FRANCE
GR.	GREECE
IT.	ITALY
NETH.	NETHERLANDS
N.Z.	NEW ZEALAND
REP. CONGO	REPUBLIC OF THE CONGO
SP.	SPAIN
U.A.E.	UNITED ARAB EMIRATES
U.K.	UNITED KINGDOM
U.S.	UNITED STATES

Europe

FINLAND

NORWAY

SWEDEN

ESTONIA

RUSSIA

LATVIA

North Sea

UNITED KINGDOM

DENMARK

LITHUANIA
Kaliningrad (Russia)

BELARUS

IRELAND

NETHERLANDS

POLAND

UKRAINE

ATLANTIC OCEAN

Channel Islands (U.K.)

BELGIUM

GERMANY

CZECH REPUBLIC SLOVAKIA

LUXEMBOURG

LIECHTENSTEIN

MOLDOVA

AUSTRIA HUNGARY

ROMANIA

SWITZERLAND

SLOVENIA CROATIA

FRANCE

SAN MARINO

BOSNIA AND HERZEGOVINA SERBIA

MONACO Corsica (Fr.)

ITALY

MONTE-NEGRO KOSOVO
NORTH MACEDONIA

BULGARIA

Black Sea

TURKEY

ANDORRA

Balearic Islands (Sp.)

VATICAN CITY
Sardinia (It.)

ALBANIA

GREECE

PORTUGAL

SPAIN

Mediterranean Sea

Gibraltar (U.K.)

Sicily (It.)

MALTA

Crete (Gr.)

0 200 400 mi
0 200 400 km
Projection: Azimuthal Equal-Area

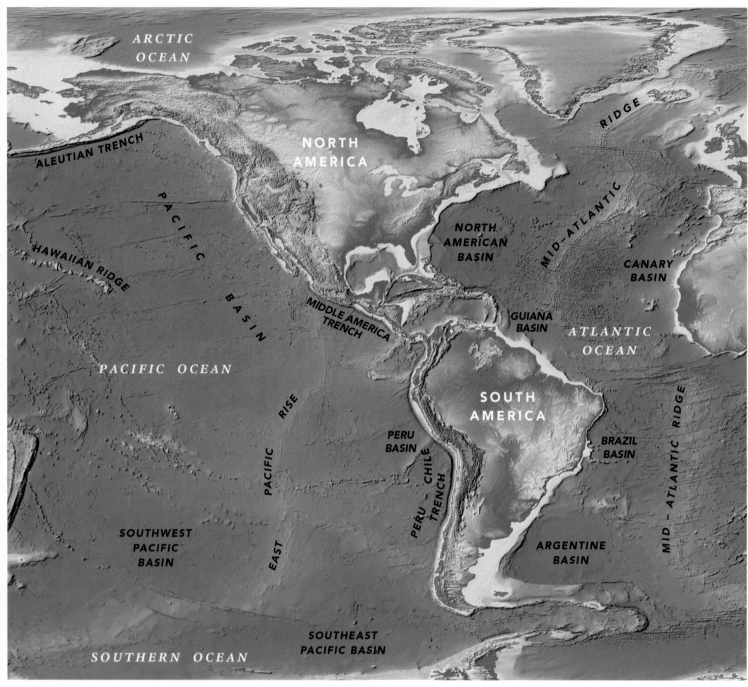

ARCTIC OCEAN

NORTH AMERICA

ALEUTIAN TRENCH

RIDGE

PACIFIC BASIN

HAWAIIAN RIDGE

NORTH AMERICAN BASIN

MID-ATLANTIC

CANARY BASIN

PACIFIC OCEAN

MIDDLE AMERICA TRENCH

GUIANA BASIN

ATLANTIC OCEAN

PACIFIC RISE

SOUTH AMERICA

PERU BASIN

PERU – CHILE TRENCH

BRAZIL BASIN

MID – ATLANTIC RIDGE

SOUTHWEST PACIFIC BASIN

EAST

ARGENTINE BASIN

SOUTHEAST PACIFIC BASIN

SOUTHERN OCEAN

Surrounding most of the continents are gently sloping areas called continental shelves, which reach depths of about 650 feet (200 meters). At the edges of the continental shelves lie steeper continental slopes leading down to the deep ocean basin, or abyss. The abyss contains many of the same features we see on land, including plains, mountains ranges (ridges), isolated mountains (known as sea mounts or guyots), and trenches. The Mid-Ocean Ridge system marks the areas where crustal plates are moving apart, and is very active geologically, as molten rock rises and erupts to create new crust. Earthquakes and volcanoes are common along many undersea trenches and ridges.

Ocean Floor

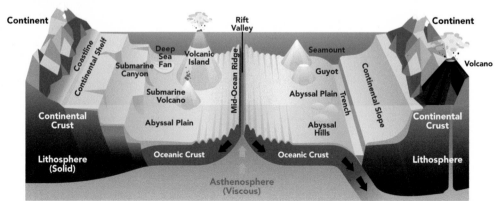

EUROPE

ASIA

AFRICA

ARABIAN BASIN

SOMALI BASIN

ANGOLA BASIN

CHAGOS TRENCH

NINETYEAST RIDGE

JAVA TRENCH

PACIFIC OCEAN

JAPAN TRENCH

KURIL TRENCH

PHILIPPINE TRENCH

MARIANA TRENCH

MID-PACIFIC MOUNTAINS

AUSTRALIA

INDIAN OCEAN

SOUTHWEST INDIAN RIDGE

KERGUELEN PLATEAU

SOUTH INDIAN BASIN

TASMAN BASIN

ENDERBY PLAIN

SOUTHERN OCEAN

Looking south towards Thingvallavatn Lake, the Almannagjá Gorge along the west side of Thingvellir National Park in Iceland marks the edge of the North American tectonic plate along the Mid-Atlantic Ridge. The park is located in the rift valley created by the separation of the North American and Eurasian tectonic plates. The plates here are pulling apart at a rate of about 2 centimeters (0.8 inches) a year, causing the land to slowly subside in this region of Iceland. The width of the Thingvellir Rift Valley is approximately 7 kilometers (4.3 miles) wide. Many hiking trails in the valley allow visitors to explore this geologic border between the two continents.

Did You Know?

According to the U.S. National Ocean Service, the average depth of the ocean is 12,100 feet (about 2.3 miles). The deepest part of the ocean is called Challenger Deep, at the southern end of the Mariana Trench. The depth of Challenger Deep is estimated to be 36,200 feet (almost 6.9 miles).

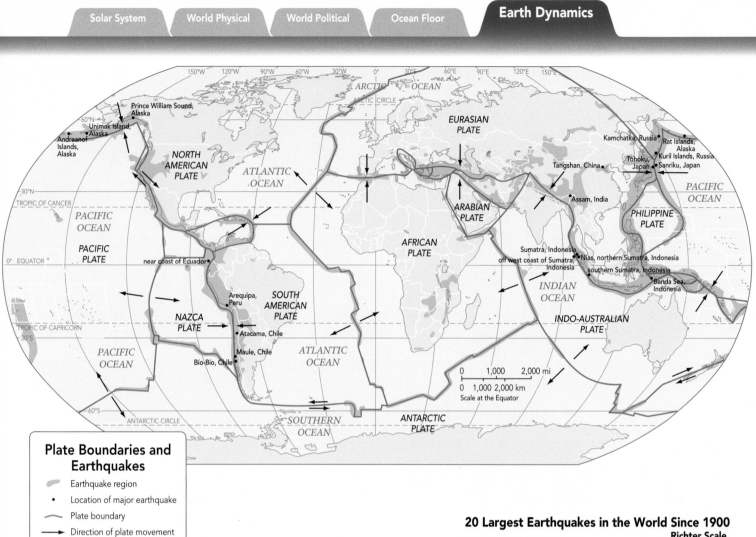

Plate Boundaries and Earthquakes

- Earthquake region
- Location of major earthquake
- Plate boundary
- Direction of plate movement

The movement of Earth's crustal plates causes the phenomena known as **earthquakes**. The surface of the Earth actually moves or quakes. An earthquake can have the destructive energy of an atomic bomb. However, thousands of earthquakes occur each day all over the world without most people realizing it.

The majority of earthquakes occur along a **fault.** A fault is usually a weak or broken area in the rocks beneath the surface of the Earth, but some, like the San Andreas Fault in California, can be seen on the surface.

The Richter Scale measures the energy of an earthquake. This measurement is obtained from the focus, or hypocenter, the spot where the first break in the rock layers occurs. The spot on the surface of the Earth, directly above the focus and nearest to the source of energy is called the epicenter.

Earthquake damage is caused by this energy, called seismic energy, moving through the rocks or along the surface. Many geographic factors, both physical and human, determine how much damage is done by these seismic waves of energy.

20 Largest Earthquakes in the World Since 1900

Date (UTC)	Location	Richter Scale Magnitude
May 22, 1960	Bío-Bío, Chile	9.5
March 28, 1964	Prince William Sound, Alaska	9.2
Dec. 26, 2004	Sumatra, Indonesia	9.1
March 11, 2011	Tōhoku, Japan	9.1
Nov. 4, 1952	Kamchatka, Russia	9.0
Feb. 27, 2010	Maule, Chile	8.8
Jan. 31, 1906	near coast of Ecuador	8.8
Feb. 4, 1965	Rat Islands, Alaska	8.7
Aug. 15, 1950	Assam, India	8.6
April 11, 2012	off west coast of Sumatra, Indonesia	8.6
March 28, 2005	Nias, northern Sumatra, Indonesia	8.6
March 9, 1957	Andreanof Islands, Alaska	8.6
April 1, 1946	Unimak Island, Alaska	8.6
Feb. 1, 1938	Banda Sea, Indonesia	8.5
Nov. 11, 1922	Atacama, Chile	8.5
Oct. 13, 1963	Kuril Islands, Russia	8.5
Feb. 3, 1923	Kamchatka, Russia	8.4
Sept. 12, 2007	southern Sumatra, Indonesia	8.4
June 23, 2001	Arequipa, Peru	8.4
March 2, 1933	Sanriku, Japan	8.4

Source: National Earthquake Information Center, U.S.G.S, 2021

Types of Plate Boundaries

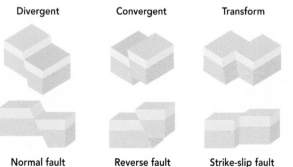

Divergent   Convergent   Transform

Normal fault   Reverse fault   Strike-slip fault

Did You Know?
The Tanghan earthquake of 1976 is likely the deadliest earthquake in history. The magnitude 7.5 quake, with an epicenter near Tangshan, China, killed 242,000 people as officially reported, though the death toll may have exceeded 600,000. Another 700,000 or more may have been injured.

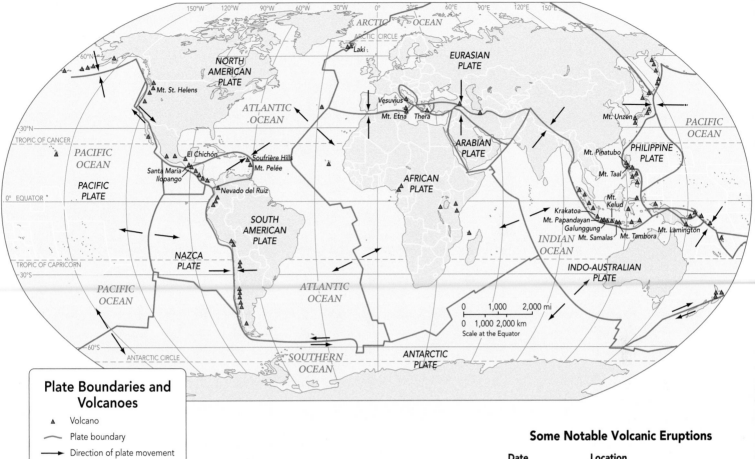

Plate Boundaries and Volcanoes

- ▲ Volcano
- ⌒ Plate boundary
- → Direction of plate movement

A **volcano** is an opening in the Earth's crust often capped by a cone-shaped hill or mountain formed from erupted lava and ash.

Volcanoes are associated with plate boundaries. Powerful forces occurring far beneath the surface at the edges of plates cause rock to melt and, at the same time, open cracks in the crust. An eruption occurs when magma (melted rock) flows, and many times explodes, through a weakness, such as a crack in the Earth's crust. Once magma is flowing on the Earth's surface it is called lava. Flowing lava can be several thousand degrees Fahrenheit.

In a few cases, volcanoes exist without being near the edge of a plate. In these cases, such as the Hawaiian Islands, a powerful and persistent flow of magma has broken through the crust.

Some Notable Volcanic Eruptions

Date	Location
around 1500 B.C.	Thera (Santorini), Greece
A.D. 79	Vesuvius, Italy
around 450	Ilopango, El Salvador
1257	Mt. Samalas, Lombok, Indonesia
1586	Mt. Kelud, Java, Indonesia
Dec. 16, 1631	Vesuvius, Italy
March–July, 1669	Mt. Etna, Italy
Aug. 11, 1772	Mt. Papandayan, Java, Indonesia
June 8, 1783	Laki, Iceland
May 21, 1792	Mt. Unzen, Japan
April 5–10, 1815	Mt. Tambora, Sumbawa, Indonesia
Oct. 8, 1822	Galunggung, Java, Indonesia
Aug. 26–28, 1883	Krakatoa, Indonesia
Aug. 25, 1902	Santa Maria, Guatemala
April–Oct., 1902	Mt. Pelée, Martinique
Jan. 30, 1911	Mt. Taal, Philippines
May 19, 1919	Mt. Kelud, Java, Indonesia
Jan. 17–21, 1951	Mt. Lamington, Papua New Guinea
May 18, 1980	Mt. St. Helens, United States
March–April, 1982	El Chichón, Mexico
Nov. 13, 1985	Nevado del Ruiz, Colombia
June 12–15, 1991	Mt. Pinatubo, Philippines
June–Sept., 1997	Soufrière Hills, Montserrat

Types of Volcanoes

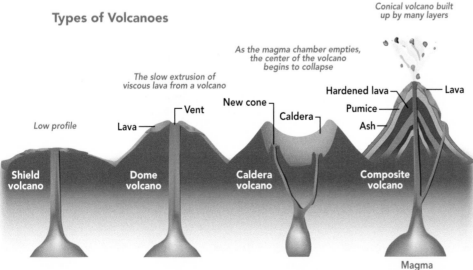

Conical volcano built up by many layers

As the magma chamber empties, the center of the volcano begins to collapse

The slow extrusion of viscous lava from a volcano

Hardened lava — Lava
Pumice
Ash

Low profile — Lava — Vent — New cone — Caldera

Shield volcano — **Dome volcano** — **Caldera volcano** — **Composite volcano**

Magma

Did You Know?

Yellowstone National Park lies in the caldera formed by the eruption of the Yellowstone Supervolcano around 640,000 years ago. Yellowstone's famous geysers, hot springs, and mud pots provide evidence of the hydrothermal and magma activity below the park's surface.

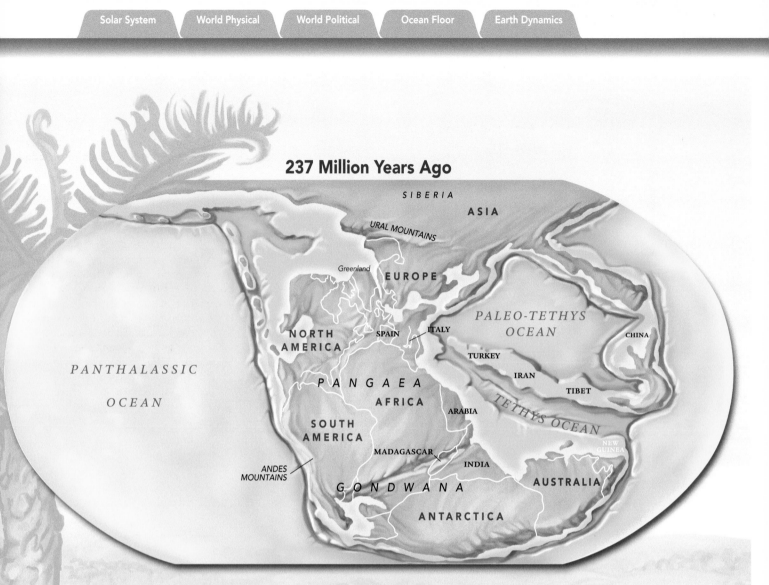

237 Million Years Ago

SIBERIA

ASIA

URAL MOUNTAINS

Greenland

EUROPE

PANTHALASSIC OCEAN

NORTH AMERICA

SPAIN

ITALY

PALEO-TETHYS OCEAN

CHINA

TURKEY

IRAN

TIBET

PANGAEA

AFRICA

ARABIA

TETHYS OCEAN

SOUTH AMERICA

MADAGASCAR

INDIA

NEW GUINEA

AUSTRALIA

ANDES MOUNTAINS

GONDWANA

ANTARCTICA

This peculiar—to our eyes—arrangement of continents with its unfamiliar oceans and seas, mountains and plains, and peninsulas and islands reminds us that the dinosaurs lived in a far different landscape than our own. As the last dinosaurs receded into memory, the future Atlantic Ocean and Mediterranean Sea were becoming more substantial and recognizable, and the continents, except for Australia and Antarctica, were nearing their present latitudes. Within the last 65 million years, most continents nestled unhurriedly into their current positions. However, the Indian sub-continent "sprinted" north, crashing into Asia and bulldozing up the Himalayas, earth's loftiest mountain range.

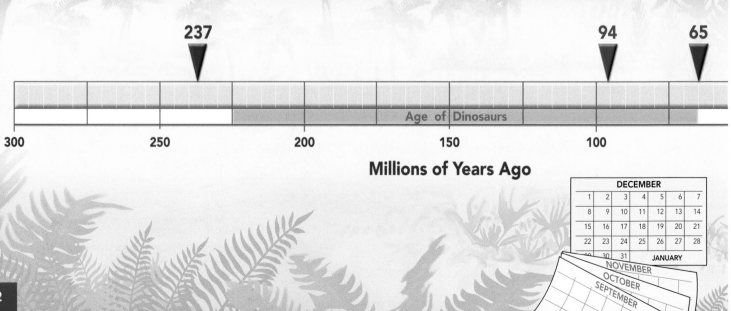

237   94   65

Age of Dinosaurs

300   250   200   150   100

Millions of Years Ago

DECEMBER						
1	2	3	4	5	6	7
8	9	10	11	12	13	14
15	16	17	18	19	20	21
22	23	24	25	26	27	28
29	30	31	JANUARY			

NOVEMBER

OCTOBER

SEPTEMBER

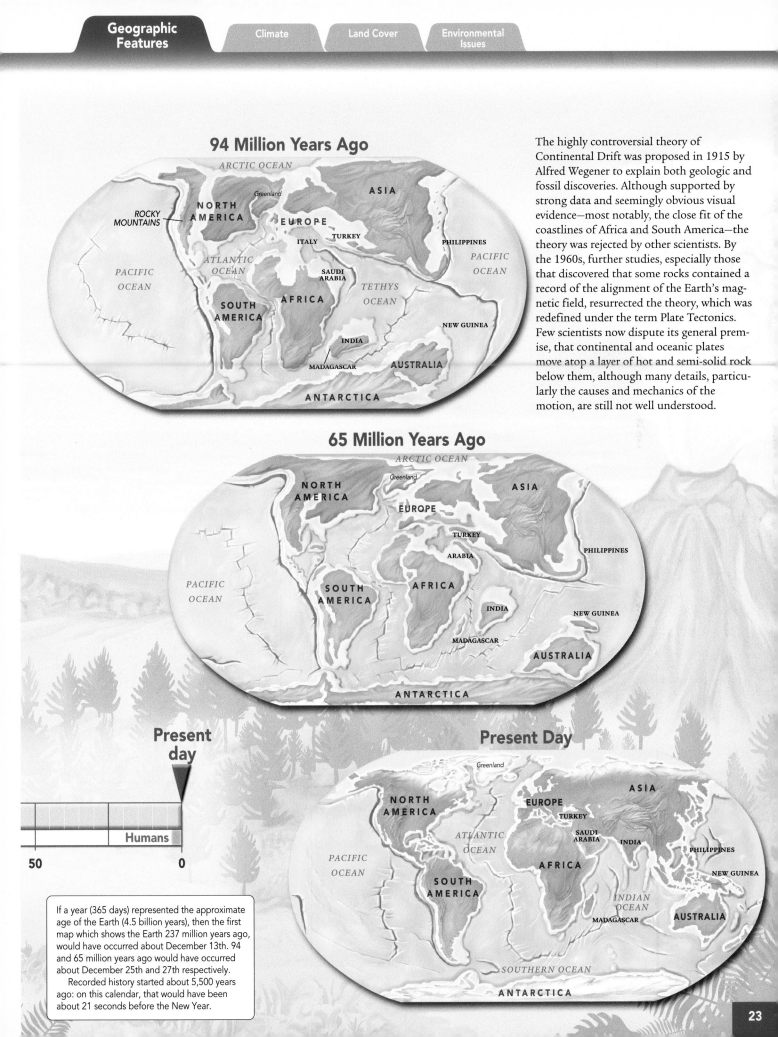

94 Million Years Ago

ARCTIC OCEAN

Greenland

NORTH AMERICA

ROCKY MOUNTAINS

EUROPE

ASIA

ITALY   TURKEY

PHILIPPINES

ATLANTIC OCEAN

PACIFIC OCEAN

SAUDI ARABIA

PACIFIC OCEAN

SOUTH AMERICA

AFRICA

TETHYS OCEAN

NEW GUINEA

INDIA

MADAGASCAR

AUSTRALIA

ANTARCTICA

The highly controversial theory of Continental Drift was proposed in 1915 by Alfred Wegener to explain both geologic and fossil discoveries. Although supported by strong data and seemingly obvious visual evidence—most notably, the close fit of the coastlines of Africa and South America—the theory was rejected by other scientists. By the 1960s, further studies, especially those that discovered that some rocks contained a record of the alignment of the Earth's magnetic field, resurrected the theory, which was redefined under the term Plate Tectonics. Few scientists now dispute its general premise, that continental and oceanic plates move atop a layer of hot and semi-solid rock below them, although many details, particularly the causes and mechanics of the motion, are still not well understood.

65 Million Years Ago

ARCTIC OCEAN

Greenland

NORTH AMERICA

EUROPE

ASIA

TURKEY

PHILIPPINES

ARABIA

PACIFIC OCEAN

SOUTH AMERICA

AFRICA

INDIA

NEW GUINEA

MADAGASCAR

AUSTRALIA

ANTARCTICA

Present day

Humans

50   0

Present Day

Greenland

NORTH AMERICA

EUROPE

ASIA

TURKEY

ATLANTIC OCEAN

SAUDI ARABIA

INDIA

PHILIPPINES

PACIFIC OCEAN

AFRICA

NEW GUINEA

SOUTH AMERICA

INDIAN OCEAN

MADAGASCAR

AUSTRALIA

SOUTHERN OCEAN

ANTARCTICA

If a year (365 days) represented the approximate age of the Earth (4.5 billion years), then the first map which shows the Earth 237 million years ago, would have occurred about December 13th. 94 and 65 million years ago would have occurred about December 25th and 27th respectively.

Recorded history started about 5,500 years ago: on this calendar, that would have been about 21 seconds before the New Year.

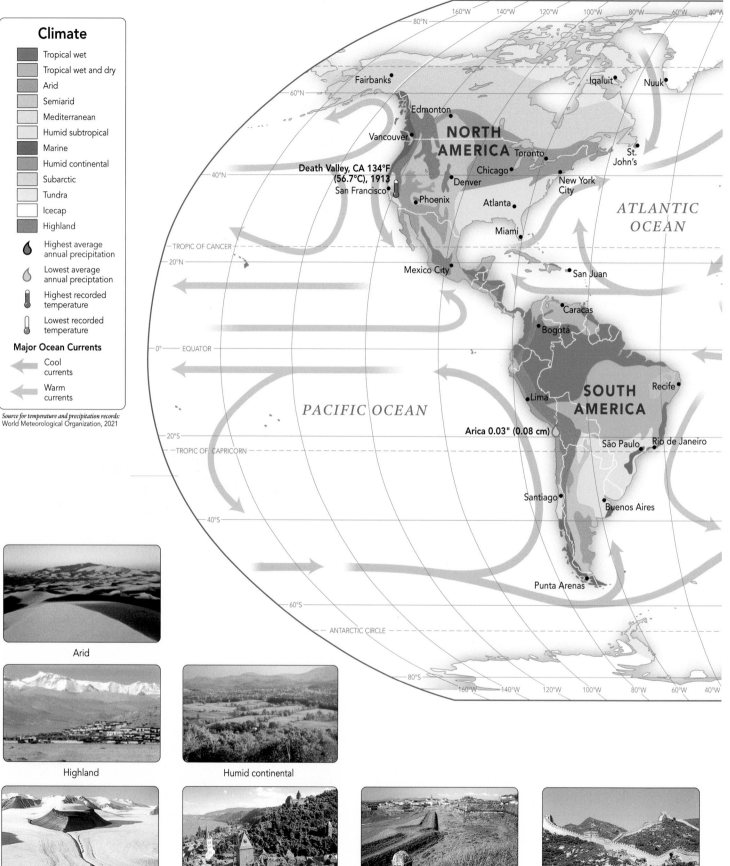

Climate

- Tropical wet
- Tropical wet and dry
- Arid
- Semiarid
- Mediterranean
- Humid subtropical
- Marine
- Humid continental
- Subarctic
- Tundra
- Icecap
- Highland

- Highest average annual precipitation
- Lowest average annual precipitation
- Highest recorded temperature
- Lowest recorded temperature

Major Ocean Currents

- Cool currents
- Warm currents

Source for temperature and precipitation records:
World Meteorological Organization, 2021

NORTH AMERICA

Fairbanks • Iqaluit • Nuuk •
Edmonton •
Vancouver • Toronto • St. John's •
Death Valley, CA 134°F (56.7°C), 1913
Chicago • New York City
San Francisco • Denver •
Phoenix • Atlanta •
Miami •

ATLANTIC OCEAN

Mexico City • San Juan •

Caracas •
Bogotá •

SOUTH AMERICA
Recife •

PACIFIC OCEAN

Lima •

Arica 0.03" (0.08 cm)

São Paulo • Rio de Janeiro •

Santiago • Buenos Aires •

Punta Arenas •

TROPIC OF CANCER
EQUATOR
TROPIC OF CAPRICORN
ANTARCTIC CIRCLE

Arid

Highland

Humid continental

Icecap

Marine

Mediterranean

Semiarid

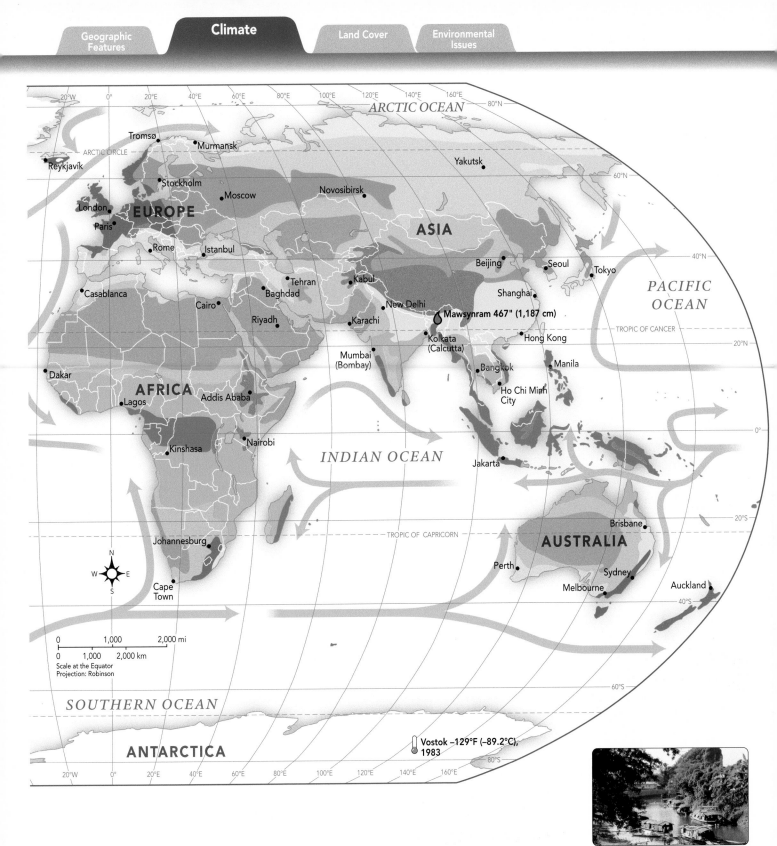

ARCTIC OCEAN

80°N

Tromsø
Murmansk
ARCTIC CIRCLE
Reykjavík
60°N
Yakutsk
Stockholm
Moscow
Novosibirsk
EUROPE
ASIA
London
Paris
40°N
Rome
Istanbul
Beijing
Seoul
Tokyo
Casablanca
Tehran
Kabul
PACIFIC OCEAN
Cairo
Baghdad
Shanghai
Riyadh
New Delhi
🌢 Mawsynram 467" (1,187 cm)
Karachi
TROPIC OF CANCER
20°N
Kolkata
(Calcutta)
Hong Kong
Dakar
Mumbai
(Bombay)
Bangkok
Manila
AFRICA
Ho Chi Minh
City
Lagos
Addis Ababa
0°
Kinshasa
Nairobi
INDIAN OCEAN
Jakarta

Brisbane
20°S
Johannesburg
TROPIC OF CAPRICORN
AUSTRALIA
N
Perth
Sydney
W E
Cape Town
Melbourne
Auckland
S
40°S

0   1,000   2,000 mi
0   1,000   2,000 km
Scale at the Equator
Projection: Robinson

60°S

SOUTHERN OCEAN

🌡 Vostok –129°F (–89.2°C), 1983

ANTARCTICA

20°W   0°   20°E   40°E   60°E   80°E   100°E   120°E   140°E   160°E   80°S

Humid subtropical

Subarctic

Tropical wet

Tropical wet and dry

Tundra

Vegetation

- Unclassified highlands or icecap
- Tundra and alpine tundra
- Coniferous forest
- Midlatitude deciduous forest
- Subtropical broadleaf evergreen forest
- Mixed forest
- Midlatitude scrubland
- Midlatitude grassland
- Desert
- Tropical seasonal and scrub
- Tropical rain forest
- Tropical savanna

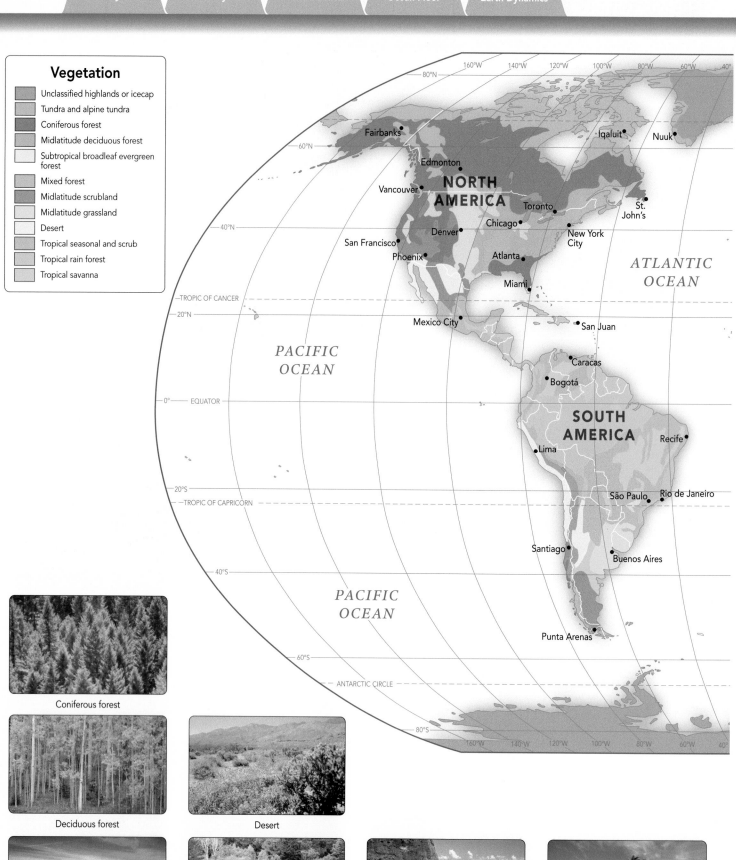

80°N · 160°W · 140°W · 120°W · 100°W · 80°W · 60°W · 40°

Fairbanks
Iqaluit
Nuuk

Edmonton
NORTH AMERICA
Vancouver
Toronto
St. John's

60°N

Denver
Chicago
New York City

40°N

San Francisco
Phoenix
Atlanta

Miami

ATLANTIC OCEAN

TROPIC OF CANCER
20°N

Mexico City
San Juan

PACIFIC OCEAN

Caracas
Bogotá

0° — EQUATOR

SOUTH AMERICA

Recife

Lima

20°S

TROPIC OF CAPRICORN

São Paulo
Rio de Janeiro

Santiago
Buenos Aires

40°S

PACIFIC OCEAN

Punta Arenas

60°S

ANTARCTIC CIRCLE

80°S · 160°W · 140°W · 120°W · 100°W · 80°W · 60°W · 40°

Coniferous forest

Deciduous forest

Desert

Midlatitude scrubland

Mixed forest

Subtropical broadleaf evergreen forest

Tropical rain forest

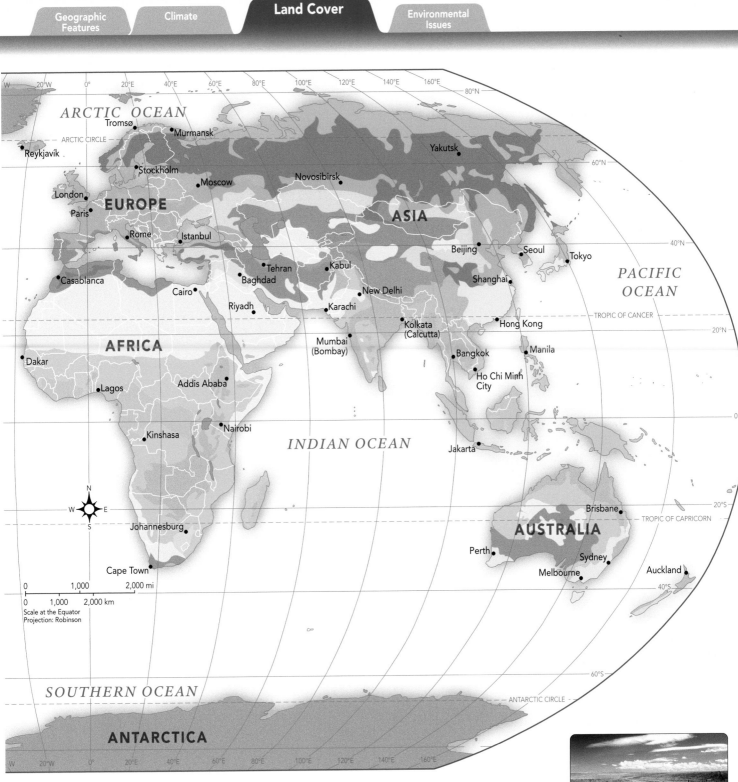

ARCTIC OCEAN

ARCTIC CIRCLE

Reykjavík
Tromsø
Murmansk
Stockholm
London
Moscow
Novosibirsk
Yakutsk
Paris
EUROPE
Rome
Istanbul
ASIA
Casablanca
Cairo
Tehran
Kabul
Beijing
Seoul
Tokyo
Baghdad
Shanghai
PACIFIC OCEAN
Riyadh
New Delhi
Karachi
Hong Kong
TROPIC OF CANCER
Dakar
AFRICA
Mumbai (Bombay)
Kolkata (Calcutta)
Bangkok
Manila
Lagos
Addis Ababa
Ho Chi Minh City
Kinshasa
Nairobi
INDIAN OCEAN
Jakarta
Johannesburg
AUSTRALIA
Brisbane
TROPIC OF CAPRICORN
Cape Town
Perth
Sydney
Auckland
Melbourne

0   1,000   2,000 mi
0   1,000   2,000 km
Scale at the Equator
Projection: Robinson

SOUTHERN OCEAN
ANTARCTIC CIRCLE

ANTARCTICA

Midlatitude grassland

Tropical savanna

Tropical seasonal and scrub

Tundra and alpine tundra

Unclassified highlands or icecap

Challenges in the 21st Century

Our Earth faces a number of environmental challenges in the 21st Century, such as: climate change, air and water pollution, deforestation, food and water scarcity, protecting biodiversity, and waste management. These problems affect all of us. Air and water pollution cause health problems. Rising world populations put stress on food, water, and fuel resources. The oceans have become dumping grounds for plastic and other waste products that damage ecosystems and threaten marine life.

Waste Management and Recycling

In 2018, the World Bank estimated that 2.01 billion metric tons of municipal solid waste (MSW) are produced annually worldwide. They estimate that by 2050, global generation of MSW will increase to 3.4 billion metric tons.

The World Bank's findings also concluded that 13.5% of today's waste is recycled and 5.5% is composted. However, they found that up to 40% of the waste generated worldwide is improperly managed.

Percent of municipal waste recycled and composted

- Germany 65%
- South Korea 59%
- Austria 58%
- Switzerland 51%
- United Kingdom 43%
- Australia 41%
- France 38%
- United States 35%
- Spain 30%
- Canada 24%
- Japan 19%
- Mexico 5%
- Turkey 1%

Source: *Municipal Waste*, OECD Environmental Statistics, 2015

Did You Know?
A 2015 study published in the scientific journal *Nature* estimated there were approximately 3,040,000,000,000 (3.04 trillion) trees around the world.

World Forest Cover

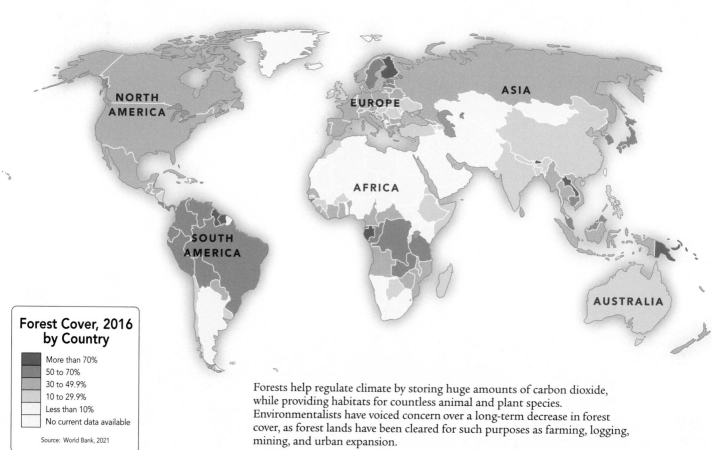

Forest Cover, 2016 by Country

- More than 70%
- 50 to 70%
- 30 to 49.9%
- 10 to 29.9%
- Less than 10%
- No current data available

Source: World Bank, 2021

Forests help regulate climate by storing huge amounts of carbon dioxide, while providing habitats for countless animal and plant species. Environmentalists have voiced concern over a long-term decrease in forest cover, as forest lands have been cleared for such purposes as farming, logging, mining, and urban expansion.

Climate Change

The Earth's climate has changed throughout history. The modern climate era began about 11,000-12,000 years ago with the end of the last ice age. Most earlier climate changes are believed to have been caused by very small variations in the Earth's orbit around the Sun. These changes affect the amount of solar energy the planet receives.

While the exact causes of the current warming trend are not completely understood, it is likely that human activities, such as industrialization and the burning of fossil fuels, are important factors. The role that society has contributed to this warming pattern is highly debated. However, there is compelling evidence that climate change is occurring. According to the National Aeronautics and Space Administration (NASA):

"The Earth has warmed about 2.12 degrees Fahrenheit since the late 1800s. Most of this warming has occurred in the last 40 years. The years 2016 and 2020 are tied for the warmest year on record.

The oceans have absorbed much of this increased heat, with the top 300 feet of ocean showing warming of over 0.6 degrees Fahrenheit since 1969.

Sea levels around the globe have risen about 8 inches in the last hundred years. The rate since 2000, however, is almost double that of the last century.

The Greenland ice sheet has lost an average of about 280 billion tons of ice per year between 1993 and 2019. Antarctica has lost about 148 billion tons of ice per year during this period."

In addition, satellite imagery shows that glaciers are retreating almost everywhere around the world. Below are side-by-side photos showing the retreat of the Muir Glacier in Alaska between 1941 and 2004, and the retreat of the Gigjoekull Glacier in Iceland between 1992 and 2007.

NASA projects that the global climate will continue to change over this century and beyond. The rate of change beyond the next few decades will largely depend on the emissions of heat-trapping gases, such as carbon dioxide, methane, and nitrous oxide. Changes in temperature and precipitation patterns are likely to bring more droughts and heat waves to areas like the southwestern United States. The Arctic Ocean is expected to become ice-free during the summer by 2050. Sea levels are expected to rise by 1 to 8 feet by 2100, significantly affecting low-lying areas—such as the island nation of Maldives in the Indian Ocean.

Source: NASA, "Global Climate Change, Vital Signs of the Planet', *climate.nasa.gov*

Picture Source: The National Snow and Ice Data Center, Glacier Photograph Collection, *nsidc.org*

Muir Glacier, Glacier Bay National Park and Preserve, Alaska

1941   2004

Gigjoekull Glacier, Iceland

1992   2007

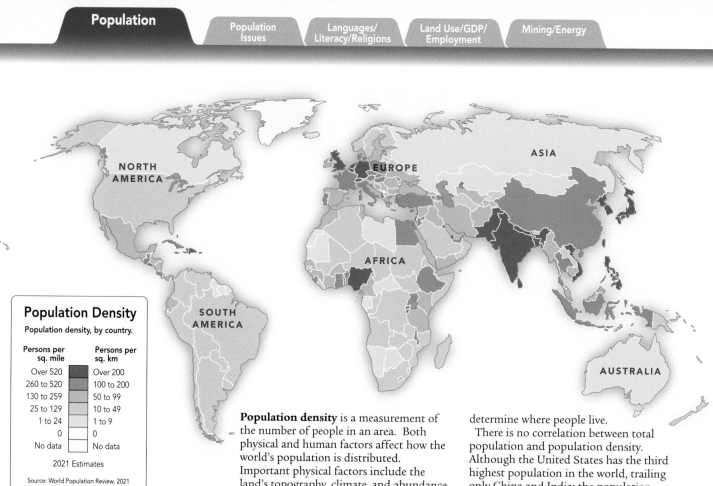

Population Density

Population density, by country.

Persons per sq. mile		Persons per sq. km
Over 520		Over 200
260 to 520		100 to 200
130 to 259		50 to 99
25 to 129		10 to 49
1 to 24		1 to 9
0		0
No data		No data

2021 Estimates

Source: World Population Review, 2021

Did You Know?
World Population Day is July 11th.
Learn why at www.un.org/observances

Population density is a measurement of the number of people in an area. Both physical and human factors affect how the world's population is distributed. Important physical factors include the land's topography, climate, and abundance of resources. Political stability and the promise of jobs and economic opportunity are examples of human factors that help determine where people live.

There is no correlation between total population and population density. Although the United States has the third highest population in the world, trailing only China and India; the population density of the United States currently ranks 174th out of 232 countries.

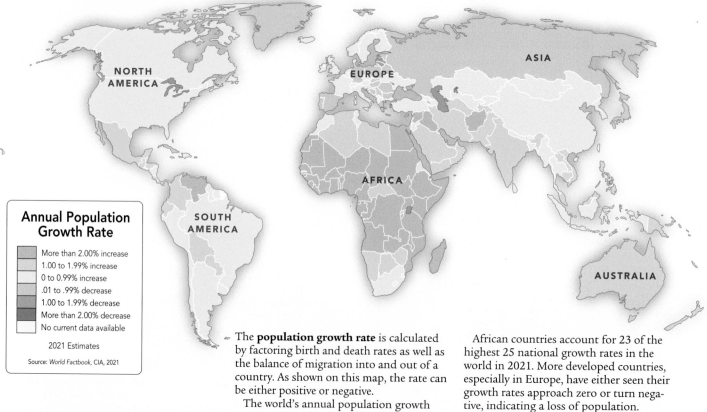

Annual Population Growth Rate

	More than 2.00% increase
	1.00 to 1.99% increase
	0 to 0.99% increase
	.01 to .99% decrease
	1.00 to 1.99% decrease
	More than 2.00% decrease
	No current data available

2021 Estimates

Source: World Factbook, CIA, 2021

The **population growth rate** is calculated by factoring birth and death rates as well as the balance of migration into and out of a country. As shown on this map, the rate can be either positive or negative.

The world's annual population growth rate is estimated to be 1.1% in 2020.

African countries account for 23 of the highest 25 national growth rates in the world in 2021. More developed countries, especially in Europe, have either seen their growth rates approach zero or turn negative, indicating a loss of population.

The green shaded area on the chart to the right indicates that there is a 95% probability that the world's population will fall within this range in the future. For the year 2100, this spread ranges from a high of 13.2 billion to a low of 9.6 billion.

Near-term fertility rates will have a significant effect on the state of the world's population in 2100, as small increases or decreases can have large impacts when projected over several generations. Varying widely by continent, currently the global fertility rate stands at 2.5 births per woman.

United Nations estimates in 2017 show that about 83 million people are being added to the world's population each year.

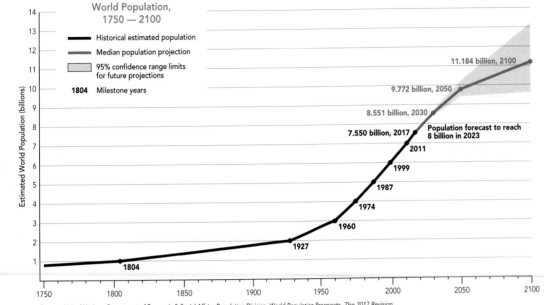

World Population, 1750 — 2100

- Historical estimated population
- Median population projection
- 95% confidence range limits for future projections
- **1804** Milestone years

11.184 billion, 2100
9.772 billion, 2050
8.551 billion, 2030
7.550 billion, 2017
Population forecast to reach 8 billion in 2023
2011
1999
1987
1974
1960
1927
1804

Sources: United Nations, Department of Economic & Social Affairs, Population Division, *World Population Prospects, The 2017 Revision*
United Nations, Population Division, *The World at Six Billion, 1999*

Africa Population Estimates (in millions)

Year	Value
2017	1,256
2030	1,704
2050	2,528
2100	4,468

Asia Population Estimates (in millions)

Year	Value
2017	4,504
2030	4,947
2050	5,257
2100	4,780

Europe Population Estimates (in millions)

Year	Value
2017	742
2030	739
2050	716
2100	653

"Europe" includes all of Russia.

Latin America & Caribbean Population Estimates (in millions)

Year	Value
2017	646
2030	718
2050	780
2100	712

"Latin America & Caribbean" includes all Caribbean island nations; all of Central America, including Mexico; and all of South America.

Northern America Population Estimates (in millions)

Year	Value
2017	361
2030	395
2050	435
2100	499

"Northern America" includes the United States, Canada, Bermuda, Greenland, and the French possession of St. Pierre & Miquelon.

Australia & Oceania Population Estimates (in millions)

Year	Value
2017	41
2030	48
2050	57
2100	72

Source: United Nations, Department of Economic & Social Affairs, Population Division, *World Population Prospects, The 2017 Revision*

Scale for this chart: 0.500" = 1 billion in population

Largest Cities (urban agglomerations)

	2018		2030 (projected)
1	Tokyo 37,468,000	1 Delhi	38,939,000
2	Delhi 28,514,000	2 Tokyo	36,574,000
3	Shangahi 25,582,000	3 Shanghai	32,869,000
4	São Paulo 21,650,000	4 Dhaka	28,076,000
5	Mexico City 21,581,000	5 Cairo	25,517,000
6	Cairo 20,076,000	6 Mumbai	24,572,000
7	Mumbai 19,980,000	7 Beijing	24,282,000
8	Beijing 19,618,000	8 Mexico City	24,111,000
9	Dhaka 19,578,000	9 São Paulo	23,824,000
10	Osaka 19,281,000	10 Kinshasa	21,914,000

Source: United Nations. Department of Social & Economic Affairs, Population Division, 2018

Given that the growth rate in India is forecast to increase while the growth rate in Japan decreases slightly, by 2030 the population of Delhi, India is forecast to surpass that of Tokyo, Japan and become the world's largest city.

At the turn of the 21st century in 2000, there were 371 cities worldwide with a population of more than 1 million. By 2018 the number of cities with at least 1 million residents had grown to 548, and by 2030, the number of cities with a population of 1 million is expected to rise to 706.

A city with more than 10 million inhabitants is often referred to as a "megacity". The number of megacities around the world is projected to rise from 33 in 2018 to 43 in 2030.

In some cases a city may lose population due to economic factors or to a natural disaster, as happened in New Orleans, Louisiana following Hurricane Katrina in 2005. In most cases, though, the lack of growth or decline in population is related to low fertility rates, especially in European cities.

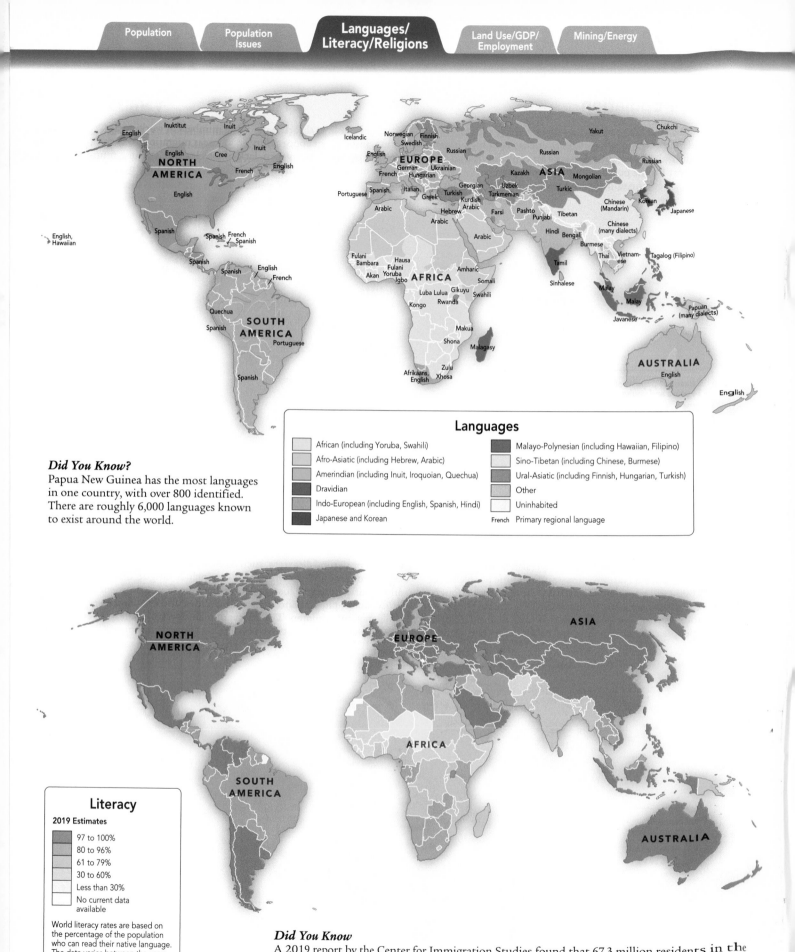

Languages

- African (including Yoruba, Swahili)
- Afro-Asiatic (including Hebrew, Arabic)
- Amerindian (including Inuit, Iroquoian, Quechua)
- Dravidian
- Indo-European (including English, Spanish, Hindi)
- Japanese and Korean
- Malayo-Polynesian (including Hawaiian, Filipino)
- Sino-Tibetan (including Chinese, Burmese)
- Ural-Asiatic (including Finnish, Hungarian, Turkish)
- Other
- Uninhabited
- French Primary regional language

Did You Know?

Papua New Guinea has the most languages in one country, with over 800 identified. There are roughly 6,000 languages known to exist around the world.

Literacy

2019 Estimates

- 97 to 100%
- 80 to 96%
- 61 to 79%
- 30 to 60%
- Less than 30%
- No current data available

World literacy rates are based on the percentage of the population who can read their native language. The data varies between the years of 2000 to 2016.

Source: *World Factbook*, CIA, 2019

Did You Know

A 2019 report by the Center for Immigration Studies found that 67.3 million residents in the United States now speak a language other than English at home. About two-thirds of that total speak Spanish at home rather than English. The state of California has the highest share of population speaking a language other than English at home at 45%.

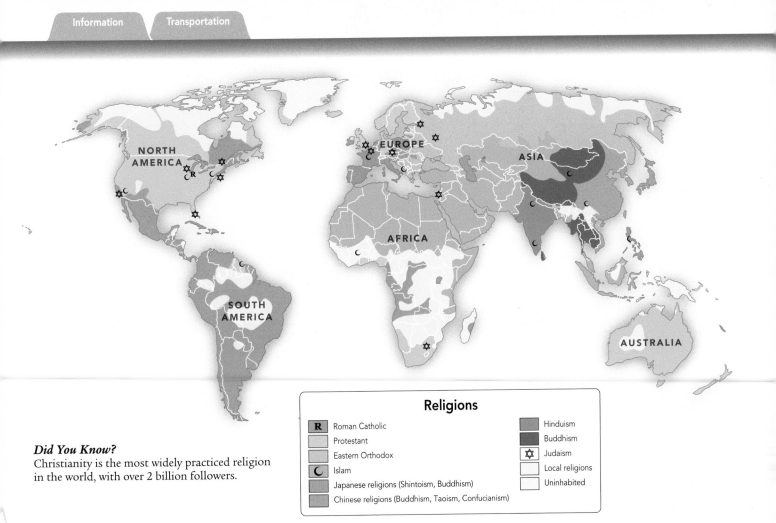

Religions

R	Roman Catholic		Hinduism
	Protestant		Buddhism
	Eastern Orthodox	✡	Judaism
☾	Islam		Local religions
	Japanese religions (Shintoism, Buddhism)		Uninhabited
	Chinese religions (Buddhism, Taoism, Confucianism)		

Did You Know?

Christianity is the most widely practiced religion in the world, with over 2 billion followers.

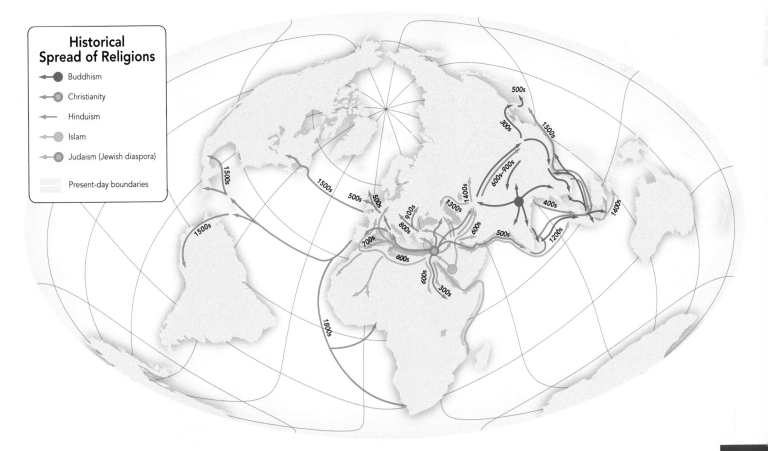

Historical Spread of Religions

- Buddhism
- Christianity
- Hinduism
- Islam
- Judaism (Jewish diaspora)
- Present-day boundaries

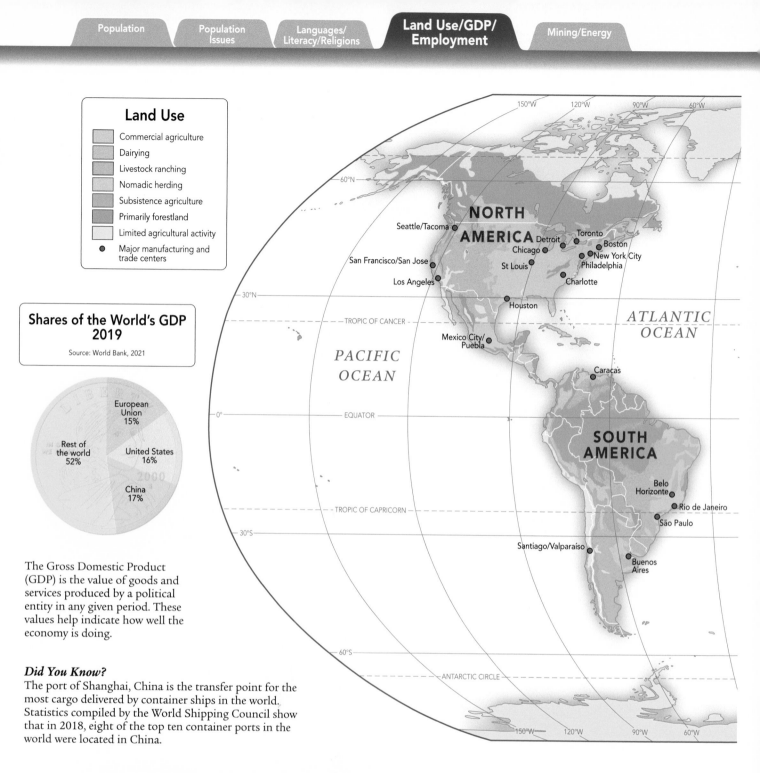

Land Use

- Commercial agriculture
- Dairying
- Livestock ranching
- Nomadic herding
- Subsistence agriculture
- Primarily forestland
- Limited agricultural activity
- ● Major manufacturing and trade centers

Shares of the World's GDP 2019

Source: World Bank, 2021

- European Union 15%
- United States 16%
- China 17%
- Rest of the world 52%

The Gross Domestic Product (GDP) is the value of goods and services produced by a political entity in any given period. These values help indicate how well the economy is doing.

Did You Know?

The port of Shanghai, China is the transfer point for the most cargo delivered by container ships in the world. Statistics compiled by the World Shipping Council show that in 2018, eight of the top ten container ports in the world were located in China.

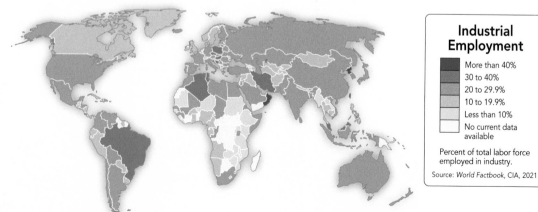

Industrial Employment

- More than 40%
- 30 to 40%
- 20 to 29.9%
- 10 to 19.9%
- Less than 10%
- No current data available

Percent of total labor force employed in industry.

Source: *World Factbook*, CIA, 2021

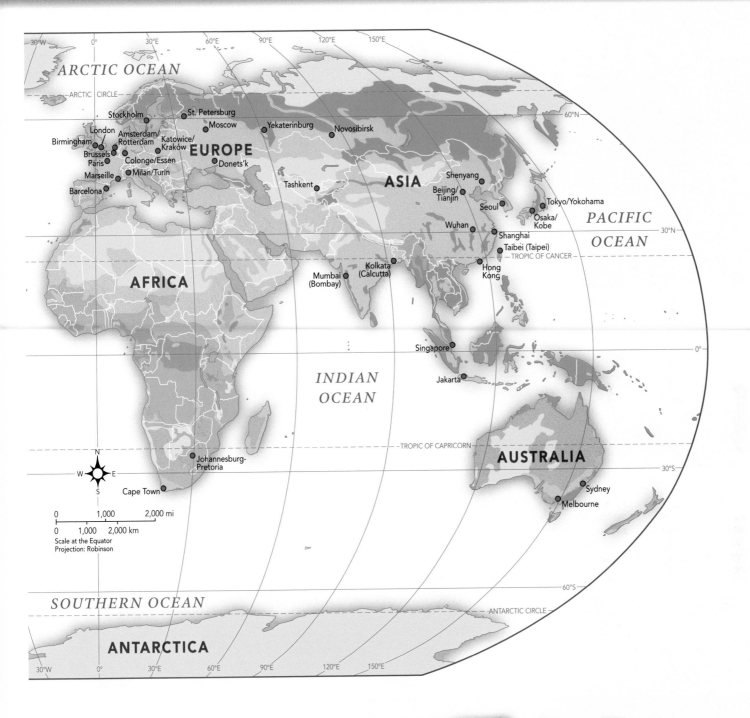

ARCTIC OCEAN

ARCTIC CIRCLE

Stockholm
St. Petersburg
Moscow
Yekaterinburg
Novosibirsk
London
Birmingham
Amsterdam/
Rotterdam
Katowice/
Kraków
Brussels
Paris
Colonge/Essen
Donets'k
EUROPE
Marseille
Milan/Turin
Barcelona
Tashkent
ASIA
Shenyang
Beijing/
Tianjin
Seoul
Tokyo/Yokohama
Osaka/
Kobe
PACIFIC
OCEAN
Wuhan
Shanghai
Taibei (Taipei)
30°N
TROPIC OF CANCER
Kolkata
(Calcutta)
Mumbai
(Bombay)
Hong
Kong

AFRICA

Singapore
Jakarta
INDIAN
OCEAN
0°

TROPIC OF CAPRICORN
AUSTRALIA
30°S
Johannesburg-
Pretoria
Sydney
Cape Town
Melbourne

N
W   E
S

0   1,000   2,000 mi
0   1,000 2,000 km
Scale at the Equator
Projection: Robinson

SOUTHERN OCEAN

60°S

ANTARCTIC CIRCLE

ANTARCTICA

60°N
30°N
TROPIC OF CANCER

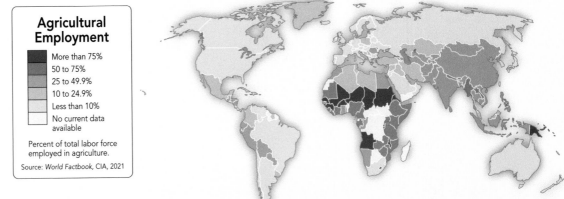

Agricultural Employment

- More than 75%
- 50 to 75%
- 25 to 49.9%
- 10 to 24.9%
- Less than 10%
- No current data available

Percent of total labor force employed in agriculture.

Source: *World Factbook*, CIA, 2021

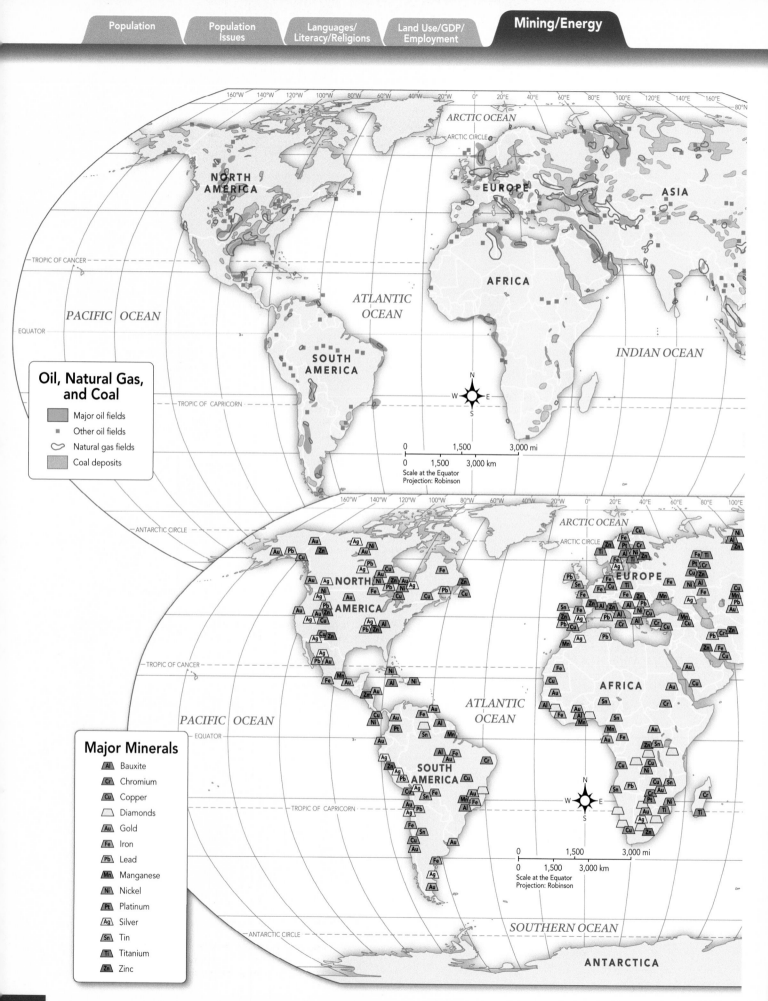

Oil, Natural Gas, and Coal

- Major oil fields
- Other oil fields
- Natural gas fields
- Coal deposits

Major Minerals

- Al Bauxite
- Cr Chromium
- Cu Copper
- ◇ Diamonds
- Au Gold
- Fe Iron
- Pb Lead
- Mn Manganese
- Ni Nickel
- Pt Platinum
- Ag Silver
- Sn Tin
- Ti Titanium
- Zn Zinc

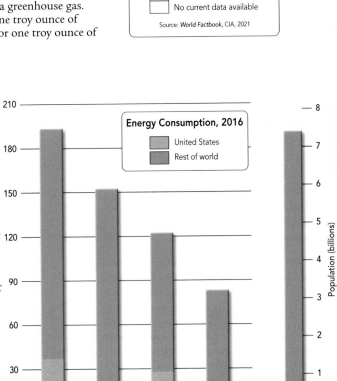

Electrical Energy Production

Billions of Kilowatt hours, 2016

- More than 1,000
- 500 to 999
- 100 to 499
- 50 to 99
- 1 to 49
- Less than 1
- No current data available

Source: *World Factbook*, CIA, 2021

Did You Know?

The most expensive precious metal in the world is rhodium. Mined primarily in South Africa, this silver-colored metal is highly reflective and resistant to corrosion. The most common use for rhodium is in the exhaust system of vehicles as it reduces the release of pollutants such as nitrous oxide—a greenhouse gas.

On April 1, 2021, the price for one troy ounce of rhodium was $26,700. The price for one troy ounce of gold on the same day was $1,716.

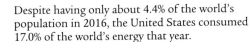

Source: U.S. Energy Information Administration, 2019

Energy Consumption, 2016
- United States
- Rest of world

Despite having only about 4.4% of the world's population in 2016, the United States consumed 17.0% of the world's energy that year.

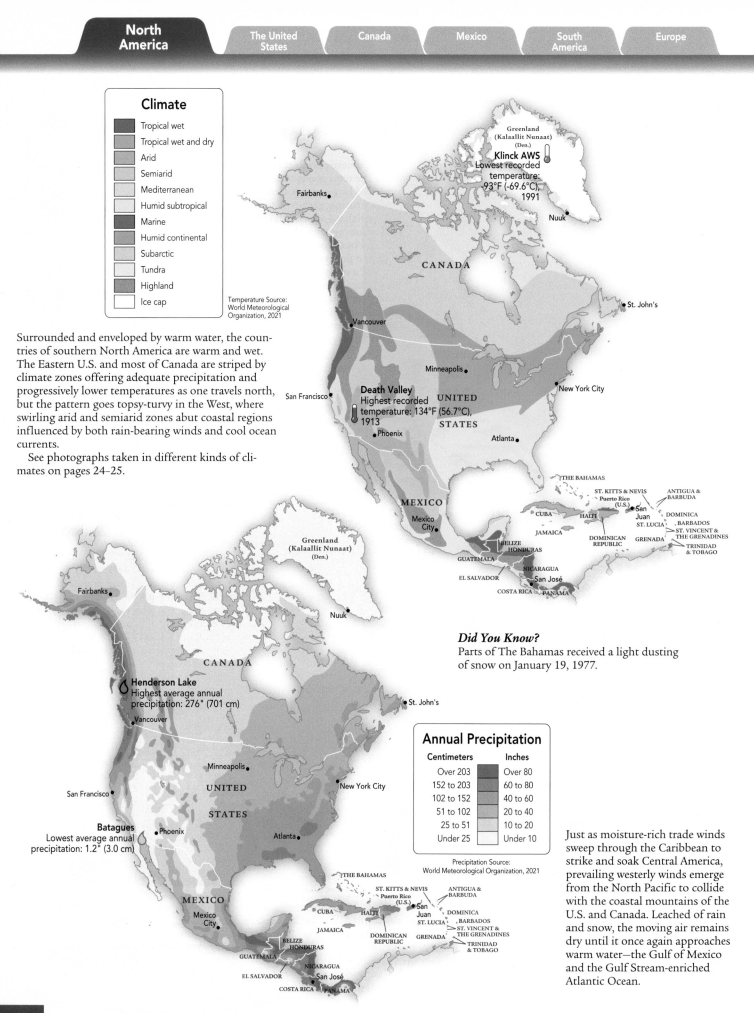

Climate

- Tropical wet
- Tropical wet and dry
- Arid
- Semiarid
- Mediterranean
- Humid subtropical
- Marine
- Humid continental
- Subarctic
- Tundra
- Highland
- Ice cap

Temperature Source:
World Meteorological
Organization, 2021

Klinck AWS
Lowest recorded temperature: -93°F (-69.6°C), 1991

Death Valley
Highest recorded temperature: 134°F (56.7°C), 1913

Surrounded and enveloped by warm water, the countries of southern North America are warm and wet. The Eastern U.S. and most of Canada are striped by climate zones offering adequate precipitation and progressively lower temperatures as one travels north, but the pattern goes topsy-turvy in the West, where swirling arid and semiarid zones abut coastal regions influenced by both rain-bearing winds and cool ocean currents.

See photographs taken in different kinds of climates on pages 24–25.

Henderson Lake
Highest average annual precipitation: 276" (701 cm)

Batagues
Lowest average annual precipitation: 1.2" (3.0 cm)

Annual Precipitation

Centimeters	Inches
Over 203	Over 80
152 to 203	60 to 80
102 to 152	40 to 60
51 to 102	20 to 40
25 to 51	10 to 20
Under 25	Under 10

Precipitation Source:
World Meteorological Organization, 2021

Did You Know?
Parts of The Bahamas received a light dusting of snow on January 19, 1977.

Just as moisture-rich trade winds sweep through the Caribbean to strike and soak Central America, prevailing westerly winds emerge from the North Pacific to collide with the coastal mountains of the U.S. and Canada. Leached of rain and snow, the moving air remains dry until it once again approaches warm water—the Gulf of Mexico and the Gulf Stream-enriched Atlantic Ocean.

Climate Graphs

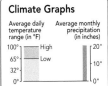

Average daily temperature range (in °F)

Average monthly precipitation (in inches)

High
Low

ATLANTA, USA

FAIRBANKS, USA

Temp. Range -21° to -1°

MEXICO CITY, Mexico

MINNEAPOLIS, USA

NUUK, Greenland

NEW YORK CITY, USA

PHOENIX, USA

ST. JOHN'S, Canada

SAN FRANCISCO, USA

SAN JOSÉ, Costa Rica

SAN JUAN, Puerto Rico

VANCOUVER, Canada

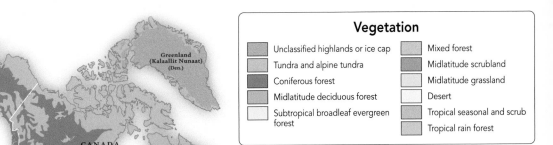

Vegetation

- Unclassified highlands or ice cap
- Tundra and alpine tundra
- Coniferous forest
- Midlatitude deciduous forest
- Subtropical broadleaf evergreen forest
- Mixed forest
- Midlatitude scrubland
- Midlatitude grassland
- Desert
- Tropical seasonal and scrub
- Tropical rain forest

Greenland (Kalaallit Nunaat) (Den.)

CANADA

UNITED STATES

MEXICO

THE BAHAMAS
ST. KITTS & NEVIS
Puerto Rico (U.S.)
ANTIGUA & BARBUDA
CUBA
HAITI
DOMINICA
JAMAICA
ST. LUCIA
BARBADOS
DOMINICAN REPUBLIC
GRENADA
ST. VINCENT & THE GRENADINES
BELIZE
HONDURAS
TRINIDAD & TOBAGO
GUATEMALA
NICARAGUA
EL SALVADOR
PANAMA
COSTA RICA

Deserts span the U.S./Mexico border, joining the tropical plant life of Central America and southern Mexico to the temperate and arctic vegetation of Canada and the U.S. Forest land predominates the continent north of Mexico, split by the arc of the Great Plains and interwoven with scrublands able to endure infrequent rainfall.

See photographs of different the kinds of vegetation on page 26–27.

Though Haiti has the highest per capita death rate from pollution in North America, at 137 per 100,000; the United States has the highest total number of premature deaths at almost 200,000 per year. The United Nations estimates that almost 9 million premature deaths occur annually due to the effects of pollution around the world.

Modern pollution, such as outdoor air pollution from industries and the burning of fossil fuels in vehicles, tends to occur in more affluent countries like the United States. Traditional pollution, such as indoor air pollution and water pollution from unsafe sanitation is typically found in more impoverished countries. While the effects from traditional pollution tend to improve as economies and standards of living improve, the resulting effects generated by modern pollution usually worsen.

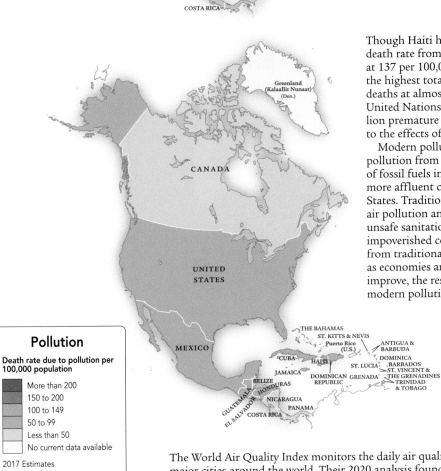

Greenland (Kalaallit Nunaat) (Den.)

CANADA

UNITED STATES

MEXICO

THE BAHAMAS
ST. KITTS & NEVIS
Puerto Rico (U.S.)
ANTIGUA & BARBUDA
CUBA
HAITI
DOMINICA
JAMAICA
ST. LUCIA
BARBADOS
DOMINICAN REPUBLIC
GRENADA
ST. VINCENT & THE GRENADINES
BELIZE
HONDURAS
TRINIDAD & TOBAGO
GUATEMALA
NICARAGUA
EL SALVADOR
PANAMA
COSTA RICA

Pollution

Death rate due to pollution per 100,000 population

- More than 200
- 150 to 200
- 100 to 149
- 50 to 99
- Less than 50
- No current data available

2017 Estimates

Air, water, lead, and occupational sources of pollution are included in the analysis.

Source: *Global Burden of Disease Study (GBD 2017)*, Institute for Health Metrics and Evaluation, published by the Global Alliance on Health and Pollution, 2019.

Did You Know?
The Ohio and Mississippi Rivers are considered to be the most polluted rivers in the United States.

The World Air Quality Index monitors the daily air quality in 380 major cities around the world. Their 2020 analysis found that Aguascalientes, Mexico had the worst air quality in North America, ranking 39th worst in the world. The same study found that Fresno, California had the worst air quality in the United States, with a world ranking of 224th.

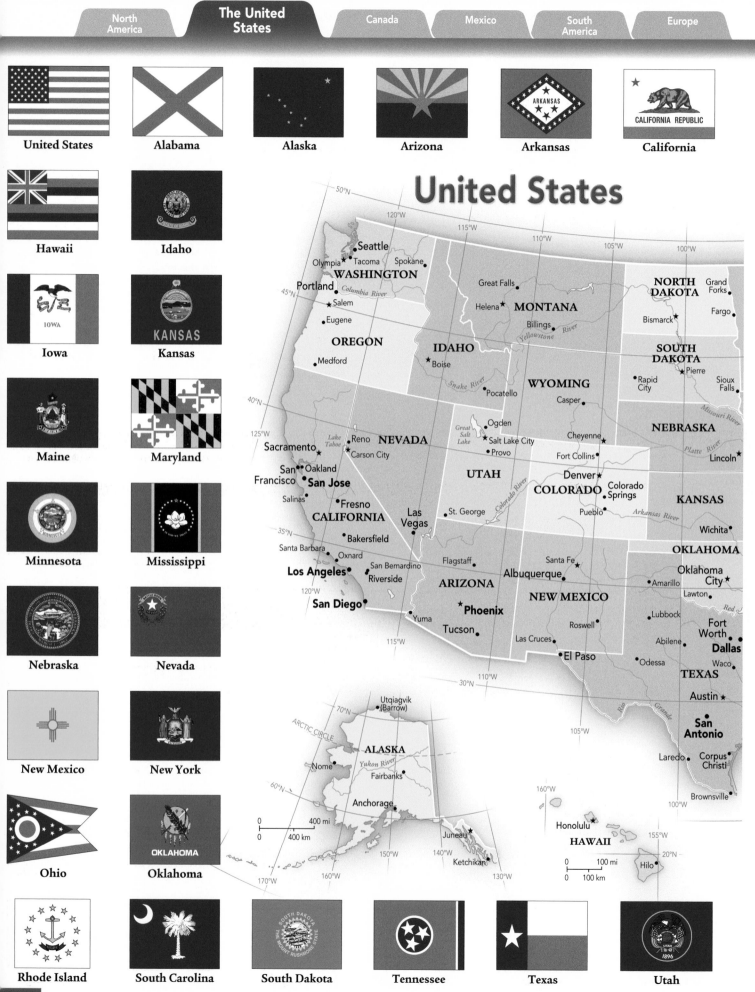

United States

Alabama

Alaska

Arizona

Arkansas

California

Hawaii

Idaho

Iowa

Kansas

Maine

Maryland

Minnesota

Mississippi

Nebraska

Nevada

New Mexico

New York

Ohio

Oklahoma

Rhode Island

South Carolina

South Dakota

Tennessee

Texas

Utah

United States

50

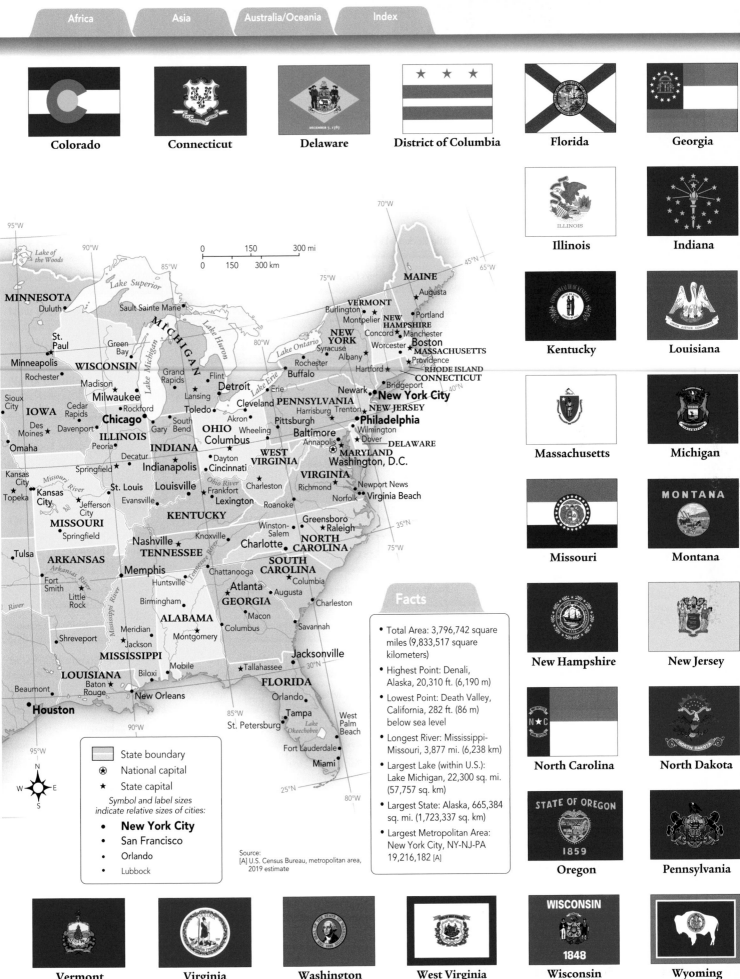

Colorado   Connecticut   Delaware   District of Columbia   Florida   Georgia

Illinois   Indiana

Kentucky   Louisiana

Massachusetts   Michigan

Missouri   Montana

New Hampshire   New Jersey

North Carolina   North Dakota

Oregon   Pennsylvania

Facts

- Total Area: 3,796,742 square miles (9,833,517 square kilometers)
- Highest Point: Denali, Alaska, 20,310 ft. (6,190 m)
- Lowest Point: Death Valley, California, 282 ft. (86 m) below sea level
- Longest River: Mississippi-Missouri, 3,877 mi. (6,238 km)
- Largest Lake (within U.S.): Lake Michigan, 22,300 sq. mi. (57,757 sq. km)
- Largest State: Alaska, 665,384 sq. mi. (1,723,337 sq. km)
- Largest Metropolitan Area: New York City, NY-NJ-PA 19,216,182 [A]

Source:
[A] U.S. Census Bureau, metropolitan area, 2019 estimate

Legend

State boundary
National capital
State capital

Symbol and label sizes indicate relative sizes of cities:

- **New York City**
- San Francisco
- Orlando
- Lubbock

Vermont   Virginia   Washington   West Virginia   Wisconsin   Wyoming

Vegetation

- Tundra and alpine tundra
- Coniferous forest
- Midlatitude deciduous forest
- Subtropical broadleaf evergreen forest
- Mixed forest
- Midlatitude scrubland
- Midlatitude grassland
- Desert
- Tropical rain forest

Coniferous forest

Desert

Midlatitude deciduous forest

Seattle

WASHINGTON

Portland

OREGON

MONTANA

Helena

NORTH DAKOTA

IDAHO

Boise

WYOMING

SOUTH DAKOTA

Reno

NEVADA

Salt Lake City

NEBRASKA

San Francisco

UTAH

Denver

COLORADO

KANSAS

CALIFORNIA

Los Angeles

ARIZONA

Phoenix

NEW MEXICO

OKLAHOMA

San Diego

Dallas

TEXAS

ALASKA

Anchorage

Honolulu

San Antonio

HAWAII

Midlatitude grassland

Midlatitude scrubland

Mixed forest

Subtropical broadleaf evergreen forest

Tropical rain forest

Tundra and alpine tundra

MINNESOTA

Lake Superior

MICHIGAN

Lake Huron

MAINE

VERMONT   •Portland

NEW HAMPSHIRE

Minneapolis•   WISCONSIN

Lake Michigan

Lake Ontario

Boston•   MASSACHUSETTS

•Buffalo   NEW YORK

RHODE ISLAND
CONNECTICUT

IOWA

Detroit•   *Lake Erie*

Chicago•

PENNSYLVANIA

•New York City   NEW JERSEY

Philadelphia•

ILLINOIS   INDIANA

OHIO

Baltimore•   — DELAWARE

Indianapolis•

Washington, D.C.•   — MARYLAND

WEST VIRGINIA

VIRGINIA

St. Louis•

Lexington•

MISSOURI

KENTUCKY

Raleigh•

Nashville•   NORTH CAROLINA

TENNESSEE

ARKANSAS

SOUTH CAROLINA

Atlanta•

MISSISSIPPI   GEORGIA

ALABAMA

LOUISIANA   FLORIDA

Houston•   •New Orleans

•Miami

North America

The United States

Canada

Mexico

South America

Europe

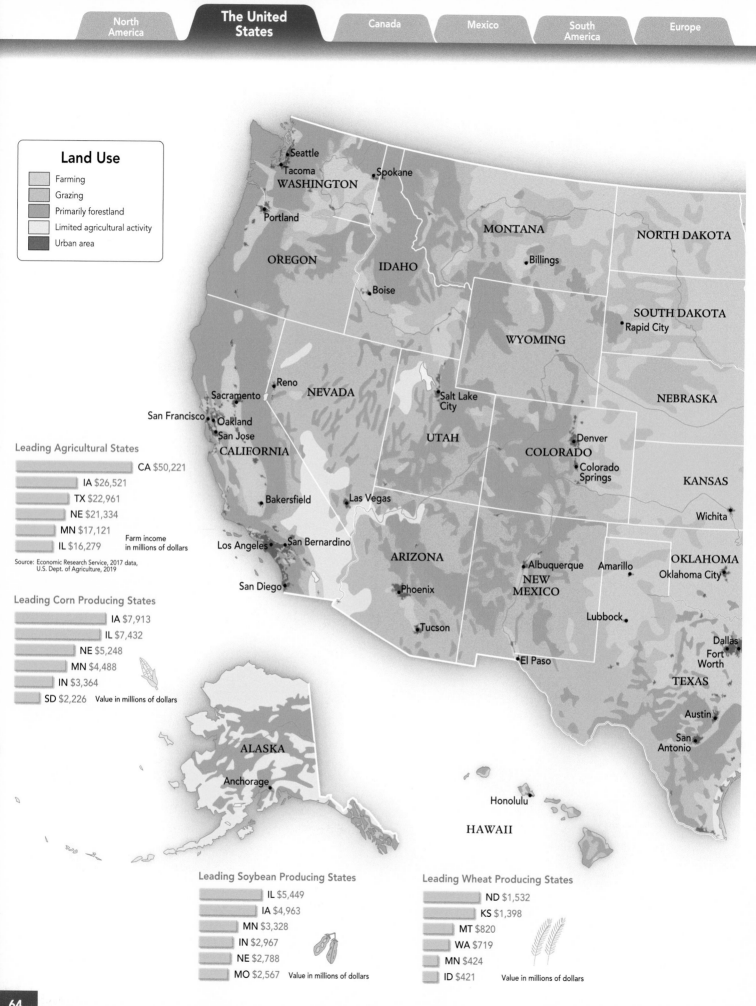

Land Use

- Farming
- Grazing
- Primarily forestland
- Limited agricultural activity
- Urban area

Leading Agricultural States

CA	$50,221
IA	$26,521
TX	$22,961
NE	$21,334
MN	$17,121
IL	$16,279

Farm income in millions of dollars

Source: Economic Research Service, 2017 data, U.S. Dept. of Agriculture, 2019

Leading Corn Producing States

IA	$7,913
IL	$7,432
NE	$5,248
MN	$4,488
IN	$3,364
SD	$2,226

Value in millions of dollars

Leading Soybean Producing States

IL	$5,449
IA	$4,963
MN	$3,328
IN	$2,967
NE	$2,788
MO	$2,567

Value in millions of dollars

Leading Wheat Producing States

ND	$1,532
KS	$1,398
MT	$820
WA	$719
MN	$424
ID	$421

Value in millions of dollars

MAINE

MINNESOTA

WISCONSIN

MICHIGAN

Lake Superior

Lake Michigan

Lake Huron

Lake Erie

Lake Ontario

VT

NH

St. Paul
Minneapolis

Green Bay

Grand Rapids

Saginaw

Flint

Milwaukee

Rockford

Detroit

IOWA

Des Moines

Chicago

South Bend

Toledo

Cleveland

Akron

Fort Wayne

OHIO

Columbus

Dayton

Cincinnati

Syracuse   Albany

Rochester   Springfield

Buffalo   NEW YORK   Hartford

Scranton

PENNSYLVANIA

Harrisburg

Pittsburgh

Boston   MASSACHUSETTS

Providence

RHODE ISLAND

CONNECTICUT

New York City

NEW JERSEY
Trenton

Philadelphia

Baltimore

Washington, D.C.

DELAWARE

MARYLAND

Omaha

Peoria

INDIANA

Indianapolis

ILLINOIS

Kansas City   St. Louis

Evansville

Louisville

Charleston

WEST VIRGINIA

Lexington

KENTUCKY

Richmond

VIRGINIA

Norfolk

MISSOURI

Tulsa

ARKANSAS

Little Rock

Nashville

TENNESSEE

Memphis

Huntsville

Knoxville

Greensboro   Raleigh

NORTH CAROLINA

Charlotte

Greenville

SOUTH CAROLINA

Columbia

Charleston

Birmingham

Atlanta

GEORGIA

MISSISSIPPI   ALABAMA

Jackson

Savannah

LOUISIANA

Mobile

Jacksonville

Beaumont   Baton Rouge

New Orleans

FLORIDA

Houston

Orlando

Tampa

St. Petersburg

West Palm Beach

Miami

Commodity Source: Economic Research Service, 2017 data, U.S. Dept. of Agriculture, 2019

Leading Cattle Producing States

NE $11,165
TX $8,828
KS $8,265
IA $4,059
CO $3,445
OK $3,259   Value in millions of dollars

Leading Hog Producing States

IA $7,119
MN $2,612
NC $2,344
IL $1,283
IN $1,227
OK $918   Value in millions of dollars

Leading Poultry Producing States

GA $4,972
NC $4,776
AR $4,631
AL $3,705
MS $2,794
TX $2,678   Value in millions of dollars

U.S. Percentage of World Production

	United States	World
Corn	34.3%	
Cotton	16.1%	
Rice	1.5%	
Soybean	33.5%	
Wheat	8.3%	

Source: World Agricultural Production; 2016/2017 data, Foreign Agricultural Service, U.S. Dept. of Agriculture, 2019

Leading Vegetable Producing States

CA $8,410
AZ $1,649
WA $1,263
FL $1,227
ID $1,048
ND $639   Value in millions of dollars

Leading Milk Producing States

CA $6,562
WI $5,444
NY $2,704
ID $2,510
TX $2,213
PA $2,021   Value in millions of dollars

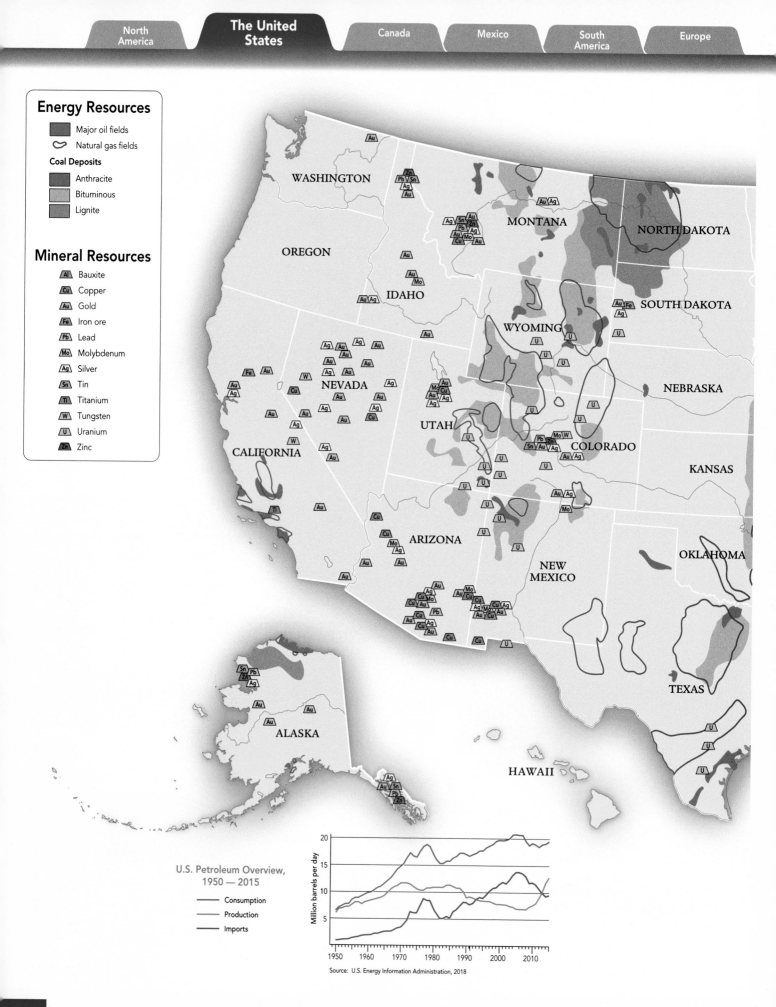

Energy Resources

- Major oil fields
- Natural gas fields

Coal Deposits
- Anthracite
- Bituminous
- Lignite

Mineral Resources

Al	Bauxite
Cu	Copper
Au	Gold
Fe	Iron ore
Pb	Lead
Mo	Molybdenum
Ag	Silver
Sn	Tin
Ti	Titanium
W	Tungsten
U	Uranium
Zn	Zinc

WASHINGTON
OREGON
MONTANA
NORTH DAKOTA
IDAHO
SOUTH DAKOTA
WYOMING
NEBRASKA
NEVADA
UTAH
COLORADO
KANSAS
CALIFORNIA
ARIZONA
NEW MEXICO
OKLAHOMA
TEXAS
ALASKA
HAWAII

U.S. Petroleum Overview, 1950 — 2015

- Consumption
- Production
- Imports

Million barrels per day

20
15
10
5

1950   1960   1970   1980   1990   2000   2010

Source: U.S. Energy Information Administration, 2018

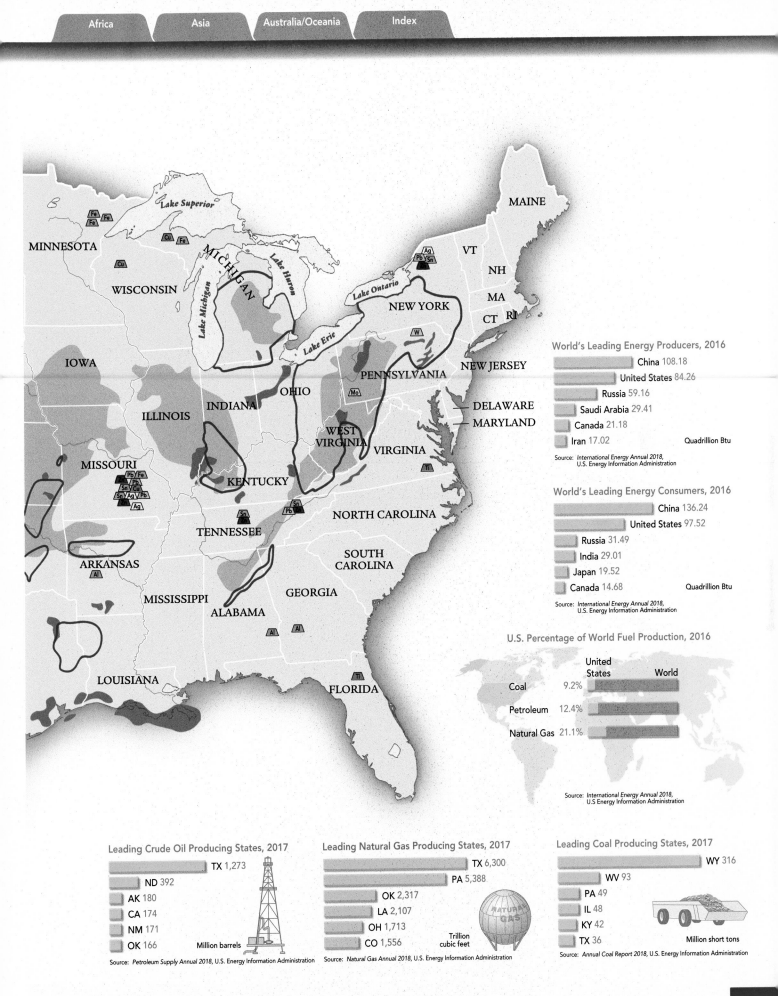

MAINE

MINNESOTA

VT

NH

WISCONSIN

MA

CT   RI

NEW YORK

Lake Superior

Fe
Fe   Fe

Cu   Fe

Cu

MICHIGAN

Lake Huron

Lake Michigan

Lake Ontario

Lake Erie

W

Ag
Pb Sn
Zn

IOWA

PENNSYLVANIA

NEW JERSEY

OHIO

Mo

DELAWARE

MARYLAND

INDIANA

ILLINOIS

WEST
VIRGINIA

VIRGINIA

MISSOURI

Pb Fe
V   Pb
Sn Cu
Zn Ag V Pb
Ag

Ti

KENTUCKY

Sn
Pb Zn

Sn
Zn

NORTH CAROLINA

TENNESSEE

ARKANSAS
Al

SOUTH
CAROLINA

GEORGIA

MISSISSIPPI

ALABAMA

Al   Al

LOUISIANA

FLORIDA

Ti

World's Leading Energy Producers, 2016

China 108.18
United States 84.26
Russia 59.16
Saudi Arabia 29.41
Canada 21.18
Iran 17.02   Quadrillion Btu

Source: *International Energy Annual 2018,*
U.S. Energy Information Administration

World's Leading Energy Consumers, 2016

China 136.24
United States 97.52
Russia 31.49
India 29.01
Japan 19.52
Canada 14.68   Quadrillion Btu

Source: *International Energy Annual 2018,*
U.S. Energy Information Administration

U.S. Percentage of World Fuel Production, 2016

		United States	World
Coal	9.2%		
Petroleum	12.4%		
Natural Gas	21.1%		

Source: *International Energy Annual 2018,*
U.S Energy Information Administration

Leading Crude Oil Producing States, 2017

TX 1,273
ND 392
AK 180
CA 174
NM 171
OK 166   Million barrels

Source: *Petroleum Supply Annual 2018,* U.S. Energy Information Administration

Leading Natural Gas Producing States, 2017

TX 6,300
PA 5,388
OK 2,317
LA 2,107
OH 1,713
CO 1,556   Trillion
                  cubic feet

Source: *Natural Gas Annual 2018,* U.S. Energy Information Administration

Leading Coal Producing States, 2017

WY 316
WV 93
PA 49
IL 48
KY 42
TX 36   Million short tons

Source: *Annual Coal Report 2018,* U.S. Energy Information Administration

67

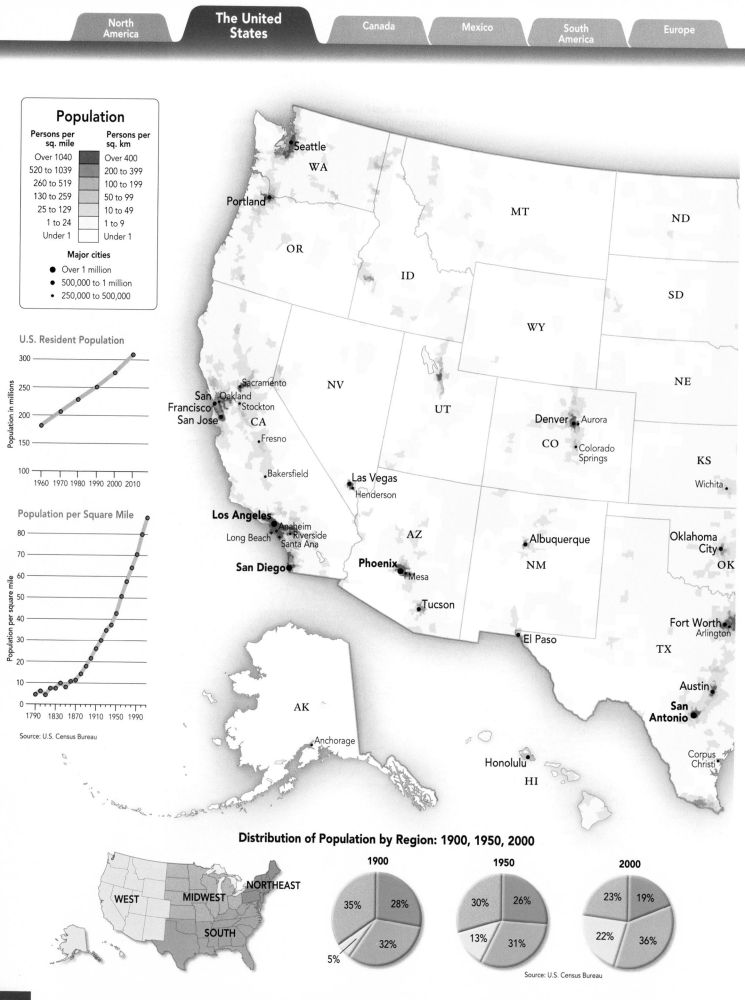

Population

Persons per sq. mile | **Persons per sq. km**

Persons per sq. mile	Persons per sq. km
Over 1040	Over 400
520 to 1039	200 to 399
260 to 519	100 to 199
130 to 259	50 to 99
25 to 129	10 to 49
1 to 24	1 to 9
Under 1	Under 1

Major cities
- Over 1 million
- 500,000 to 1 million
- 250,000 to 500,000

U.S. Resident Population

Population in millions

1960 1970 1980 1990 2000 2010

Population per Square Mile

Population per square mile

1790 1830 1870 1910 1950 1990

Source: U.S. Census Bureau

Distribution of Population by Region: 1900, 1950, 2000

WEST | MIDWEST | NORTHEAST | SOUTH

1900
35% | 28% | 32% | 5%

1950
30% | 26% | 13% | 31%

2000
23% | 19% | 22% | 36%

Source: U.S. Census Bureau

70

Minneapolis • •St. Paul

MN

WI

MI

ME

VT

NH

Boston

NY

MA

CT RI

Milwaukee •

Detroit •

Buffalo •

Newark •

New York City •

IA

Chicago •

Toledo •

Cleveland •

PA

NJ

Philadelphia •

Omaha •

Fort Wayne •

OH

Pittsburgh •

IL

IN

Columbus •

MD Baltimore •

DE

Indianapolis •

Cincinnati •

Washington, D.C. •

Kansas City •

WV

St. Louis •

Louisville •

Lexington •

VA

Virginia Beach •

MO

KY

Tulsa •

Nashville •

Greensboro • NC Raleigh •

TN

Charlotte •

AR

Memphis •

SC

Atlanta •

Plano •

MS

AL

GA

Dallas

LA

Jacksonville •

FL

Houston

New Orleans •

Tampa •

Miami •

U.S. Center of Population

The center of U.S. population is the center of "population gravity," or the point on which the U. S. would balance if it were a rigid plane, assuming all individuals weigh the same and exert influence proportional to their distance from a central point.

25 Largest Cities, 2010

	City	Population 2010	2000	Change
1	New York	8,175,133	8,008,278	2.08%
2	Los Angeles	3,792,621	3,694,820	2.65%
3	Chicago	2,695,598	2,896,016	-6.92%
4	Houston	2,099,451	1,953,631	7.46%
5	Philadelphia	1,526,006	1,517,550	0.56%
6	Phoenix	1,445,632	1,321,045	9.43%
7	San Antonio	1,327,407	1,144,646	15.97%
8	San Diego	1,307,402	1,223,400	6.87%
9	Dallas	1,197,816	1,188,580	0.78%
10	San Jose	945,942	894,943	5.70%
11	Jacksonville	821,784	735,617	11.71%
12	Indianapolis	820,445	791,926	3.60%
13	San Francisco	805,235	776,733	3.67%
14	Austin	790,390	656,562	20.38%
15	Columbus	787,033	711,470	10.62%
16	Fort Worth	741,206	534,694	38.62%
17	Charlotte	731,424	540,828	35.24%
18	Detroit	713,777	951,270	-24.97%
19	El Paso	649,121	563,662	15.16%
20	Memphis	646,889	650,100	-0.49%
21	Baltimore	620,961	651,154	-4.64%
22	Boston	617,594	589,141	4.83%
23	Seattle	608,660	563,374	8.04%
24	Washington	601,723	572,059	5.19%
25	Nashville	601,222	569,891	5.50%

Source: U.S. Census Bureau

Source: U.S. Census Bureau

United States Population Estimates (in millions)

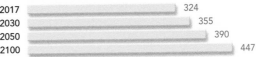

2017	324
2030	355
2050	390
2100	447

Source: United Nations, Department of Economic & Social Affairs, Population Division, *World Population Prospects, The 2017 Revision*

The population of the United States stood at 308.7 million in the 2010 census and at 281.4 million in the 2000 census.

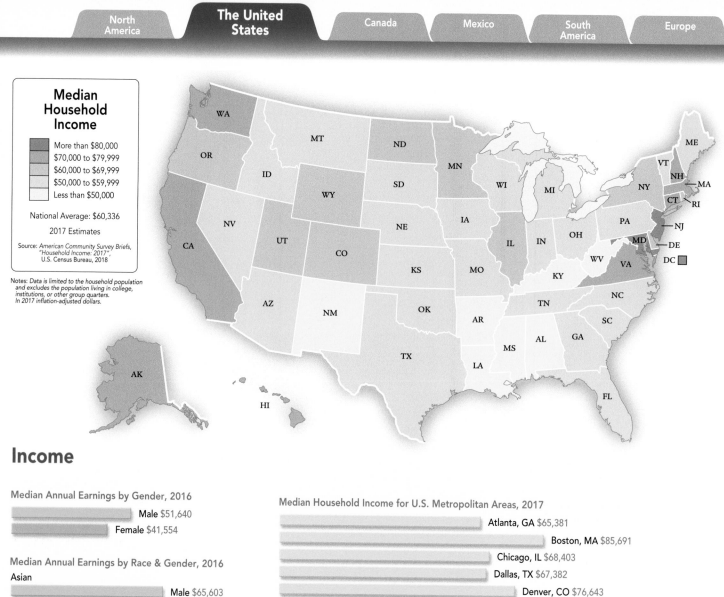

Median Household Income

- More than $80,000
- $70,000 to $79,999
- $60,000 to $69,999
- $50,000 to $59,999
- Less than $50,000

National Average: $60,336

2017 Estimates

Source: American Community Survey Briefs, "Household Income: 2017", U.S. Census Bureau, 2018

Notes: Data is limited to the household population and excludes the population living in college, institutions, or other group quarters. In 2017 inflation-adjusted dollars.

Income

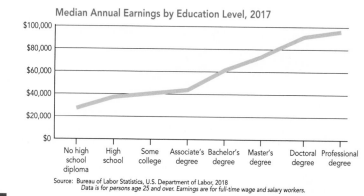

Median Annual Earnings by Gender, 2016

Male $51,640
Female $41,554

Median Annual Earnings by Race & Gender, 2016

Asian
Male $65,603
Female $50,615

White (not Hispanic)
Male $57,925
Female $45,741

Black
Male $41,293
Female $36,227

Hispanic
Male $37,354
Female $31,522

Source: Women's Bureau, U.S. Department of Labor, 2017

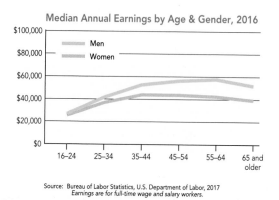

Median Household Income for U.S. Metropolitan Areas, 2017

Atlanta, GA $65,381
Boston, MA $85,691
Chicago, IL $68,403
Dallas, TX $67,382
Denver, CO $76,643
Houston, TX $63,802
Los Angeles, CA $69,992
New York, NY $75,368
Philadelphia, PA $68,572
Phoenix, AZ $61,506
San Diego, CA $76,207
San Francisco, CA $101,714
Seattle, WA $82,133
Washington, DC $99,669

Source: American Community Survey Briefs, "Household Income: 2017", U.S. Census Bureau, 2018

Median Annual Earnings by Education Level, 2017

(x-axis: No high school diploma, High school, Some college, Associate's degree, Bachelor's degree, Master's degree, Doctoral degree, Professional degree)

Source: Bureau of Labor Statistics, U.S. Department of Labor, 2018
Data is for persons age 25 and over. Earnings are for full-time wage and salary workers.

Median Annual Earnings by Age & Gender, 2016

Men
Women

(x-axis: 16–24, 25–34, 35–44, 45–54, 55–64, 65 and older)

Source: Bureau of Labor Statistics, U.S. Department of Labor, 2017
Earnings are for full-time wage and salary workers.

Poverty

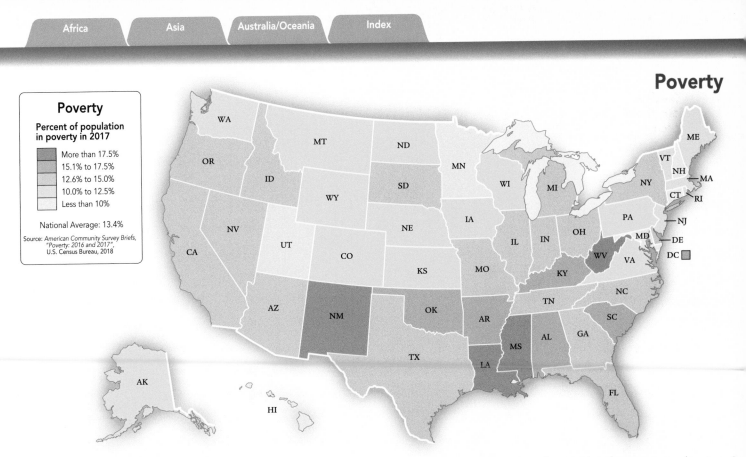

Poverty

Percent of population in poverty in 2017

- More than 17.5%
- 15.1% to 17.5%
- 12.6% to 15.0%
- 10.0% to 12.5%
- Less than 10%

National Average: 13.4%

Source: *American Community Survey Briefs, "Poverty: 2016 and 2017"*, U.S. Census Bureau, 2018

Poverty is calculated by comparing annual income to a set of dollar values that vary by family size, number of children, and the age of the householder; the amount calculated is called a poverty threshold. Should a family's pre-tax income fall below the dollar value of their threshold, the family is considered to be in poverty.

2017 marked the fifth consecutive year that the poverty rate in the United States had declined, since a peak of 15.9% in 2012. Even with that improvement, however, over 42 million Americans still lived below their poverty threshold in 2017.

Unemployment

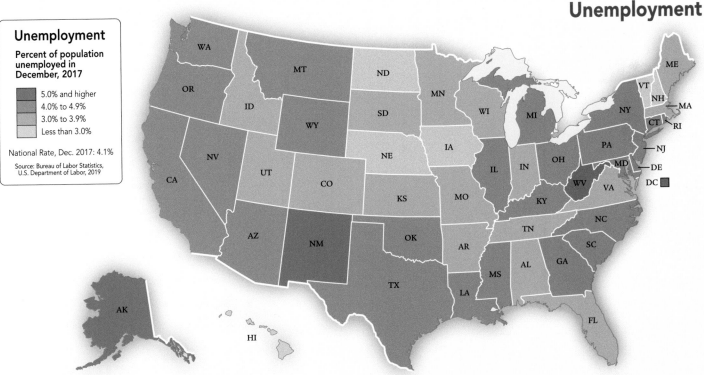

Unemployment

Percent of population unemployed in December, 2017

- 5.0% and higher
- 4.0% to 4.9%
- 3.0% to 3.9%
- Less than 3.0%

National Rate, Dec. 2017: 4.1%

Source: Bureau of Labor Statistics, U.S. Department of Labor, 2019

An area's **unemployment rate** equals the number of unemployed persons divided by the labor force. The labor force is the sum of unemployed and employed persons. Unemployment means the loss of wages and purchasing power for an individual or family. This loss can trigger joblessness for other workers.

Unemployment is a key economic indicator used by all levels of government to track the health of the economy. In December 2017, there were roughly 6.6 million people unemployed among the 160.6 million Americans in the labor force.

The highest rate of unemployment in the United States was 24.9% in 1933, during the Great Depression.

Canada

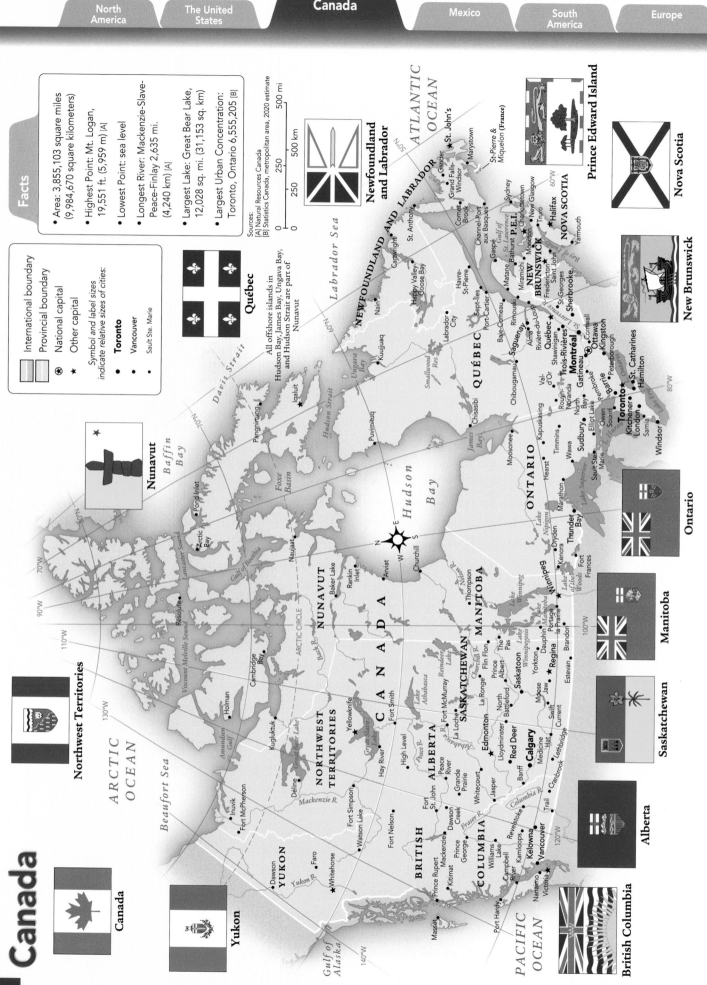

Canada

Yukon

Northwest Territories

British Columbia

Alberta

Saskatchewan

Manitoba

Ontario

Nunavut

Québec

Newfoundland and Labrador

New Brunswick

Prince Edward Island

Nova Scotia

Facts

- Area: 3,855,103 square miles (9,984,670 square kilometers)
- Highest Point: Mt. Logan, 19,551 ft. (5,959 m) [A]
- Lowest Point: sea level
- Longest River: Mackenzie-Slave-Peace-Finlay 2,635 mi. (4,240 km) [A]
- Largest Lake: Great Bear Lake, 12,028 sq. mi. (31,153 sq. km)
- Largest Urban Concentration: Toronto, Ontario 6,555,205 [B]

Sources:
[A] Natural Resources Canada
[B] Statistics Canada, metropolitan area, 2020 estimate

All offshore islands in Hudson Bay, James Bay, Ungava Bay, and Hudson Strait are part of Nunavut

International boundary
Provincial boundary
★ National capital
★ Other capital

Symbol and label sizes indicate relative sizes of cities:

Toronto
Vancouver
• Sault Ste. Marie

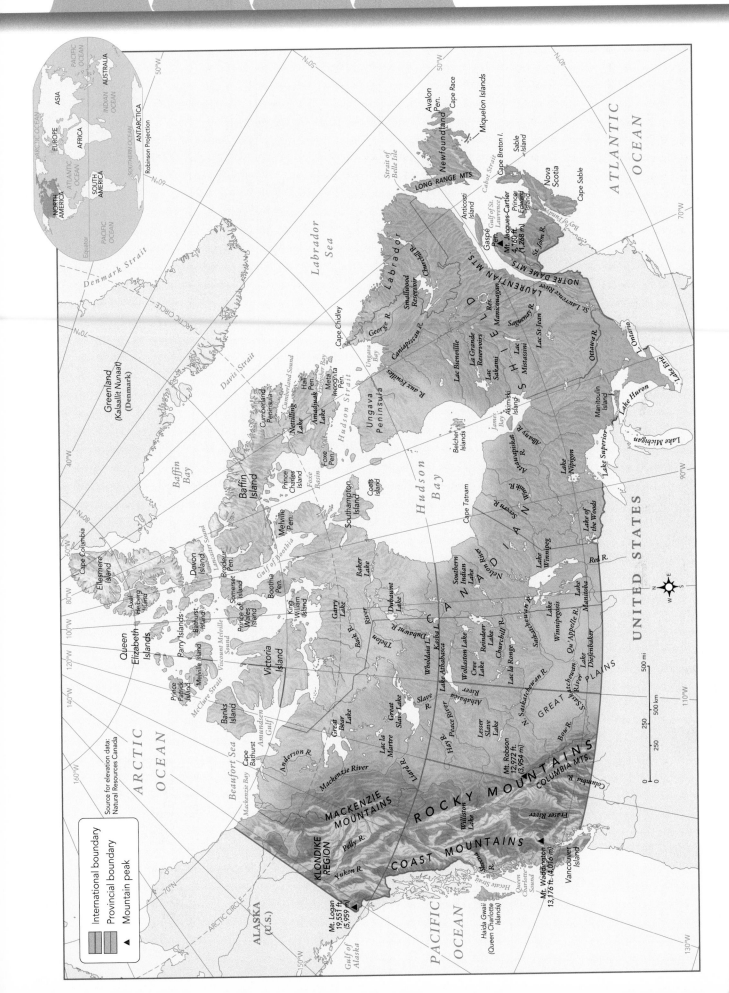

Mexico

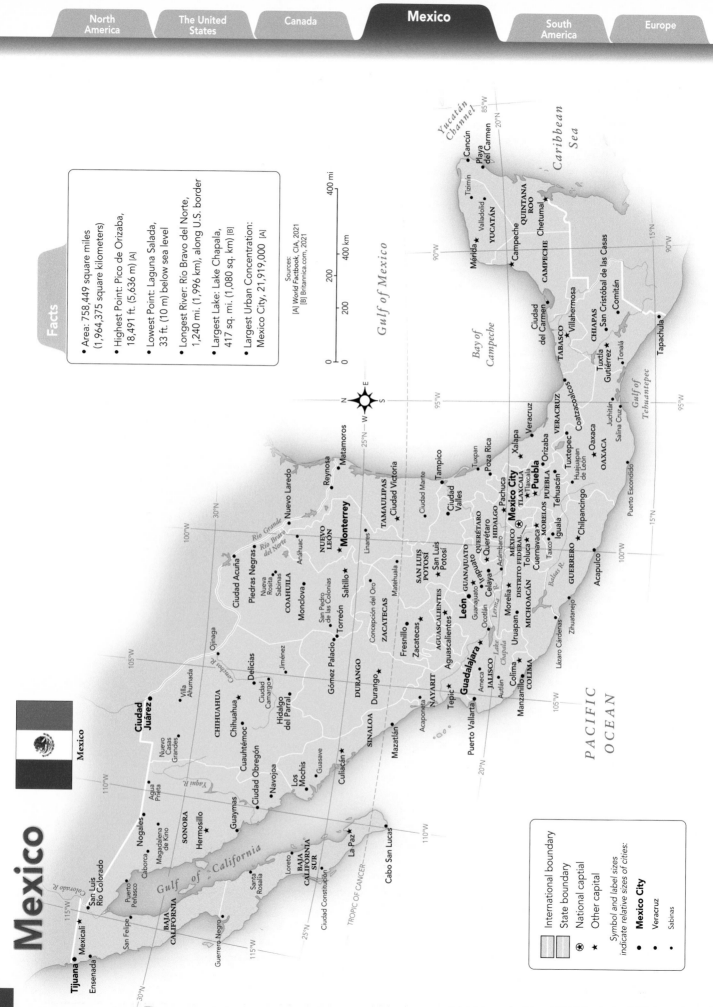

Mexico

Facts

- Area: 758,449 square miles (1,964,375 square kilometers)
- Highest Point: Pico de Orizaba, 18,491 ft. (5,636 m) [A]
- Lowest Point: Laguna Salada, 33 ft. (10 m) below sea level
- Longest River: Río Bravo del Norte, 1,240 mi. (1,996 km), along U.S. border
- Largest Lake: Lake Chapala, 417 sq. mi. (1,080 sq. km) [B]
- Largest Urban Concentration: Mexico City, 21,919,000 [A]

Sources:
[A] World Factbook, CIA, 2021
[B] Britannica.com, 2021

International boundary
State boundary
National capital
Other capital
Symbol and label sizes indicate relative sizes of cities:

Mexico City
Veracruz
Sabinas

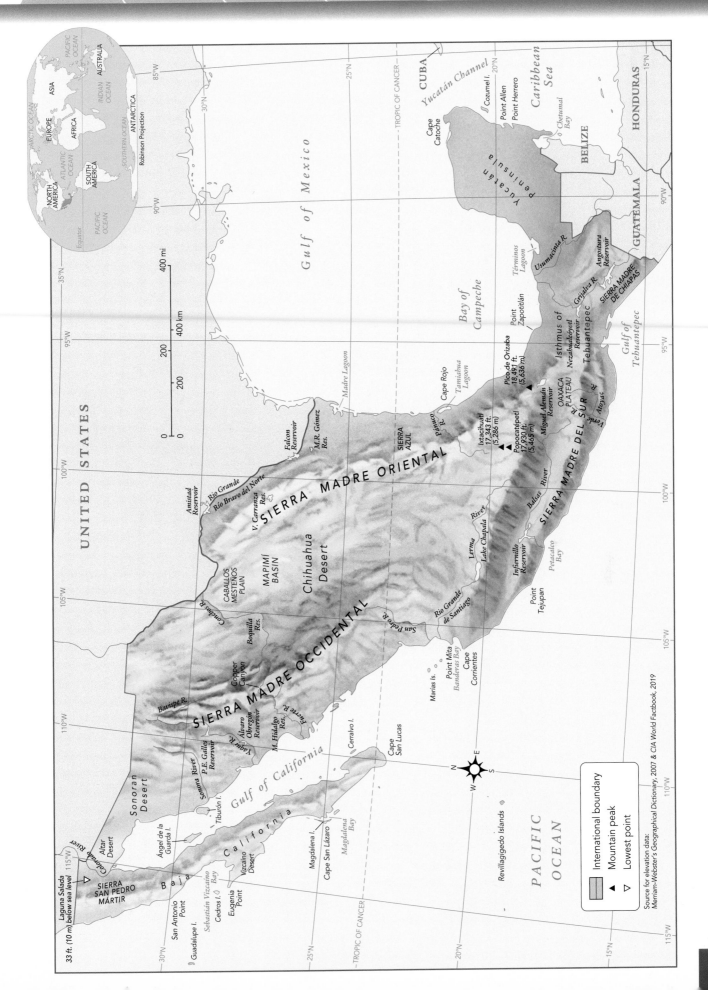

PACIFIC OCEAN
EUROPE
ASIA
ARCTIC OCEAN
NORTH AMERICA
ATLANTIC OCEAN
AFRICA
INDIAN OCEAN
AUSTRALIA
SOUTH AMERICA
PACIFIC OCEAN
ANTARCTICA
SOUTHERN OCEAN
Equator
Robinson Projection

UNITED STATES

Gulf of Mexico

TROPIC OF CANCER

CUBA

Yucatán Channel

Cozumel I.
Point Allen
Point Herrero

Caribbean Sea

Cape Catoche

Chetumal Bay

BELIZE

Yucatán Peninsula

HONDURAS

GUATEMALA

Términos Lagoon

Usumacinta R.

Angostura Reservoir

SIERRA MADRE DE CHIAPAS

Bay of Campeche

Point Zapotitlán

Grijalva R.

Gulf of Tehuantepec

Isthmus of Tehuantepec

Nezahualcóyotl Reservoir

Cape Rojo

Tamiahua Lagoon

Pánuco R.

Pico de Orizaba 18,491 ft. (5,636 m)

Miguel Alemán Reservoir

OAXACA PLATEAU

Verde

Atoyac

Madre Lagoon

SIERRA AZUL

Ixtacihuatl 17,343 ft. (5,286 m)

Popocatépetl 17,930 ft. (5,465 m)

SIERRA MADRE DEL SUR

Falcon Reservoir

M.R. Gómez Res.

SIERRA MADRE ORIENTAL

Balsas River

Amistad Reservoir

Río Grande
Río Bravo del Norte

V. Carranza Res.

Lerma

Lake Chapala

River

Infiernillo Reservoir

Petacalco Bay

400 mi
400 km
200
200
0
0

Conchos R.

CABALLOS MESTEÑOS PLAIN

MAPIMÍ BASIN

Chihuahua Desert

Río Grande de Santiago

San Pedro R.

Point Tejupan

Boquilla Res.

SIERRA MADRE OCCIDENTAL

Copper Canyon

Bavispe R.

Alvaro Obregón Reservoir

Fuerte R.

M. Hidalgo Res.

Cerralvo I.

Cape San Lucas

Marías Is.

Point Mita
Banderas Bay

Cape Corrientes

PACIFIC OCEAN

Revillagigedo Islands

N
E
W
S

Sonora River

P.E. Gallés Reservoir

Yaqui R.

Sonoran Desert

Tiburón I.

Gulf of California

Angel de la Guarda I.

Cedros I.

Sebastián Vizcaíno Bay

Vizcaíno Desert

Magdalena I.

Cape San Lázaro

Magdalena Bay

Baja California

Altar Desert

Colorado River

Laguna Salada
33 ft. (10 m) below sea level

SIERRA SAN PEDRO MÁRTIR

San Antonio Point

Eugenia Point

Guadalupe I.

TROPIC OF CANCER

International boundary
Mountain peak
Lowest point

Source for elevation data:
Merriam-Webster's Geographical Dictionary, 2007 & CIA World Factbook, 2019

South America

Caribbean Sea

Legend:
- International boundary
- ⊛ National capital
- ★ Other capital

Symbol and label sizes indicate relative sizes of cities:
- **Rio de Janeiro**
- Maturín
- Punta Arenas

VENEZUELA
- Barranquilla
- Cartagena
- Maracaibo
- Valencia
- Caracas
- Cumaná
- Barquisimeto
- Maturín
- Sincelejo
- Valera
- Maracay
- Montería
- Mérida
- Ciudad Bolívar
- Cúcuta
- San Cristóbal
- Ciudad Guayana
- **Medellín**
- Bucaramanga
- Barrancabermeja
- Manizales
- Puerto Ayacucho
- Pereira
- **Bogotá**
- Armenia
- Ibagué
- Buenaventura
- **Cali**
- **COLOMBIA**
- Neiva
- Pasto
- Florencia
- Esmeraldas
- **Quito**
- **ECUADOR**
- **Guayaquil**
- Cuenca
- Machala
- Tumbes
- Iquitos
- Piura
- **PERU**
- Chiclayo
- Cajamarca
- Trujillo
- Pucallpa
- Chimbote
- Huánuco
- **Callao**
- Huancayo
- **Lima**
- Ayacucho
- Ica
- Cuzco
- **Arequipa**
- Tacna
- Arica

GUYANA
- Georgetown
- Paramaribo
- Cayenne
- **SURINAME**
- **FRENCH GUIANA (France)**
- Boa Vista
- Macapá

BRAZIL
- **Manaus**
- Santarém
- **Belém**
- **São Luís**
- Parnaíba
- Marabá
- Imperatriz
- **Fortaleza**
- Teresina
- Floriano
- Juàzeiro do Norte
- Natal
- Campina Grande
- João Pessoa
- Petrolina
- **Recife**
- Gurupi
- **Maceió**
- Feira de Santana
- Aracaju
- **Salvador**
- Ilhéus
- Vitória da Conquista
- Montes Claros
- **Goiânia**
- **Brasília**
- Jataí
- **Uberlândia**
- Governador Valadares
- Cuiabá
- Corumbá
- **Belo Horizonte**
- Campo Grande
- São José do Rio Prêto
- **Vitória**
- Dourados
- Bauru
- Ribeirão Prêto
- Volta Redonda
- **Campinas**
- Londrina
- **São Paulo**
- Santos
- Niterói
- **Rio de Janeiro**
- Foz do Iguaçu
- **Curitiba**
- Joinville
- Florianópolis
- Passo Fundo

BOLIVIA
- Benjamin Constant
- Cruzeiro do Sul
- Rio Branco
- Pôrto Velho
- Guajará-Mirim
- Riberalta
- Trinidad
- Puerto Maldonado
- Lake Titicaca
- **La Paz**
- Cochabamba
- **Santa Cruz**
- Oruro
- Lake Poopó
- Potosí
- Sucre
- Tarija

PARAGUAY
- Calama
- Iquique
- Antofagasta
- Salta
- San Salvador de Jujuy
- Concepción
- **Asunción**
- Ciudad del Este
- San Miguel de Tucumán
- Encarnación
- Copiapó
- Resistencia
- Corrientes
- Catamarca
- Santiago del Estero
- Reconquista
- La Rioja

CHILE
- La Serena
- **Córdoba**
- Santa Fe
- Santa Maria
- **Porto Alegre**
- Rancagua
- **Mendoza**
- **Rosario**
- Paraná
- Rivera
- Pelotas
- Valparaíso
- **Santiago**
- Río Cuarto
- **Buenos Aires**
- Salto
- Melo
- **URUGUAY**
- Talca
- La Plata
- **Montevideo**
- Chillán
- Santa Rosa
- **ARGENTINA**
- Mar del Plata
- Concepción
- Temuco
- Neuquén
- Bahía Blanca
- Necochea
- Valdivia
- San Carlos de Bariloche
- Viedma
- Puerto Montt
- Esquel
- Rawson
- Comodoro Rivadavia
- Río Gallegos
- Stanley
- **Falkland Islands (U.K.) (Islas Malvinas)**
- Punta Arenas
- Ushuaia

Islands:
- **Galápagos Islands (Ecuador)**
- San Ambrosio Island (Chile)
- San Félix Island (Chile)
- Juan Fernández Islands (Chile)

Oceans:
- PACIFIC OCEAN
- ATLANTIC OCEAN

Rivers:
- Orinoco R.
- Río Negro
- Amazon (Solimões) R.
- Tapajós R.
- Xingú R.
- Tocantins R.
- São Francisco R.
- Marañón R.
- Ucayali R.
- Juruá R.
- Purus R.
- Madeira R.
- Guaporé R.
- Beni R.
- Araguaia R.
- Grande R.
- Paraná R.
- Paraguay R.
- Pilcomayo R.
- Uruguay R.
- Río de la Plata

Scale:
0 — 300 — 600 mi
0 — 300 — 600 km

N W E S (compass)

Sources and notes:
[A] *World Almanac*, 2019
[B] *World Factbook*, CIA, 2021

Facts

- **Area:** 6,886,332 square miles (17,783,718 square kilometers) [A]
- **Highest Point:** Mt. Aconcagua, Argentina, 22,831 ft (6,959 m) [A]
- **Lowest Point:** Laguna del Carbón, Argentina, 344 ft (105 m) below sea level [B]
- **Longest River:** Amazon, 3,900 mi (6,276 km) [A]
- **Largest Lake:** Lake Maracaibo, Venezuela, 5,217 sq. mi (13,512 sq. km) [A]
- **Largest Country:** Brazil, 3,287,957 sq. mi (8,515,770 sq. km) (slightly smaller than the United States) [B]
- **Largest Urban Concentration:** São Paulo, Brazil, 21,650,000 (2018 estimate) [A]

ARCTIC OCEAN
NORTH AMERICA EUROPE ASIA
ATLANTIC OCEAN
Equator
PACIFIC OCEAN AFRICA
SOUTH AMERICA INDIAN OCEAN AUSTRALIA
SOUTHERN OCEAN
ANTARCTICA
Robinson Projection

NORTH AMERICA

Caribbean Sea

Gulf of Panama

Galápagos Islands

EQUATOR

Gulf of Guayaquil
Pariñas Pt.

PACIFIC OCEAN

Lake Maracaibo
LLANOS
Orinoco River
Angel Falls ≈
GUIANA HIGHLANDS
Orinoco River
Rio Negro
Cauca River
Magdalena River
Putumayo River
AMAZON BASIN
Amazon (Solimões) River
Juruá River
Purus River
Marañón River
Ucayali River
Amazon River
Madeira River
Tapajós River
Teles Pires
Xingu River
Tocantins River
Araguaia River
Parnaiba River
São Francisco River

ATLANTIC OCEAN
Cape São Roque

▲ Mt. Huascarán 22,205 ft. (6,768 m)

Paracas Peninsula
Volcán Misti 19,101 ft. (5,822 m) ▲
Beni River
Lake Titicaca
▲ Mt. Illimani 21,201 ft. (6,462 m)
ALTIPLANO
Lake Poopó
Guaporé River
Mamoré River
MATO GROSSO PLATEAU
BRAZILIAN HIGHLANDS

ANDES

Atacama Desert

San Félix I. San Ambrosio I.

GRAN CHACO
Paraguay River
Pilcomayo River
Salado River
Paraná River
Grande River
SERRA DO MAR
Iguazú Falls
Paraná River
Uruguay River

TROPIC OF CAPRICORN

Juan Fernández Is.
▲ Mt. Aconcagua 22,831 ft. (6,959 m)

Río de la Plata

ATLANTIC OCEAN

Chiloé I.

PAMPAS
Colorado River
Negro River
Gulf of San Matías

Los Chonos Archipelago
Gulf of San Jorge

Patagonia

ANDES

0 300 600 mi
0 300 600 km

N
W E
S

▽ Laguna del Carbón 344 ft (105 m) below sea level

Strait of Magellan
Falkland Islands (Islas Malvinas)
Tierra del Fuego
Cape Horn
South Georgia

International boundary
▲ Mountain peak
▽ Lowest point
≈ Falls

Sources for elevation data:
World Factbook, CIA, 2019
World Almanac, 2019

A ▬▬▬ B

Elevation Profile

Paracas Peninsula Lake Titicaca Andes Mountains   Mato Grosso Plateau   Brazilian Highlands
20,000 ft.
10,000 ft.
5,000 ft.
Sea level
A   B

Largest Cities in South America (urban agglomerations)

2018

1 São Paulo, BRA 21,650,000
2 Buenos Aires, ARG . . 14,967,000
3 Rio de Janeiro, BRA . 13,293,000
4 Bogotá, COL 10,574,000
5 Lima, PER 10,391,000
6 Santiago, CHL 6,680,000
7 Belo Horizonte, BRA . . 5,972,000
8 Brasília, BRA 4,470,000
9 Porto Alegre, BRA . . . 4,094,000
10 Recife, BRA 4,028,000
11 Fortaleza, BRA 3,977,000
12 Medellín, COL 3,934,000
13 Salvador, BRA 3,754,000
14 Curitiba, BRA 3,579,000
15 Asunción, PRY 3,222,000
16 Campinas, BRA 3,210,000
17 Caracas, VEN 2,935,000
18 Guayaquil, ECU 2,899,000
19 Cali, COL 2,726,000
20 Goiânia, BRA 2,565,000

2030 (projected)

1 São Paulo, BRA 23,824,000
2 Buenos Aires, ARG . . 16,456,000
3 Rio de Janeiro, BRA . 14,408,000
4 Bogotá, COL 12,343,000
5 Lima, PER 12,266,000
6 Santiago, CHL 7,243,000
7 Belo Horizonte, BRA . . 6,583,000
8 Brasília, BRA 5,199,000
9 Recife, BRA 4,509,000
10 Fortaleza, BRA 4,446,000
11 Porto Alegre, BRA . . . 4,416,000
12 Medellín, COL 4,344,000
13 Salvador, BRA 4,181,000
14 Curitiba, BRA 4,040,000
15 Asunción, PRY 3,920,000
16 Campinas, BRA 3,627,000
17 Guayaquil, ECU 3,511,000
18 Caracas, VEN 3,164,000
19 Goiânia, BRA 3,056,000
20 Cali, COL 3,039,000

Source: United Nations. Department of Social & Economic Affairs, Population Division, 2018

Estimated 2021 Population
(in millions)

1	Brazil	214.0
2	Colombia	51.3
3	Argentina	45.6
4	Peru	33.4
5	Venezuela	28.7
6	Chile	19.2
7	Ecuador	17.9
8	Bolivia	11.8
9	Paraguay	7.2
10	Uruguay	3.5
	all others in South America	1.7

Source: World Population Review, 2021

Estimated 2021 Population Density
(in persons per square mile)

1	Ecuador	167.4
2	Colombia	116.3
3	Venezuela	81.1
4	Peru	67.2
5	Chile	65.8
6	Brazil	65.1
7	Uruguay	49.9
8	Paraguay	46.0
9	Argentina	42.5
10	Bolivia	27.9

Ripening coffee cherries on coffee trees in Colombia. Coffee cherries turn red when ripe and can be harvested by hand or machine. Each cherry contains two seeds, known as beans. Once the seeds are extracted from the cherry, the beans are dried, milled, roasted, and ground into the coffee beans available to brew around the world.

According to the International Coffee Organization, Brazil and Colombia rank first and third in world coffee exports, capturing about half of the world market in 2020. Coffee production in Ecuador, Peru, and Venezuela is primarily grown for internal use. The United States, Germany, and France were the largest importers of coffee, by dollar value, in 2020.

Two indigenous Quechua women, dressed in traditional clothing, are pictured with two llamas (left, held by the woman dressed in red) and one alpaca (right, with the woman in blue) near Cuzco, Peru. Through history, both alpacas and llamas have been used by people living in the central Andean Mountains in Bolivia, Ecuador, and Peru in a variety of roles, such as their meat for food, their fibers for clothing, and their image as a religious and artistic symbol.

Though similar in appearance, there are a number of ways to tell the difference between alpacas and llamas. Comparing their size, hair, and facial shapes provide important clues. First, llamas are typically much larger, up to twice the weight of an alpaca. Their larger size made llamas more useful as pack animals. Second, the wool from alpacas is noticeably finer, softer, and considered more valuable than the coarse wool found on llamas. And finally, llamas have a longer muzzle with short, thin fur on their face compared to the round, fluffy, smoothed face of an alpaca.

The Casa Rosada ("Pink House, in English), known officially as the Casa de Gobierno ("Government House"), serves as the office of the President of Argentina in the capital city of Buenos Aires.

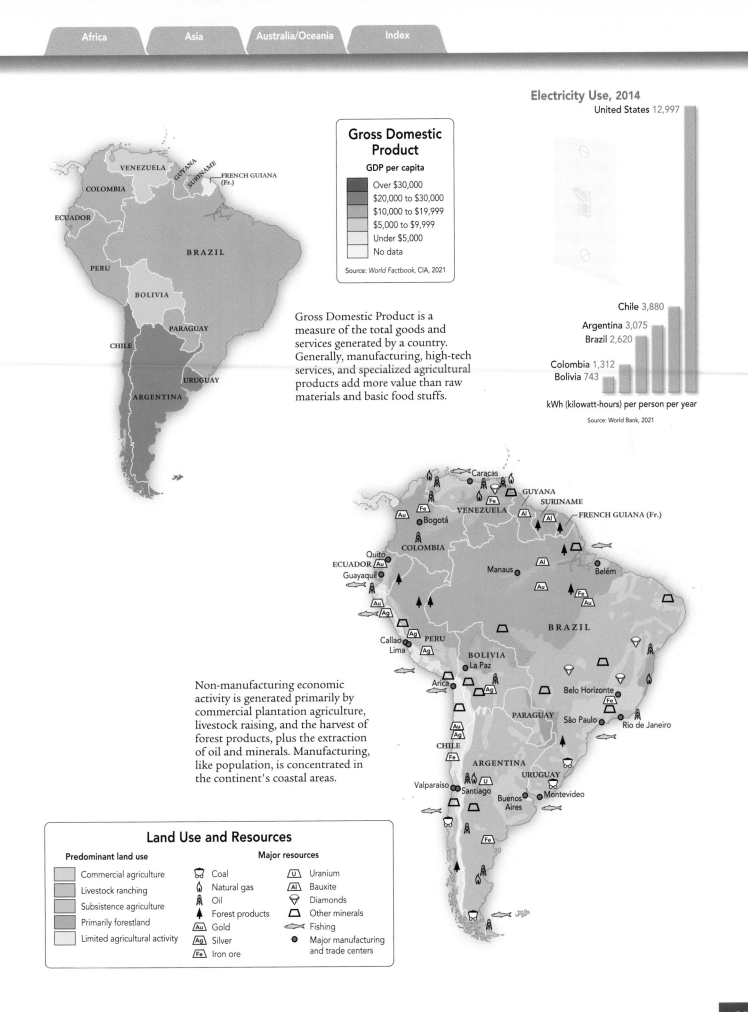

Gross Domestic Product

GDP per capita

- Over $30,000
- $20,000 to $30,000
- $10,000 to $19,999
- $5,000 to $9,999
- Under $5,000
- No data

Source: *World Factbook*, CIA, 2021

Gross Domestic Product is a measure of the total goods and services generated by a country. Generally, manufacturing, high-tech services, and specialized agricultural products add more value than raw materials and basic food stuffs.

Electricity Use, 2014

- United States 12,997
- Chile 3,880
- Argentina 3,075
- Brazil 2,620
- Colombia 1,312
- Bolivia 743

kWh (kilowatt-hours) per person per year

Source: World Bank, 2021

Non-manufacturing economic activity is generated primarily by commercial plantation agriculture, livestock raising, and the harvest of forest products, plus the extraction of oil and minerals. Manufacturing, like population, is concentrated in the continent's coastal areas.

Land Use and Resources

Predominant land use

- Commercial agriculture
- Livestock ranching
- Subsistence agriculture
- Primarily forestland
- Limited agricultural activity

Major resources

- Coal
- Natural gas
- Oil
- Forest products
- Au Gold
- Ag Silver
- Fe Iron ore
- U Uranium
- Al Bauxite
- Diamonds
- Other minerals
- Fishing
- Major manufacturing and trade centers

81

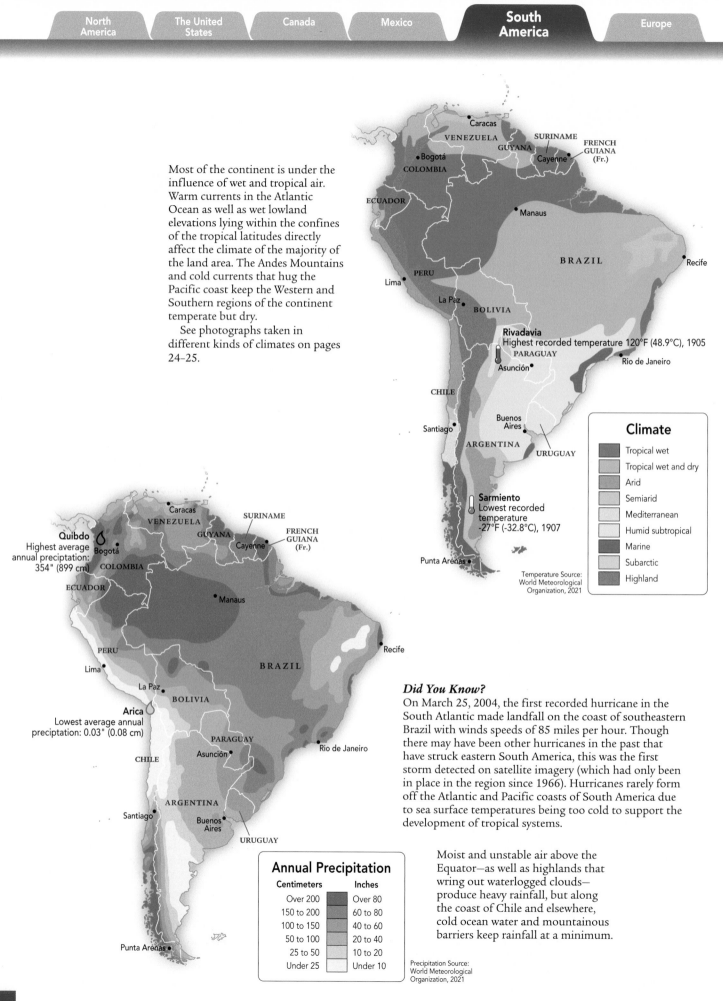

Most of the continent is under the influence of wet and tropical air. Warm currents in the Atlantic Ocean as well as wet lowland elevations lying within the confines of the tropical latitudes directly affect the climate of the majority of the land area. The Andes Mountains and cold currents that hug the Pacific coast keep the Western and Southern regions of the continent temperate but dry.

See photographs taken in different kinds of climates on pages 24–25.

Rivadavia
Highest recorded temperature 120°F (48.9°C), 1905

Sarmiento
Lowest recorded temperature
-27°F (-32.8°C), 1907

Temperature Source:
World Meteorological
Organization, 2021

Climate

- Tropical wet
- Tropical wet and dry
- Arid
- Semiarid
- Mediterranean
- Humid subtropical
- Marine
- Subarctic
- Highland

Quibdo
Highest average annual precipitation:
354" (899 cm)

Arica
Lowest average annual precipitation: 0.03" (0.08 cm)

Annual Precipitation

Centimeters	Inches
Over 200	Over 80
150 to 200	60 to 80
100 to 150	40 to 60
50 to 100	20 to 40
25 to 50	10 to 20
Under 25	Under 10

Precipitation Source:
World Meteorological
Organization, 2021

Did You Know?

On March 25, 2004, the first recorded hurricane in the South Atlantic made landfall on the coast of southeastern Brazil with winds speeds of 85 miles per hour. Though there may have been other hurricanes in the past that have struck eastern South America, this was the first storm detected on satellite imagery (which had only been in place in the region since 1966). Hurricanes rarely form off the Atlantic and Pacific coasts of South America due to sea surface temperatures being too cold to support the development of tropical systems.

Moist and unstable air above the Equator—as well as highlands that wring out waterlogged clouds—produce heavy rainfall, but along the coast of Chile and elsewhere, cold ocean water and mountainous barriers keep rainfall at a minimum.

Climate Graphs

Average daily temperature range (in °F) | Average monthly precipitation (in inches)

100° / 65° / 32° / 0° — High, Low | 20" / 10" / 0"

ASUNCIÓN, Paraguay

BOGOTÁ, Colombia

BUENOS AIRES, Argentina

CARACAS, Venezuela

CAYENNE, French Guiana

LA PAZ, Bolivia

LIMA, Peru

MANAUS, Brazil

PUNTA ARENAS, Chile

RECIFE, Brazil

RIO DE JANEIRO, Brazil

SANTIAGO, Chile

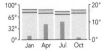

South America is dominated by tropical vegetation, including Earth's most extensive rain forest. Farther south, a vast grassland, the Pampas, fades gradually into the dry and meager vegetation of Patagonia.

See photographs of the different kinds of vegetation on pages 26–27.

Vegetation

- Unclassified highlands or ice cap
- Midlatitude deciduous forest
- Mixed forest
- Midlatitude scrubland
- Midlatitude grassland
- Desert
- Tropical seasonal and scrub
- Tropical rain forest
- Tropical savanna

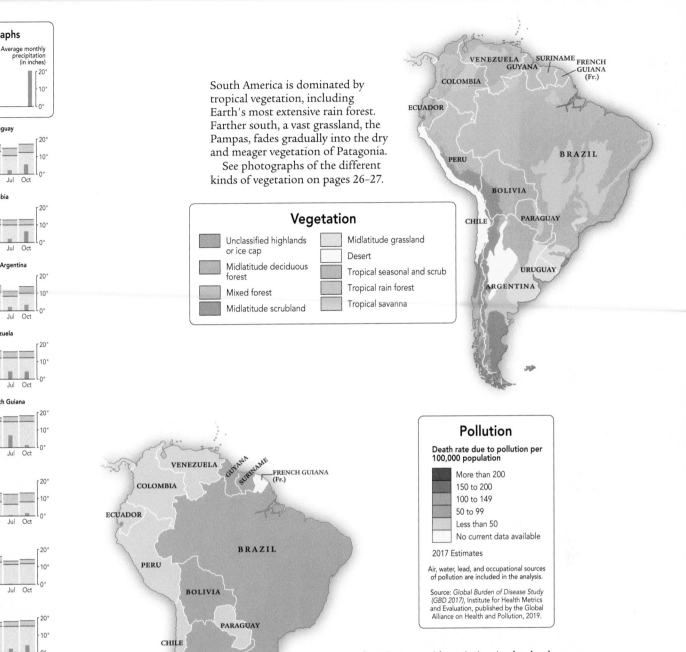

Pollution

Death rate due to pollution per 100,000 population

- More than 200
- 150 to 200
- 100 to 149
- 50 to 99
- Less than 50
- No current data available

2017 Estimates

Air, water, lead, and occupational sources of pollution are included in the analysis.

Source: *Global Burden of Disease Study (GBD 2017)*, Institute for Health Metrics and Evaluation, published by the Global Alliance on Health and Pollution, 2019.

There is not a wide variation in the death rates per 100,000 people among the nations of South America due to pollution. Brazil has the highest number of premature deaths at just over 100,000 per year—the second highest in the Western Hemisphere behind only the United States.

The effects of the deforestation of the Amazon Basin are well documented in terms of the loss of habitat for a variety of native plant and animal species. Additionally, improper mining activities, poor agricultural practices, and the rapid industrialization of major cities are other environmental issues that result in large areas of air and water contamination in South America.

The World Air Quality Index monitors the daily air quality in 380 major cities around the world. Their 2020 analysis found that Osorno, Chile had the worst air quality in South America, ranking 101st worst in the world. The air quality in the Chilean cities of Rancagua, Santiago, Puerto Montt, and Temuco measured only slightly better than in Osorno.

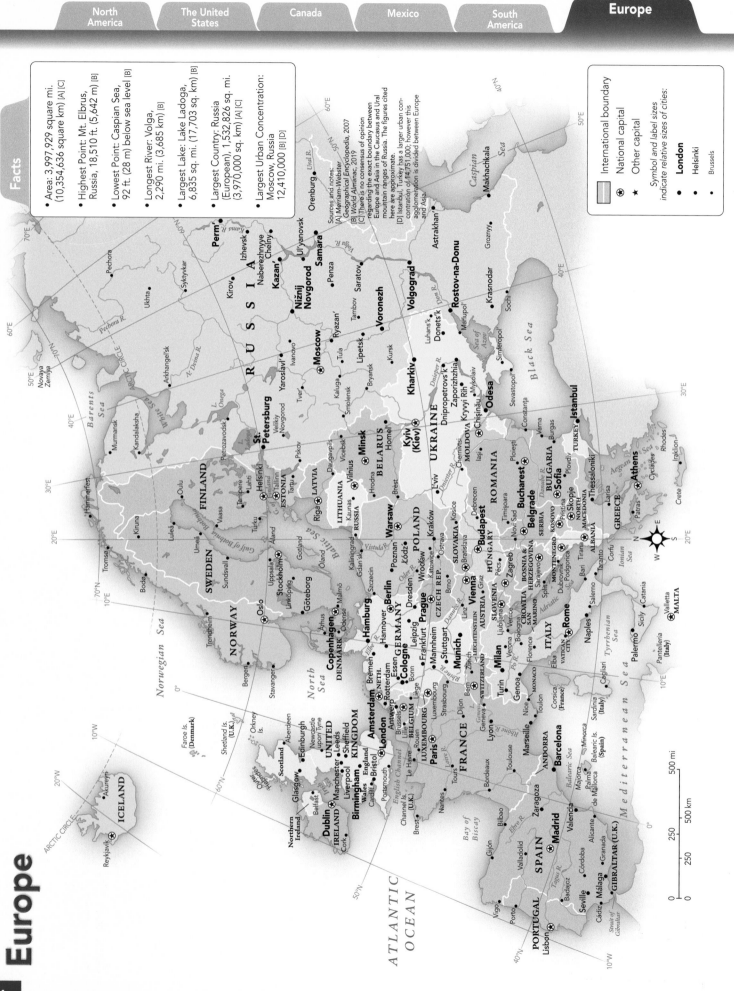

Europe

- Area: 3,997,929 square mi. (10,354,636 square km) [A] [C]
- Highest Point: Mt. Elbrus, Russia, 18,510 ft. (5,642 m) [B]
- Lowest Point: Caspian Sea, 92 ft. (28 m) below sea level [B]
- Longest River: Volga, 2,290 mi. (3,685 km) [B]
- Largest Lake: Lake Ladoga, 6,835 sq. mi. (17,703 sq. km) [B]
- Largest Country: Russia (European), 1,532,826 sq. mi. (3,970,000 sq. km) [A] [C]
- Largest Urban Concentration: Moscow, Russia 12,410,000 [B] [D]

Sources and notes:
[A] Merriam-Webster Geographical Encyclopedia, 2007
[B] World Almanac, 2019
[C] There is no consensus of opinion regarding the exact boundary between Europe and Asia in the Caucasus and Ural mountain ranges of Russia. The figures cited here are approximate.
[D] Istanbul, Turkey has a larger urban concentration of 14,751,000; however this agglomeration is divided between Europe and Asia.

Legend

- International boundary
- ⊛ National capital
- ★ Other capital
- *Symbol and label sizes indicate relative sizes of cities:*
  - ● **London**
  - ● Helsinki
  - • Brussels

84

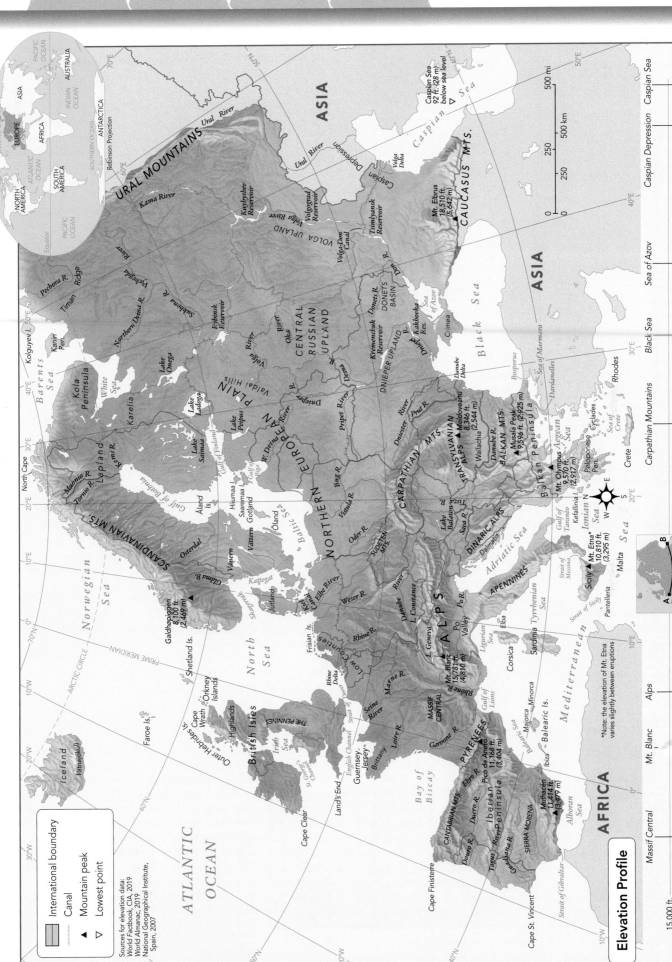

ASIA

ASIA

AFRICA

Caspian Sea
92 ft. (28 m)
below sea level

Mt. Elbrus
18,510 ft.
(5,642 m)

CAUCASUS MTS.

URAL MOUNTAINS

Ural River
Ural River

Kama River

Kuybyshev
Reservoir

Volgograd
Reservoir

Volga-Don
Canal

Tsimlyansk
Reservoir

Caspian Depression

Volga
Delta

VOLGA UPLAND

Pechora R.

Timan Ridge

Vychegda River

Northern Dvina R.

Sukhona R.

V_lian
Reservoir

Oka River

Volga River

Desna

Don R.

Donets R.

DONETS BASIN

Kremenchuk
Reservoir

DNIEPER UPLAND

CENTRAL RUSSIAN UPLAND

Kolguyev I.

Kanin
Pen.

Barents Sea

Kola
Peninsula

White Sea

Karelia

Lake
Onega

Lake
Ladoga

Lake
Peipus

Lake
Saimaa

NORTHERN EUROPEAN PLAIN

Valdai Hills

Dnieper River

Pripet River

Bug R.

Dniester

Prut R.

Danube
River

Danube
Delta

Black Sea

Kabardino
Res.

Crimea

Sea
of
Azov

Sea of Azov

North Cape

Lapland

Kemi R.

Muonio R.

Tornio R.

Gulf of Finland

Gulf of Bothnia

Hiiumaa I.

Saaremaa I.

Aland
Isls.

Gotland

Oland

Baltic Sea

Vistula R.

Oder R.

W. Dvina River

CARPATHIAN MTS.

TRANSYLVANIAN ALPS

Moldoveanu
8,346 ft.
(2,544 m)

Wallachia

BALKAN MTS.

Musala Peak
9,596 ft. (2,925 m)

Balkan Peninsula

Bosporus

Sea of Marmara

Dardanelles

Mt. Olympus
9,570 ft.
(2,917 m)

Peloponese
Pen.

Cyclades

Sea of
Crete

Crete

Rhodes

SCANDINAVIAN MTS.

Galdhøpiggen
8,100 ft.
(2,469 m)

Glama R.

Osterdal

Vänern

Vättern

Kattegat

Skagerrak

Judland

Kiel
Canal

Elbe River

Weser R.

Rhine R.

Frisian Isls.

Rhine
Delta

Low Countries

Marne R.

Seine
River

Danube

River

Tisza R.

Sava R.

Drava R.

Lake
Balaton

DINARIC ALPS

Dalmatia

Adriatic Sea

APENNINES

Gulf of
Taranto

Ionian
Sea

Kefallinia I.

Ionian
Sea

Strait of
Messina

Mt. Etna*
10,810 ft.
(3,295 m)

Sicily

Pantelleria

Strait of Sicily

Malta

Mediterranean

Mt. Blanc
15,781 ft.
(4,810 m)

ALPS

L. Geneva

L. Constance

Po R.

Po
Valley

Rhône R.

Ligurian
Sea

Elba

Corsica

Sardinia

Tyrrhenian
Sea

North Cape

Shetland Is.

Cape
Wrath

Orkney
Islands

Faroe Is.

Iceland

Vatnajökull

ATLANTIC OCEAN

Norwegian Sea

ARCTIC CIRCLE

PRIME MERIDIAN

North Sea

British Isles

Highlands

THE PENNINES

Outer Hebrides Is.

Irish Sea

St. George's Channel

English Channel

Strait of Dover

Guernsey
Jersey

Brittany

Loire R.

Garonne R.

MASSIF
CENTRAL

PYRENEES

Pico de Aneto
11,168 ft.
(3,404 m)

CANTABRIAN MTS.

Duero R.

Douro R.

Iberian Peninsula

Tagus River

Guadiana R.

SIERRA MORENA

Mulhacén
11,414 ft.
(3,479 m)

Alborán
Sea

Balearic Sea

Minorca

Majorca

Balearic Is.

Ibiza

Land's End

Cape Clear

Cape Finisterre

Cape St. Vincent

Bay of
Biscay

Gulf of
Lions

Ebro R.

Strait of Gibraltar

N
W E
S

Sources for elevation data:
World Factbook, CIA, 2019
World Almanac, 2019
National Geographic Institute,
Spain, 2007

International boundary
Canal
▲ Mountain peak
▽ Lowest point

ARCTIC OCEAN
EUROPE ASIA
ATLANTIC OCEAN
AFRICA
SOUTH AMERICA
NORTH AMERICA
PACIFIC OCEAN
INDIAN OCEAN
AUSTRALIA
ANTARCTICA
SOUTHERN OCEAN
PACIFIC OCEAN
Equator
Robinson Projection

*Note: the elevation of Mt. Etna
varies slightly between eruptions

Elevation Profile

Massif Central	Mt. Blanc	Alps	Carpathian Mountains	Crete	Black Sea	Sea of Azov	Caspian Depression	Caspian Sea

15,000 ft.
10,000 ft.
5,000 ft.
Sea level

A ————— B

500 mi
500 km
250
250
0

The Neva River in St. Petersburg, Russia captures the reflection of the Hermitage Museum. This building, formerly known as the Winter Palace, served as the official residence of the Romanov dynasty from 1732 to 1917. The museum collection is now the home to over three million works of art and cultural objects, having started as the private art collection of Empress Catherine the Great during her reign in the second half of the 17th century.

Largest Cities in Europe (urban agglomerations)

	2018		2030 (projected)
1	Moscow, RUS 12,410,000	1 Moscow, RUS 12,796,000
2	Paris, FRA 10,901,000	2 Paris, FRA 11,710,000
3	London, GBR 9,046,000	3 London, GBR 10,228,000
4	Madrid, ESP 6,497,000	4 Madrid, ESP 6,907,000
5	Barcelona, ESP 5,494,000	5 Barcelona, ESP 5,812,000
6	St. Petersburg, RUS . . 5,383,000	6 St. Petersburg, RUS . . 5,630,000
7	Rome, ITA 4,210,000	7 Rome, ITA 4,413,000
8	Berlin, DEU 3,552,000	8 Berlin, DEU 3,606,000
9	Athens, GRC. 3,156,000	9 Milan, ITA. 3,209,000
10	Milan, ITA. 3,132,000	10 Athens, GRC. 3,163,000
11	Kyiv, UKR 2,957,000	11 Lisbon, PRT 3,085,000
12	Lisbon, PRT 2,927,000	12 Kyiv, UKR 3,004,000
13	Birmingham, GBR 2,570,000	13 Birmingham, GBR 2,802,000
14	Naples, ITA 2,198,000	14 Naples, ITA 2,207,000
15	Minsk, BLR 2,005,000	15 Minsk, BLR 2,086,000
16	Vienna, AUT 1,901,000	16 Vienna, AUT 2,080,000
17	Bucharest, ROU 1,821,000	17 Lyon, FRA 1,847,000
18	Hamburg, DEU 1,793,000	18 Turin, ITA 1,834,000
19	Turin, ITA 1,786,000	19 Stockholm, SWE. 1,814,000
20	Warsaw, POL 1,768,000	20 Warsaw, POL 1,800,000

Source: United Nations. Department of Social & Economic Affairs, Population Division, 2018

Estimated 2021 Population
(in millions)

1	Russia	145.9
2	Germany	83.9
3	United Kingdom	68.2
4	France	65.4
5	Italy	60.4
6	Spain	46.7
7	Ukraine	43.5
8	Poland	37.8
9	Romania	19.1
10	Netherlands	17.2
	all others in Europe	152.0

Estimated 2021 Population Density
(in persons per square mile)

1	Monaco	50,660.0
2	Vatican City	4,709.1
3	Malta	3,629.2
4	San Marino	1,444.3
5	Netherlands	1,062.8
6	Belgium	986.9
7	Luxembourg	635.8
8	Liechtenstein	619.2
9	Germany	608.5
10	Switzerland	546.8

Source: World Population Review, 2021

The bronze statue, "Spirit of American Youth Rising from the Waves" faces towards the English Channel at the Normandy American Cemetery and Memorial in Colleville-sur-Mer, France. The site overlooks Omaha Beach, one of five beaches code-named for the landings by American, British, Canadian, and other Allied forces in Normandy on D-Day, June 6, 1944 during the Second World War. According to the American Battle Monuments Commission, "the symbolic figure is a reminder of the youth of the D-Day troops and the heroism they displayed".

The Rock of Monaco, also known as La Rocher, originally served as a fortress for the city-state of Genoa. In 1297, the fortress was seized by Francesco Grimaldi, starting the Grimaldi dynasty which has ruled the Principality of Monaco for over 700 years. Located on the Mediterranean Sea and surrounded by France, the mild climate and lenient tax laws have made Monaco a famous tourist destination and the most densely populated country in the world despite its size of less than 1 square mile.

The six countries of Andorra, Liechtenstein, Malta, Monaco, San Marino, and Vatican City are referred to as European microstates. Though "microstate" is not firmly defined, it is generally understood that it is an internationally-recognized sovereign state with a very small population or very small land area. A microstate's larger neighbor typically plays a significant role in its defense, economy, or governance.

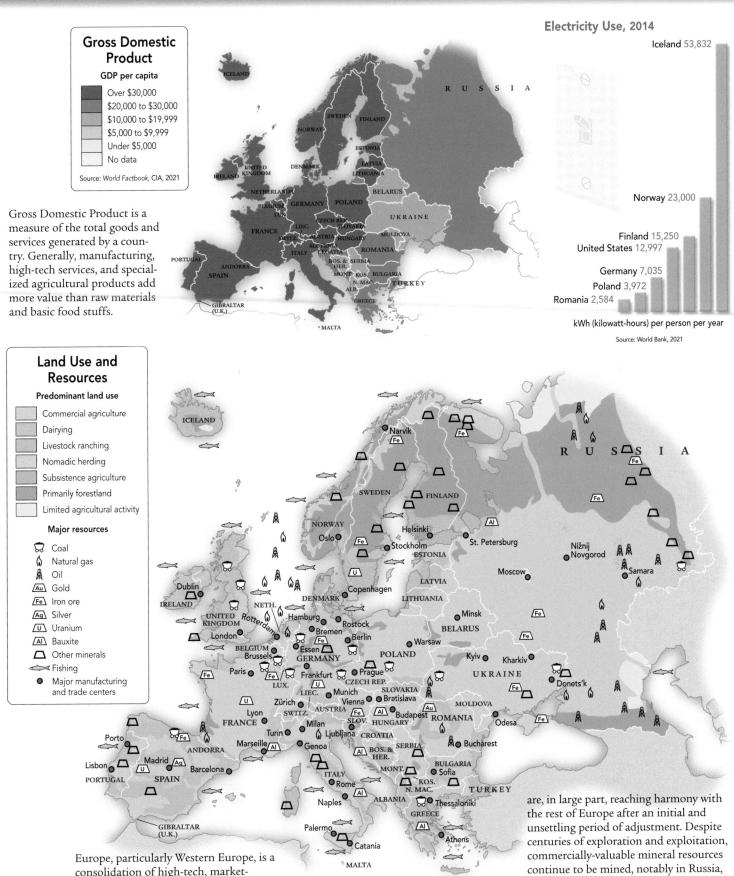

Gross Domestic Product

GDP per capita

- Over $30,000
- $20,000 to $30,000
- $10,000 to $19,999
- $5,000 to $9,999
- Under $5,000
- No data

Source: *World Factbook*, CIA, 2021

Gross Domestic Product is a measure of the total goods and services generated by a country. Generally, manufacturing, high-tech services, and specialized agricultural products add more value than raw materials and basic food stuffs.

Electricity Use, 2014

- Iceland 53,832
- Norway 23,000
- Finland 15,250
- United States 12,997
- Germany 7,035
- Poland 3,972
- Romania 2,584

kWh (kilowatt-hours) per person per year

Source: World Bank, 2021

Land Use and Resources

Predominant land use

- Commercial agriculture
- Dairying
- Livestock ranching
- Nomadic herding
- Subsistence agriculture
- Primarily forestland
- Limited agricultural activity

Major resources

- Coal
- Natural gas
- Oil
- Au Gold
- Fe Iron ore
- Ag Silver
- U Uranium
- Al Bauxite
- Other minerals
- Fishing
- ● Major manufacturing and trade centers

Europe, particularly Western Europe, is a consolidation of high-tech, market-driven, globally connected economies, where manufacturing and commercial agriculture predominate. Crucial to continental economic integration is the European Union, a partnership of twenty-seven member nations whose combined economic clout rivals the United States. Russia and former Soviet-satellite nations are, in large part, reaching harmony with the rest of Europe after an initial and unsettling period of adjustment. Despite centuries of exploration and exploitation, commercially-valuable mineral resources continue to be mined, notably in Russia, Ukraine, and Scandinavia. The bountiful oil and gas fields of the North Sea are one of the most important and most recent discoveries.

87

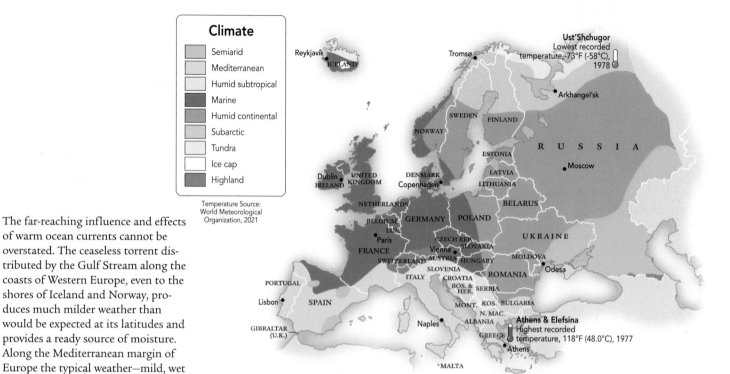

Climate

- Semiarid
- Mediterranean
- Humid subtropical
- Marine
- Humid continental
- Subarctic
- Tundra
- Ice cap
- Highland

Temperature Source:
World Meteorological
Organization, 2021

Ust'Shchugor
Lowest recorded
temperature, -73°F (-58°C),
1978

Athens & Elefsina
Highest recorded
temperature, 118°F (48.0°C), 1977

The far-reaching influence and effects of warm ocean currents cannot be overstated. The ceaseless torrent distributed by the Gulf Stream along the coasts of Western Europe, even to the shores of Iceland and Norway, produces much milder weather than would be expected at its latitudes and provides a ready source of moisture. Along the Mediterranean margin of Europe the typical weather—mild, wet winters and hot, dry summers—has been defined as a climate category that is now used worldwide.

See photographs taken in different kinds of climates on pages 24–25.

Did You Know?

The winter of 1950-51 became known as the "Winter of Terror" in the Swiss-Austrian Alps due to a previously unrecorded number of avalanches in the area. Over the course of three months, a series of 649 avalanches killed 265 people. The Swiss town of Andermatt was struck by six avalanches in less than an hour, killing 13 people. Snow avalanches are responsible for an average of 100 deaths in Europe each year.

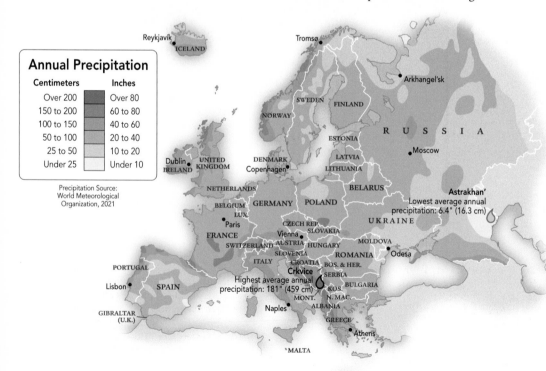

Annual Precipitation

Centimeters	Inches
Over 200	Over 80
150 to 200	60 to 80
100 to 150	40 to 60
50 to 100	20 to 40
25 to 50	10 to 20
Under 25	Under 10

Precipitation Source:
World Meteorological
Organization, 2021

Astrakhan'
Lowest average annual
precipitation: 6.4" (16.3 cm)

Crkvice
Highest average annual
precipitation: 181" (459 cm)

Though regionally formidable mountains rise to extract snow and rain, no continental-scale alpine barrier exists—thereby permitting moisture-laden, westerly winds springing from warm oceanic waters to distribute precipitation uniformly across Europe. However, by the time these currents of air reach the landlocked heart of Eastern Europe, northeast of the Black Sea, much of the moisture has already been spent.

Climate Graphs

Average daily temperature range (in °F) — High, Low
Average monthly precipitation (in inches)

ARKHANGELSK, Russia

ATHENS, Greece

COPENHAGEN, Denmark

DUBLIN, Ireland

LISBON, Portugal

MOSCOW, Russia

NAPLES, Italy

ODESA, Ukraine

PARIS, France

REYKJAVÍK, Iceland

TROMSØ, Norway

VIENNA, Austria

Vegetation

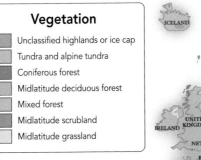

- Unclassified highlands or ice cap
- Tundra and alpine tundra
- Coniferous forest
- Midlatitude deciduous forest
- Mixed forest
- Midlatitude scrubland
- Midlatitude grassland

Forests, nourished by plentiful precipitation, dominate in Europe, but grassland and scrubland thrive where rainfall becomes sparse or is seasonal. Deciduous trees disappear as the winters grow harsh, replaced by vast and hardy stands of coniferous forest that are merely the western end of an immense belt stretching across Russia to the Pacific Ocean.

See photographs of the different kinds of vegetation on pages 26–27.

Pollution

Death rate due to pollution per 100,000 population

- More than 200
- 150 to 200
- 100 to 149
- 50 to 99
- Less than 50
- No current data available

2017 Estimates

Air, water, lead, and occupational sources of pollution are included in the analysis.

Source: *Global Burden of Disease Study (GBD 2017)*, Institute for Health Metrics and Evaluation, published by the Global Alliance on Health and Pollution, 2019.

This map clearly indicates a pattern that pollution has much less of an effect on health in the Scandinavian countries of northern Europe than in southeastern Europe, especially Serbia. The rate of 175 deaths per 100,000 people in Serbia is not only the highest in Europe, but also among the top ten highest in the world.

Emissions from the many aging cars, trucks, and factories in Europe have led to problems with air pollution and acid rain over large areas of central Europe. The inefficiency of electricity-generating and distribution plants in Serbia is believed to be a major contributor to the country's poor air quality.

The World Air Quality Index monitors the daily air quality in 380 major cities around the world. Their 2020 analysis found that Tuzla, Bosnia & Herzegovina had the poorest air quality in Europe, ranking 72nd worst in the world.

Africa

Legend
- International boundary
- ⊛ National capital
- ★ Other capital

Symbol and label sizes indicate relative sizes of cities:
- ● **Johannesburg**
- • Tripoli
- · Malabo

Facts

- Area: 11,494,808 square miles (29,771,416 square kilometers) [A]

- Highest Point: Mt. Kilimanjaro, Tanzania 19,341 ft. (5,895 m) [B]

- Lowest Point: Lake Assal, Djibouti 509 ft. (155 m) below sea level [B]

- Longest River: Nile 4,160 mi. (6,695 km) [A]

- Largest Lake: Lake Victoria, Uganda/Kenya/Tanzania 26,828 sq. mi. (69,484 sq. km) [A]

- Largest Country: Algeria 919,595 sq. mi. (2,381,740 sq. km) [B]

- Largest Urban Concentration: Cairo, Egypt 20,076,000 (2018 estimate) [A]

Sources and notes:
[A] *World Almanac*, 2019
[B] *World Factbook*, CIA, 2021

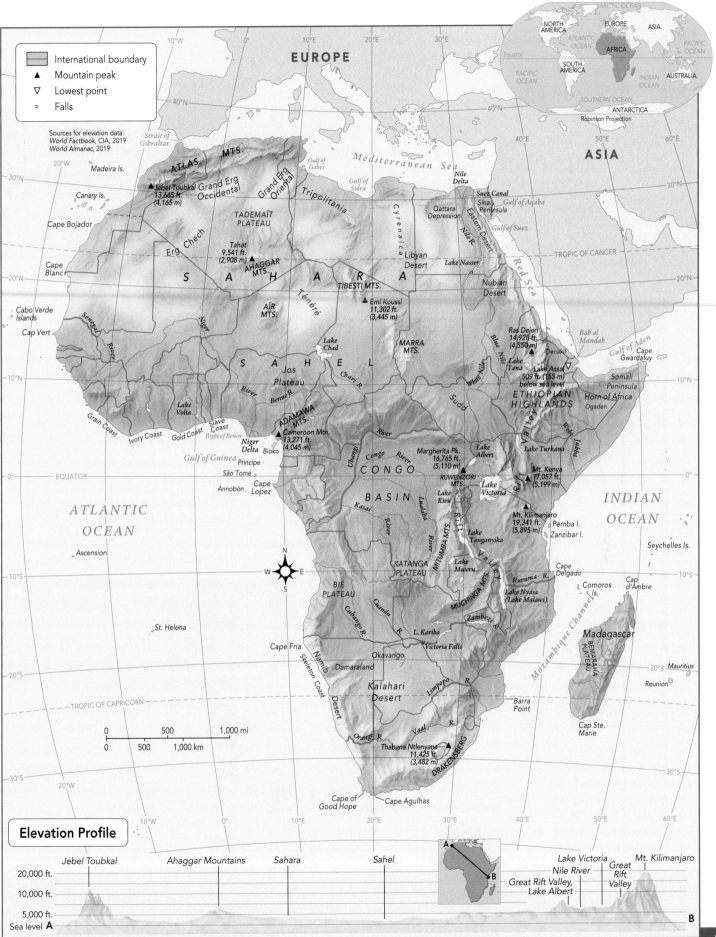

International boundary
▲ Mountain peak
▽ Lowest point
≈ Falls

Sources for elevation data:
World Factbook, CIA, 2019
World Almanac, 2019

Robinson Projection

EUROPE

ASIA

Mediterranean Sea

Strait of Gibraltar
Gulf of Gabes
Gulf of Sidra

Madeira Is.
Canary Is.
Cape Bojador
Cape Blanc

ATLAS MTS.
▲ Jebel Toubkal 13,665 ft. (4,165 m)
Grand Erg Occidental
Grand Erg Oriental
Tripolitania
Cyrenaica
Nile Delta
Suez Canal
Sinai Peninsula
Gulf of Aqaba
Gulf of Suez

TADEMAÏT PLATEAU
Erg Chech
Tahat 9,541 ft. (2,908 m) ▲
AHAGGAR MTS.
S A H A R A
Libyan Desert
Eastern Desert
Qattara Depression
Lake Nasser
Nubian Desert
Red Sea

TIBESTI MTS.
Emi Koussi 11,302 ft. (3,445 m) ▲
Ténéré
AÏR MTS.
MARRA MTS.
Ras Dejen 14,928 ft. (4,550 m) ▲
Denakil
Bab al Mandab
Gulf of Aden
Cape Gwardafuy

Cabo Verde Islands
Cap Vert
Senegal River
Niger River
Lake Chad
S A H E L
Jos Plateau
Chari R.
Blue Nile
White Nile
Lake Tana
Lake Assal 509 ft. (155 m) below sea level ▽
Somali Peninsula
Horn of Africa
Ogaden
ETHIOPIAN HIGHLANDS

Grain Coast
Ivory Coast
Gold Coast
Slave Coast
Lake Volta
Benue R.
ADAMAWA MTS.
Cameroon Mtn. 13,271 ft. (4,045 m) ▲
Bioko
Niger Delta
Bight of Benin
Gulf of Guinea
Príncipe
São Tomé
Annobón
Cape Lopez

Ubangi River
Congo River
CONGO BASIN
Kasai River
Lualaba River
Margherita Pk. 16,765 ft. (5,110 m) ▲
RUWENZORI MTS.
Lake Albert
Lake Kivu
Lake Victoria
Lake Turkana
Mt. Kenya 17,057 ft. (5,199 m) ▲
Rift Valley
Wobi Jubba

Mt. Kilimanjaro 19,341 ft. (5,895 m) ▲
Pemba I.
Zanzibar I.

ATLANTIC OCEAN

Ascension

EQUATOR

INDIAN OCEAN

Seychelles Is.

MITUMBA MTS.
Lake Tanganyika
Lake Mweru
KATANGA PLATEAU
BIÉ PLATEAU
Valley
Cape Delgado
Comoros Is.
Cap d'Ambre

St. Helena
Cuango R.
Cuando
MUCHINGA MTS.
Ruvuma R.
Lake Nyasa (Lake Malawi)
Zambezi R.
L. Kariba
Victoria Falls ≈
Okavango
Namib Desert
Skeleton Coast
Cape Fria
Damaraland
Madagascar
BEMARAHA PLATEAU
Mauritius
Reunion

Kalahari Desert
Limpopo R.
Barra Point
Mozambique Channel

TROPIC OF CAPRICORN

Orange R.
Vaal R.
Thabana Ntlenyana 11,425 ft. (3,482 m) ▲
DRAKENSBERG

Cape of Good Hope
Cape Agulhas
Cap Ste. Marie

0   500   1,000 mi
0   500   1,000 km

Elevation Profile

20,000 ft.
10,000 ft.
5,000 ft.
Sea level **A**

Jebel Toubkal
Ahaggar Mountains
Sahara
Sahel
Great Rift Valley, Lake Albert
Nile River
Lake Victoria
Great Rift Valley
Mt. Kilimanjaro
B

Largest Cities in Africa (urban agglomerations)

	2018			2030 (projected)	
1	Cairo, EGY	20,076,000	1	Cairo, EGY	25,517,000
2	Lagos, NGA	13,463,000	2	Kinshasa, COD	21,914,000
3	Kinshasa, COD	13,171,000	3	Lagos, NGA	20,600,000
4	Luanda, AGO	7,774,000	4	Luanda, AGO	12,129,000
5	Dar es Salaam, TZA	6,048,000	5	Dar es Salaam, TZA	10,789,000
6	Khartoum, SDN	5,534,000	6	Khartoum, SDN	8,023,000
7	Johannesburg, ZAF	5,486,000	7	Addis Ababa, ETH	7,352,000
8	Alexandria, EGY	5,086,000	8	Abidjan, CIV	7,136,000
9	Abidjan, CIV	4,921,000	9	Nairobi, KEN	7,031,000
10	Cape Town, ZAF	4,430,000	10	Johannesburg, ZAF	6,978,000
11	Addis Ababa, ETH	4,400,000	11	Alexandria, EGY	6,417,000
12	Nairobi, KEN	4,386,000	12	Yaoundé, CMR	5,734,000
13	Kano, NGA	3,820,000	13	Kano, NGA	5,551,000
14	Ekurhuleni, ZAF	3,741,000	14	Kampala, UGA	5,506,000
15	Casablanca, MAR	3,684,000	15	Cape Town, ZAF	5,468,000
16	Yaoundé, CMR	3,656,000	16	Antananarivo, MDG	5,189,000
17	Doula, CMR	3,412,000	17	Abuja, NGA	5,119,000
18	Ibadan, NGA	3,383,000	18	Doula, CMR	5,112,000
19	Durban, ZAF	3,134,000	19	Ibadan, NGA	4,956,000
20	Kumasi, GHA	3,065,000	20	Kumasi, GHA	4,681,000

Source: United Nations. Department of Social & Economic Affairs, Population Division, 2018

Hieroglyph of Thoth, the ibis-headed god of knowledge, carved on the outer wall of the Temple of Horus in Edfu, Egypt. Starting around 3000 BC, ancient Egyptians developed the hieroglyphic, or pictorial, form of writing to record important events and stories about their gods and Pharaohs.

The Great Mosque in Djenné, Mali is one of the most famous landmarks in Africa. Designated a World Heritage Site in 1988, the mosque is the largest earthen structure in the world. The walls require annual repair due to erosion caused by rainfall.

Estimated 2021 Population (in millions)			Estimated 2021 Population Density (in persons per square mile)		
1	Nigeria	211.4	1	Mayotte (Fr.)	1,935.7
2	Ethiopia	117.9	2	Mauritius	1,616.8
3	Egypt	104.3	3	Rwanda	1,305.6
4	Dem. Rep. of Congo	92.4	4	Comoros	1,235.8
5	Tanzania	61.5	5	Burundi	1,140.4
6	South Africa	60.0	6	Reunion (Fr.)	930.0
7	Kenya	55.0	7	Gambia	602.6
8	Uganda	47.1	8	São Tomé & Príncipe	600.1
9	Sudan	44.9	9	Nigeria	592.7
10	Algeria	44.6	10	Seychelles	566.7
all others in Africa		534.4			

Source: World Population Review, 2021

The Door of No Return in Ouidah, Benin stands as a memorial to all of the men, women, and children who were captured and sent to the Americas as slaves. The monument depicts rows of men and women–bound and chained together–walking towards the ships that would have been stationed just off this beach. Historians estimate that 12.5 million Africans were shipped to slave markets in North and South America and the Caribbean. It is believed that around 2 million enslaved Africans died during the Atlantic crossing.

Gross Domestic Product is a measure of the total goods and services generated by a country. Generally, manufacturing, high-tech services, and specialized agricultural products add more value than raw materials and basic food stuffs.

Mauritius and Seychelles now lead Africa in GDP per capita at over $20,000 per year. The development of the tourist sector in both countries played a key role in their economic transformation. They now seek to diversify their economies in order to sustain growth.

Electricity Use, 2014

United States 12,997

South Africa 4,198

Botswana 1,816

Zambia 717

Cameroon 275

Ethiopia 69

kWh (kilowatt-hours) per person per year

Source: World Bank, 2021

Gross Domestic Product

GDP per capita

- Over $30,000
- $20,000 to $30,000
- $10,000 to $19,999
- $5,000 to $9,999
- Under $5,000
- No data

Source: *World Factbook*, CIA, 2021

Agriculture supplies the livelihood for the vast majority of Africans. Agricultural exports include coffee, cocoa beans, peanuts, palm oil, and spices. These important export crops are mainly cultivated on plantations and large farms. Areas of subsistence farming supply the needs of local communities.

Unfortunately, poor soils and unfavorable climate conditions, as well as political unrest and unstable economies, all have an adverse impact on agricultural activity and therefore the standard of living.

Minerals account for more then one half of Africa's exports. Oil, diamonds, gold, cobalt, and several other minerals are leading exports. However, important mineral deposits are limited to a handful of countries.

Manufacturing has been slow to develop on the continent. Lack of money and skilled labor are the main deterrents.

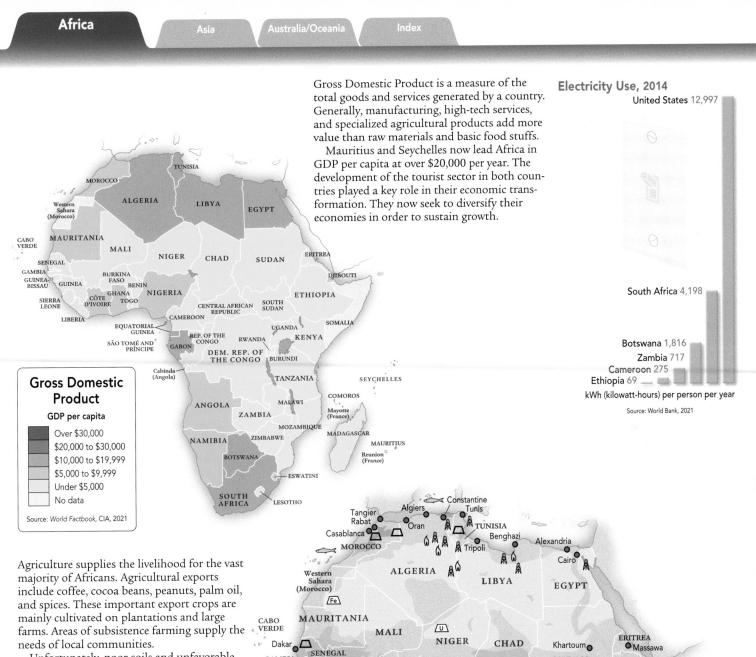

Land Use and Resources

Predominant land use

- Commercial agriculture
- Livestock ranching
- Subsistence agriculture
- Nomadic herding
- Primarily forestland
- Limited agricultural activity

Major resources

- Coal
- Natural gas
- Oil
- Au Gold
- Fe Iron ore
- Pt Platinum
- U Uranium
- Al Bauxite
- Diamonds
- Other minerals
- Fishing
- Major manufacturing and trade centers

The climate of Africa is clearly a study in geographic contrasts. Perpetually wet and tropical areas surrounding the Equator quickly acquire seasonal variety as you move north and south. Roaming even farther leads to the vast, hot and arid zones of northern and southern Africa. The influence of neighboring water bodies is limited to small regions of northern Africa, namely Morocco, Algeria, and Libya, where the mild currents of the Mediterranean Sea temper the climate, and eastern South Africa, where the mixture of warm currents flowing close to shore and the seasonal onshore winds striking the Drakensberg uplands provide for a moist and temperate marine coast climate.

See photographs taken in different kinds of climates on pages 24–25.

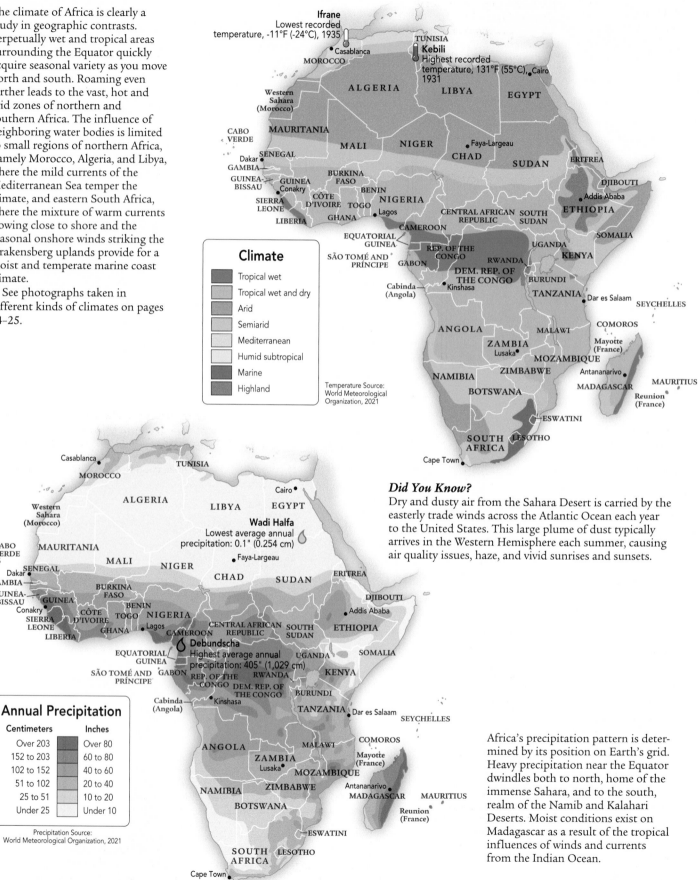

Climate

- Tropical wet
- Tropical wet and dry
- Arid
- Semiarid
- Mediterranean
- Humid subtropical
- Marine
- Highland

Temperature Source: World Meteorological Organization, 2021

Ifrane
Lowest recorded temperature, -11°F (-24°C), 1935

Kebili
Highest recorded temperature, 131°F (55°C), 1931

Wadi Halfa
Lowest average annual precipitation: 0.1" (0.254 cm)

Debundscha
Highest average annual precipitation: 405" (1,029 cm)

Annual Precipitation

Centimeters	Inches
Over 203	Over 80
152 to 203	60 to 80
102 to 152	40 to 60
51 to 102	20 to 40
25 to 51	10 to 20
Under 25	Under 10

Precipitation Source: World Meteorological Organization, 2021

Did You Know?
Dry and dusty air from the Sahara Desert is carried by the easterly trade winds across the Atlantic Ocean each year to the United States. This large plume of dust typically arrives in the Western Hemisphere each summer, causing air quality issues, haze, and vivid sunrises and sunsets.

Africa's precipitation pattern is determined by its position on Earth's grid. Heavy precipitation near the Equator dwindles both to north, home of the immense Sahara, and to the south, realm of the Namib and Kalahari Deserts. Moist conditions exist on Madagascar as a result of the tropical influences of winds and currents from the Indian Ocean.

94

Climate Graphs

Average daily temperature range (in °F)   Average monthly precipitation (in inches)

100° [High] 20°
65°   10°
32° [Low]
0°   0°

ADDIS ABABA, Ethiopia

100°   20°
65°   10°
32°
0°   Jan Apr Jul Oct   0°

ANTANANARIVO, Madagascar

100°   20°
65°   10°
32°
0°   Jan Apr Jul Oct   0°

CAIRO, Egypt

100°   20°
65°   10°
32°
0°   Jan Apr Jul Oct   0°

CAPE TOWN, South Africa

100°   20°
65°   10°
32°
0°   Jan Apr Jul Oct   0°

CASABLANCA, Morocco

100°   20°
65°   10°
32°
0°   Jan Apr Jul Oct   0°

CONAKRY, Guinea

100°   51.1   20°
65°   10°
32°
0°   Jan Apr Jul Oct   0°

DAKAR, Senegal

100°   20°
65°   10°
32°
0°   Jan Apr Jul Oct   0°

DAR ES SALAAM, Tanzania

100°   20°
65°   10°
32°
0°   Jan Apr Jul Oct   0°

FAYA-LARGEAU, Chad

100°   20°
65°   10°
32°
0°   Jan Apr Jul Oct   0°

KINSHASA, Dem. Rep. of the Congo

100°   20°
65°   10°
32°
0°   Jan Apr Jul Oct   0°

LAGOS, Nigeria

100°   20°
65°   10°
32°
0°   Jan Apr Jul Oct   0°

LUSAKA, Zambia

100°   20°
65°   10°
32°
0°   Jan Apr Jul Oct   0°

The dense, tropical rain forest surrounding the Equator is offset by the contrastingly sparse vegetation on the rest of the continent. Vast areas consist of grassland and scrub vegetation with trees only occasionally dotting the landscape. Evergreen and mixed forests of more temperate climates are limited to the Mediterranean areas of Morocco and Algeria, the Ethiopian Highlands, and Kenya.

See photographs of the different kinds of vegetation on pages 26–27.

Vegetation

- Coniferous forest
- Mixed forest
- Midlatitude scrubland
- Midlatitude grassland
- Desert
- Tropical seasonal and scrub
- Tropical rain forest
- Tropical savanna

The World Air Quality Index monitors the daily air quality in 380 major cities around the world. Their 2020 analysis found that Kampala, Uganda had the poorest air quality in Africa, ranking 11th worst in the world.

Pollution

Death rate due to pollution per 100,000 population

- More than 200
- 150 to 200
- 100 to 149
- 50 to 99
- Less than 50
- No current data available

2017 Estimates

Air, water, lead, and occupational sources of pollution are included in the analysis.

Source: *Global Burden of Disease Study (GBD 2017)*, Institute for Health Metrics and Evaluation, published by the Global Alliance on Health and Pollution, 2019.

Traditional pollution sources, such as indoor air pollution and unsanitary water sources, correlate highly with poverty. Sub-Saharan Africa is one of the poorest regions in the world. Though the continent has made some progress in terms of development, meeting basic human needs, such as access to clean water and food security, have so far eluded many African countries.

Chad has the highest rate of pollution-related deaths in the world at 287 per 100,000 population. The Central African Republic, Niger, Madagascar, South Sudan, and Somalia join Chad as having amongst the top ten highest rates in the world.

Asia

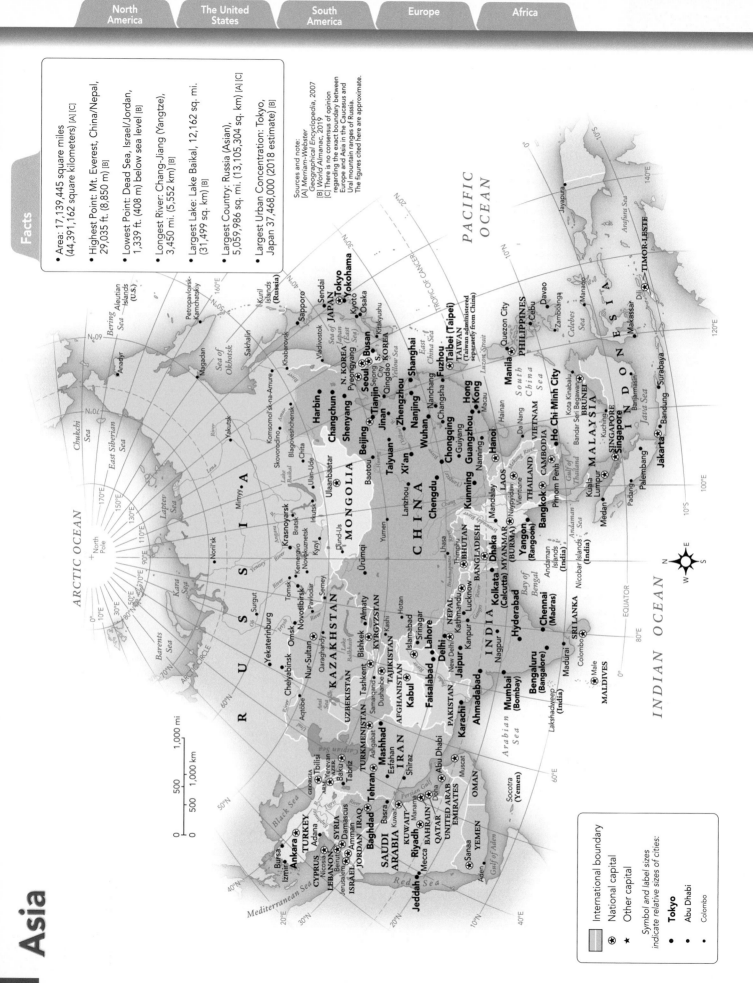

Facts

- Area: 17,139,445 square miles (44,391,162 square kilometers) [A] [C]
- Highest Point: Mt. Everest, China/Nepal, 29,035 ft. (8,850 m) [B]
- Lowest Point: Dead Sea, Israel/Jordan, 1,339 ft. (408 m) below sea level [B]
- Longest River: Chang-Jiang (Yangtze), 3,450 mi. (5,552 km) [B]
- Largest Lake: Lake Baikal, 12,162 sq. mi. (31,499 sq. km) [B]
- Largest Country: Russia (Asian), 5,059,986 sq. mi. (13,105,304 sq. km) [A] [C]
- Largest Urban Concentration: Tokyo, Japan 37,468,000 (2018 estimate) [B]

Sources and note:
[A] Merriam-Webster Geographical Encyclopedia, 2007
[B] World Almanac, 2019
[C] There is no consensus of opinion regarding the exact boundary between Europe and Asia in the Caucasus and Ural mountain ranges of Russia. The figures cited here are approximate.

International boundary
⊛ National capital
★ Other capital
Symbol and label sizes
indicate relative sizes of cities:

- **Tokyo**
- Abu Dhabi
- Colombo

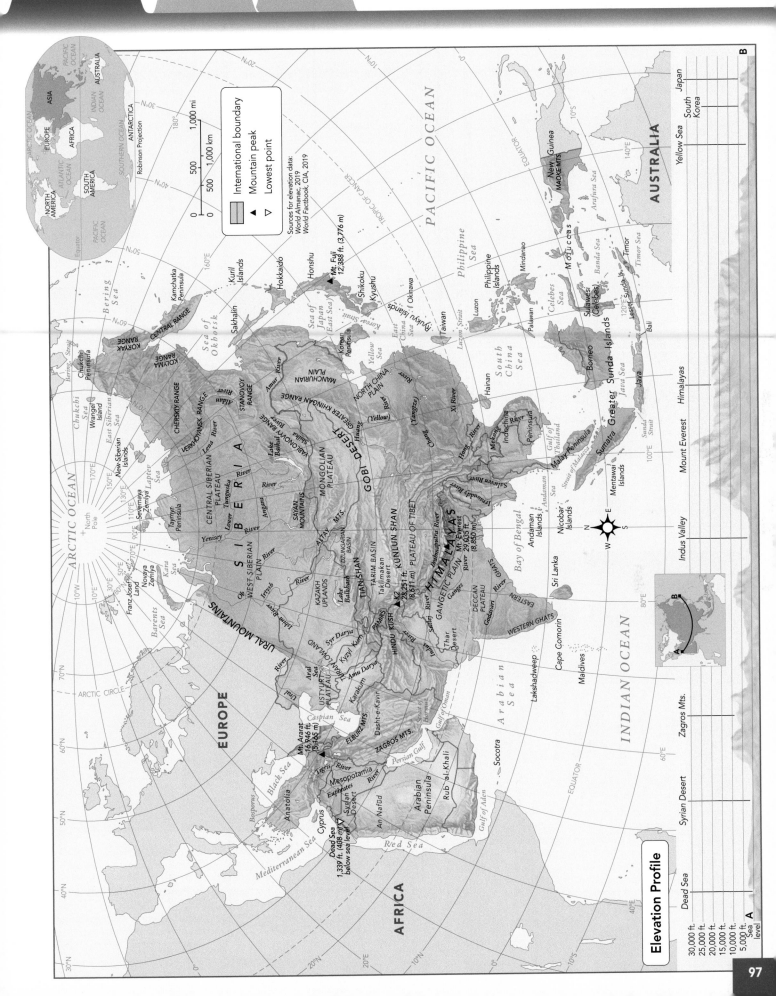

ARCTIC OCEAN

North Pole

ASIA

EUROPE

AFRICA

PACIFIC OCEAN

S I B E R I A

CHERSKIY RANGE

VERKHOYANSK RANGE

CENTRAL SIBERIAN PLATEAU

KORYAK RANGE

KOLYMA RANGE

CENTRAL RANGE

STANOVOY RANGE

YABLONOVYY RANGE

WEST SIBERIAN PLAIN

SAYAN MOUNTAINS

ALTAY MTS.

MONGOLIAN PLATEAU

GREATER KHINGAN RANGE

GOBI DESERT

MANCHURIAN PLAIN

NORTH CHINA PLAIN

URAL MOUNTAINS

KAZAKH UPLANDS

DZUNGARIAN BASIN

TIAN SHAN

TARIM BASIN

Taklimakan Desert

KUNLUN SHAN

PLATEAU OF TIBET

PAMIRS

HINDU KUSH

HIMALAYAS

GANGETIC PLAIN

USTYURT PLATEAU

TURAN LOWLAND

Kyzyl Kum

Karakum

Thar Desert

DECCAN PLATEAU

WESTERN GHATS

EASTERN GHATS

ELBURZ MTS.

ZAGROS MTS.

Dasht-e-Kavir

Mesopotamia

Anatolia

Syrian Desert

An Nafūd

Arabian Peninsula

Rubʻ al-Khali

Himalayas

Indochina Peninsula

Malay Peninsula

Greater Sunda Islands

Sumatra

Java

Borneo

MAOKE MTS.

New Guinea

AUSTRALIA

Rivers / Seas / Lakes:

Bering Strait, Bering Sea, Chukchi Sea, East Siberian Sea, Laptev Sea, Kara Sea, Barents Sea, Sea of Okhotsk, Sea of Japan (East Sea), Yellow Sea, East China Sea, Korea Strait, Philippine Sea, South China Sea, Celebes Sea, Banda Sea, Arafura Sea, Timor Sea, Java Sea, Bay of Bengal, Andaman Sea, Arabian Sea, Gulf of Thailand, Strait of Malacca, Sunda Strait, Gulf of Oman, Persian Gulf, Strait of Hormuz, Red Sea, Gulf of Aden, Mediterranean Sea, Black Sea, Bosporus, Caspian Sea, Aral Sea, Lake Balkhash, Lake Baikal

Lena River, Tunguska River, Angara River, Yenisey River, Ob River, Irtysh River, Ishim River, Ural River, Syr Darya, Amu Darya, Indus River, Ganges River, Sutlej River, Brahmaputra River, Irrawaddy River, Salween River, Mekong River, Hong River, Xi River, Chang (Yangtze) River, Huang (Yellow) River, Amur River, Shilka River, Aldan River, Kolyma River, Godavari River, Tigris River, Euphrates River, Tobol River

Islands/Peninsulas: Kamchatka Peninsula, Chukchi Peninsula, Wrangel Island, New Siberian Islands, Severnaya Zemlya, Novaya Zemlya, Franz Josef Land, Taymyr Peninsula, Sakhalin, Kuril Islands, Hokkaido, Honshu, Shikoku, Kyushu, Ryukyu Islands, Okinawa, Taiwan, Hainan, Luzon, Mindanao, Palawan, Philippine Islands, Sulawesi (Celebes), Moluccas, Bali, Lesser Sunda Is., Mentawai Islands, Nicobar Islands, Andaman Islands, Sri Lanka, Maldives, Lakshadweep, Socotra, Cyprus, Cape Comorin, Korean Peninsula, Arabian Peninsula, Anatolia

▲ Mt. Fuji 12,388 ft. (3,776 m)

▲ K2 28,251 ft. (8,611 m)

▲ Mt. Everest 29,035 ft. (8,850 m)

▲ Mt. Ararat 16,946 ft. (5,165 m)

▽ Dead Sea 1,339 ft. (408 m) below sea level

South Korea

Japan

PACIFIC OCEAN

INDIAN OCEAN

EQUATOR

TROPIC OF CANCER

ARCTIC CIRCLE

Legend:
International boundary
▲ Mountain peak
▽ Lowest point

Sources for elevation data:
World Almanac, 2019
World Factbook, CIA, 2019

Robinson Projection

1,000 mi

1,000 km

500

0

N
W E
S

Elevation Profile

30,000 ft.
25,000 ft.
20,000 ft.
15,000 ft.
10,000 ft.
5,000 ft.
Sea level

A   Dead Sea   Syrian Desert   Zagros Mts.   Indus Valley   Himalayas   Mount Everest   Yellow Sea   South Korea   Japan   B

A — B

Largest Cities in Asia (urban agglomerations)

2018		2030 (projected)	
1 Tokyo, JPN	37,468,000	1 Delhi, IND	38,939,000
2 Delhi, IND	28,514,000	2 Tokyo, JPN	36,574,000
3 Shanghai, CHN	25,582,000	3 Shanghai, CHN	32,869,000
4 Mumbai, IND	19,980,000	4 Dhaka, BGD	28,076,000
5 Beijing, CHN	19,618,000	5 Mumbai, IND	24,572,000
6 Dhaka, BGD	19,578,000	6 Beijing, CHN	24,282,000
7 Osaka, JPN	19,281,000	7 Karachi, PAK	20,432,000
8 Karachi, PAK	15,400,000	8 Chongqing, CHN	19,649,000
9 Chongqing, CHN	14,838,000	9 Osaka, JPN	18,658,000
10 Kolkata, IND	14,681,000	10 Kolkata, IND	17,584,000
11 Manila, PHL	13,482,000	11 Lahore, PAK	16,883,000
12 Tianjin, CHN	13,215,000	12 Manila, PHL	16,841,000
13 Guangzhou, CHN	12,638,000	13 Bengaluru, IND	16,227,000
14 Shenzhen, CHN	11,908,000	14 Guangzhou, CHN	16,024,000
15 Lahore, PAK	11,738,000	15 Tianjin, CHN	15,745,000
16 Bengaluru, IND	11,440,000	16 Shenzhen, CHN	14,537,000
17 Jakarta, IDN	10,517,000	17 Chennai, IND	13,814,000
18 Chennai, IND	10,456,000	18 Hyderabad, IND	12,714,000
19 Bangkok, THA	10,156,000	19 Jakarta, IDN	12,687,000
20 Seoul, KOR	9,963,000	20 Bangkok, THA	12,101,000

Source: United Nations. Department of Social & Economic Affairs, Population Division, 2018

Estimated 2021 Population
(in millions)

1	China	1,444.2
2	India	1,393.4
3	Indonesia	276.4
4	Pakistan	225.2
5	Bangladesh	166.3
6	Japan	126.1
7	Philippines	111.0
8	Vietnam	98.2
9	Iran	85.0
10	Thailand	70.0
	all others in Asia	682.6

Source: World Population Review, 2021

Estimated 2021 Population Density
(in persons per square mile)

1	Macau	56,841.4
2	Singapore	21,510.4
3	Hong Kong	17,719.2
4	Bahrain	5,919.1
5	Maldives	4,693.2
6	Bangladesh	2,918.8
7	Taiwan	1,707.1
8	Lebanon	1,677.4
9	South Korea	1,326.0
10	India	1,097.7

Mount Everest, the world's highest peak at 29,035 ft. (8,850 m.), viewed from Gokyo Ri, a mountain peak at 17,575 ft. (5,357 m.) in northeastern Nepal. The Tibetan prayer flags in the foreground are meant to carry blessings and Buddhist teachings on peace and compassion to the countryside. The flags are always displayed in the same order, each color symbolizing a different element in nature: blue for sky, white for wind, red for fire, green for water, and yellow for earth. It's believed that health and harmony are produced by the arrangement of the strings of flags. (*at right*)

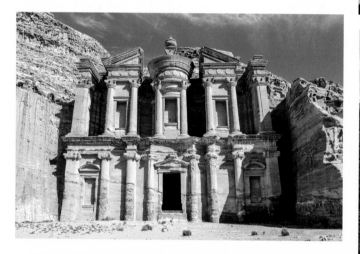

Al-Dayr ("the Monastery"), at Petra, Jordan. Cut out of the surrounding rock, the structure was to serve as the facade for a tomb; later it was used as a Byzantine church. Located along an ancient trade route, the city prospered over two thousand years ago with a population that may have approached 30,000. Changes in trade routes and damage to the city by earthquakes led to Petra's decline by around 551. After the Crusades, Petra was unknown to the European world until it was rediscovered by a Swiss traveler in 1812.

The Great Wall of China at Simatai, China, northeast of Beijing. The Great Wall is made up of several walls, built over northern China, beginning almost 3,000 years ago. Though widely known as a defensive fortification system against invasions from the north, walls were also used by ancient Chinese city-states as a source of protection from each other. Likely the largest building project ever undertaken, the total length of all the known sections of the Great Wall is 13,171 miles (21,196 kilometers).

Gross Domestic Product is a measure of the total goods and services generated by a country. Generally, manufacturing, high-tech services, and specialized agricultural products add more value than raw materials and basic food stuffs. The high-tech and oil producing countries on the fringes of Asia are the exceptions in this generally poor continent.

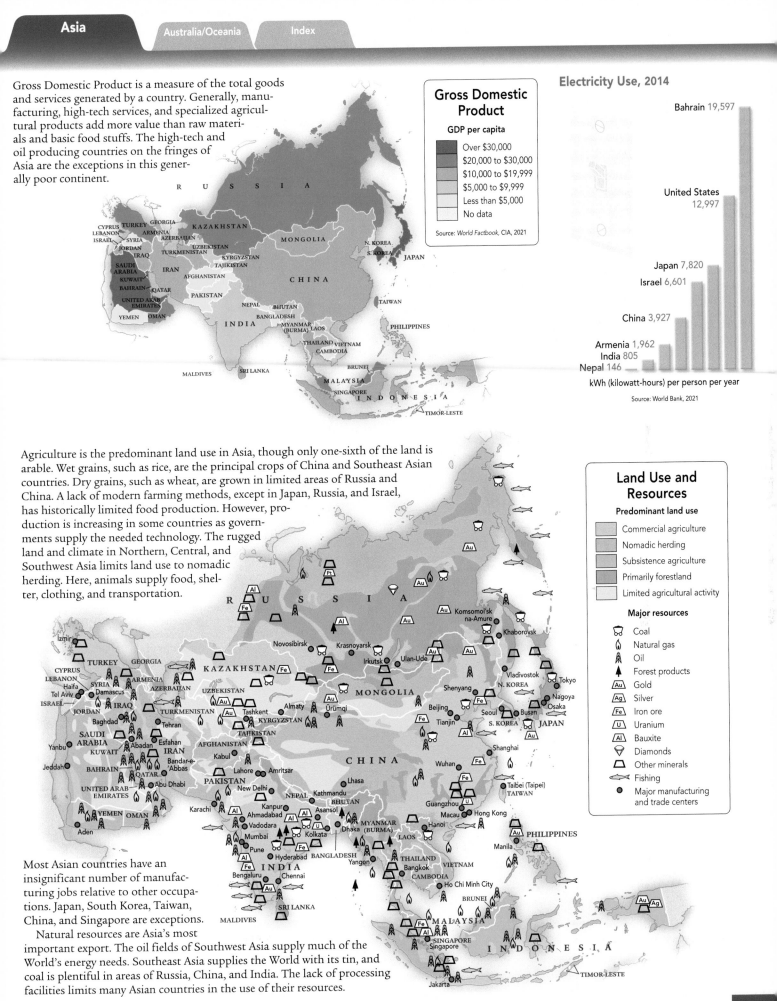

Gross Domestic Product

GDP per capita

Over $30,000
$20,000 to $30,000
$10,000 to $19,999
$5,000 to $9,999
Less than $5,000
No data

Source: *World Factbook*, CIA, 2021

Electricity Use, 2014

Bahrain 19,597
United States 12,997
Japan 7,820
Israel 6,601
China 3,927
Armenia 1,962
India 805
Nepal 146

kWh (kilowatt-hours) per person per year

Source: World Bank, 2021

Agriculture is the predominant land use in Asia, though only one-sixth of the land is arable. Wet grains, such as rice, are the principal crops of China and Southeast Asian countries. Dry grains, such as wheat, are grown in limited areas of Russia and China. A lack of modern farming methods, except in Japan, Russia, and Israel, has historically limited food production. However, production is increasing in some countries as governments supply the needed technology. The rugged land and climate in Northern, Central, and Southwest Asia limits land use to nomadic herding. Here, animals supply food, shelter, clothing, and transportation.

Land Use and Resources

Predominant land use

Commercial agriculture
Nomadic herding
Subsistence agriculture
Primarily forestland
Limited agricultural activity

Major resources

Coal
Natural gas
Oil
Forest products
Au Gold
Ag Silver
Fe Iron ore
U   Uranium
Al Bauxite
Diamonds
Other minerals
Fishing
Major manufacturing and trade centers

Most Asian countries have an insignificant number of manufacturing jobs relative to other occupations. Japan, South Korea, Taiwan, China, and Singapore are exceptions.

Natural resources are Asia's most important export. The oil fields of Southwest Asia supply much of the World's energy needs. Southeast Asia supplies the World with its tin, and coal is plentiful in areas of Russia, China, and India. The lack of processing facilities limits many Asian countries in the use of their resources.

Australia/Oceania

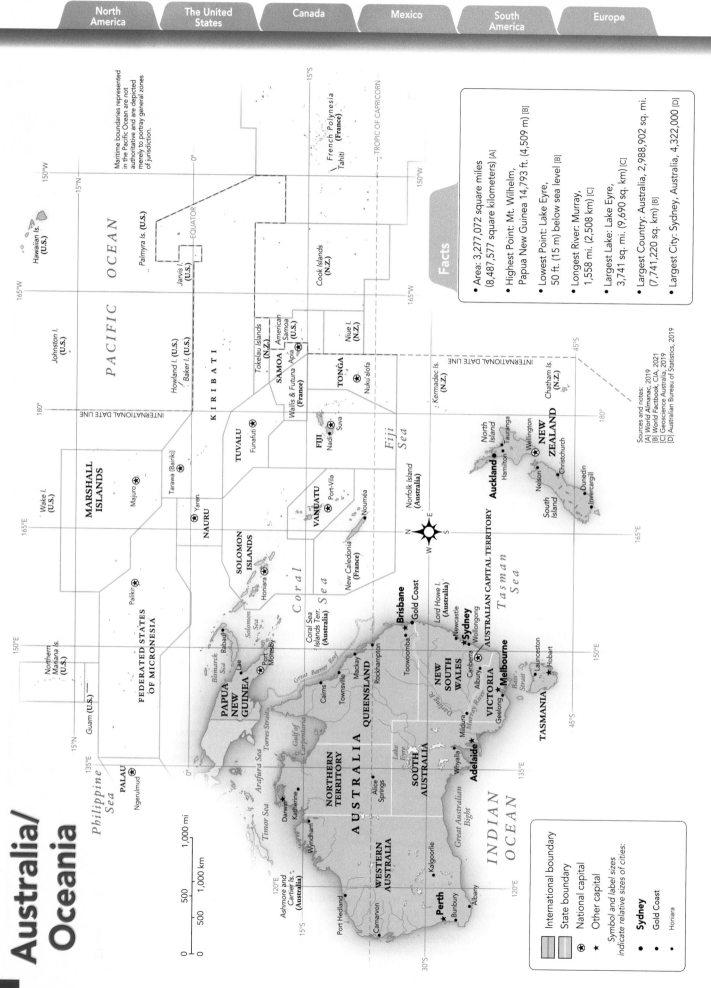

Maritime boundaries represented in the Pacific Ocean are not authoritative and are depicted merely to portray general zones of jurisdiction.

Facts

- Area: 3,277,072 square miles (8,487,577 square kilometers) [A]
- Highest Point: Mt. Wilhelm, Papua New Guinea 14,793 ft. (4,509 m) [B]
- Lowest Point: Lake Eyre, 50 ft. (15 m) below sea level [B]
- Longest River: Murray, 1,558 mi. (2,508 km) [C]
- Largest Lake: Lake Eyre, 3,741 sq. mi. (9,690 sq. km) [C]
- Largest Country: Australia, 2,988,902 sq. mi. (7,741,220 sq. km) [B]
- Largest City: Sydney, Australia, 4,322,000 [D]

Sources and notes:
[A] World Almanac, 2019
[B] World Factbook, CIA, 2021
[C] Geoscience Australia, 2019
[D] Australian Bureau of Statistics, 2019

International boundary
State boundary
⊛ National capital
★ Other capital

Symbol and label sizes indicate relative sizes of cities:

● **Sydney**
● Gold Coast
· Honiara

102

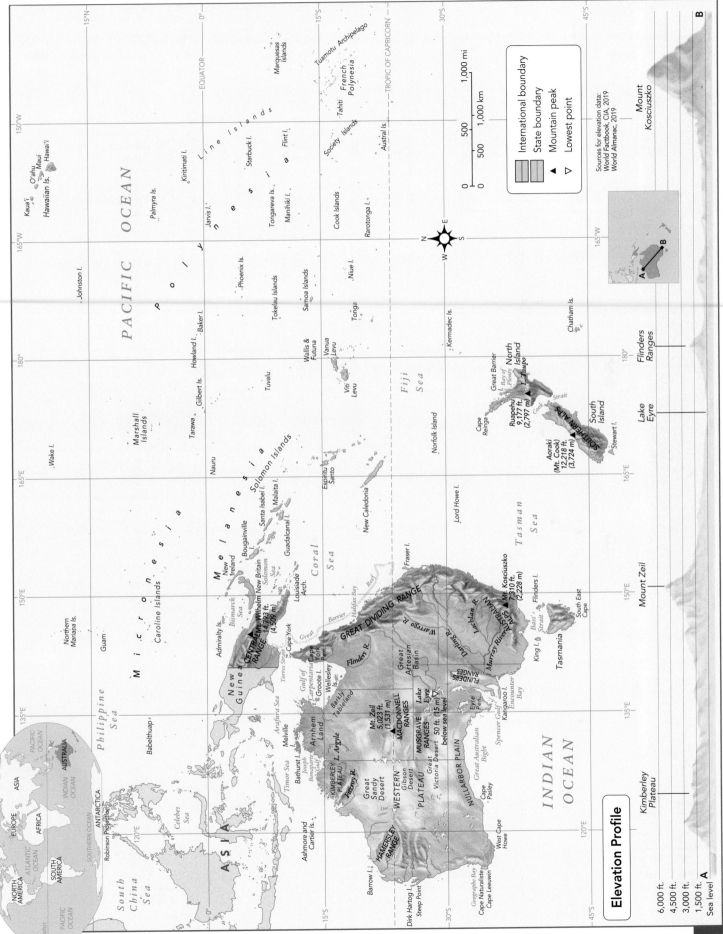

PACIFIC OCEAN

Kaua'i
O'ahu
Maui
Hawaiian Is.
Hawai'i

Johnston I.

Palmyra Is.

Line Islands

Kiritimati I.

Jarvis I.

Starbuck I.

Flint I.

Marquesas Islands

Tuamotu Archipelago

French Polynesia

Tahiti

Society Islands

Austral Is.

P o l y n e s i a

Phoenix Is.

Howland I.

Baker I.

Tokelau Islands

Tongareva I.

Manihiki I.

Samoa Islands

Cook Islands

Rarotonga I.

Niue I.

Tonga

TROPIC OF CAPRICORN

EQUATOR

Wake I.

Marshall Islands

Nauru

Tarawa

Gilbert Is.

Tuvalu

Wallis & Futuna

Vanua Levu

Viti Levu

Fiji Sea

Kermadec Is.

Chatham Is.

Northern Mariana Is.

Guam

Caroline Islands

M i c r o n e s i a

Admiralty Is.

New Ireland

Mt. Wilhelm 14,793 ft. (4,509 m)
CENTRAL RANGE

New Britain

Bismarck Sea

Bougainville

Solomon Islands

Santa Isabel I.

Malaita I.

Solomon Sea

Guadalcanal I.

Louisiade Arch.

M e l a n e s i a

Espiritu Santo

New Caledonia

Norfolk Island

Lord Howe I.

Tasman Sea

North Island

Ruapehu 9,177 ft. (2,797 m)

L. Taupo

Cook Strait

Bay of Plenty

Cape Reinga

Aoraki (Mt. Cook) 12,218 ft. (3,724 m)

SOUTHERN ALPS

South Island

Stewart I.

Philippine Sea

Babelthuap

New Guinea

Torres Strait

Cape York

Gulf of Carpentaria

Arafura Sea

Timor Sea

Ashmore and Cartier Is.

Melville I.

Bathurst I.

Arnhem Land

Groote I.

Wellesley Is.

Barkly Tableland

Cape York Pen.

Coral Sea

Great Barrier Reef

Halifax Bay

Fraser I.

GREAT DIVIDING RANGE

Warrego R.

Flinders R.

Great Artesian Basin

Darling R.

Lachlan R.

Murray River

Mt. Kosciuszko 7,310 ft. (2,228 m)

AUSTRALIAN ALPS

Bass Strait

King I.

Flinders I.

South East Cape

Tasmania

Kimberley Plateau

L. Argyle

Fitzroy R.

Great Sandy Desert

WESTERN PLATEAU

Gibson Desert

Mt. Zeil 5,023 ft. (1,531 m)
MACDONNELL RANGES

MUSGRAVE RANGES

Lake Eyre 50 ft. (15 m) below sea level

FLINDERS RANGES

Bonaparte Gulf

HAMERSLEY RANGE

KIMBERLEY PLATEAU

Victoria Desert

Great Victoria Desert

NULLARBOR PLAIN

Great Australian Bight

Spencer Gulf

Eyre Pen.

Kangaroo I.

Encounter Bay

Cape Pasley

West Cape Howe

Geographe Bay

Cape Naturaliste

Cape Leeuwin

Dirk Hartog I.

Steep Point

Barrow I.

INDIAN OCEAN

Joseph Bonaparte Gulf

A S I A

South China Sea

Celebes Sea

INDIAN OCEAN

ANTARCTICA

Robinson Projection

ARCTIC OCEAN

EUROPE

ASIA

ATLANTIC OCEAN

AFRICA

INDIAN OCEAN

AUSTRALIA

SOUTHERN OCEAN

NORTH AMERICA

PACIFIC OCEAN

SOUTH AMERICA

PACIFIC OCEAN

Equator

International boundary

State boundary

▲ Mountain peak

▽ Lowest point

Sources for elevation data:
World Factbook, CIA, 2019
World Almanac, 2019

0   500   1,000 mi
0   500   1,000 km

N E W S

Elevation Profile

6,000 ft.
4,500 ft.
3,000 ft.
1,500 ft.
Sea level

A   Kimberley Plateau   Mount Zeil   Lake Eyre   Flinders Ranges   Mount Kosciuszko   B

Largest Cities in Australia & Oceania (urban agglomerations)

2018

1 Sydney, AUS 4,792,000
2 Melbourne, AUS 4,771,000
3 Brisbane, AUS 2,338,000
4 Perth, AUS 1,991,000
5 Auckland, NZL 1,557,000
6 Adelaide, AUS 1,320,000

2030 (projected)

1 Melbourne, AUS 5,736,000
2 Sydney, AUS 5,566,000
3 Brisbane, AUS 2,724,000
4 Perth, AUS 2,299,000
5 Auckland, NZL 1,791,000
6 Adelaide, AUS 1,472,000

Source: United Nations. Department of Social & Economic Affairs, Population Division, 2018

Estimated 2021 Population
(in millions)

1	Australia	25.50
2	Papua New Guinea	8.95
3	New Zealand	4.82
4	Fiji	0.90
5	Solomon Islands	0.69
6	Vanuatu	0.31
7	New Caledonia (Fr.)	0.29
8	French Polynesia (Fr.)	0.28
9	Samoa	0.20
10	Guam (U.S.)	0.19
	all others in Oceania	1.09

Source: World Population Review, 2021

Estimated 2021 Population Density
(in persons per square mile)

1	Nauru	1,341.4
2	Tuvalu	1,188.5
3	Marshall Islands	853.0
4	Guam (U.S.)	802.8
5	Amer. Samoa (U.S.)	717.1
6	Micronesia	428.9
7	Kiribati	387.7
8	Tonga	370.2
9	N. Mariana Is. (U.S.)	323.3
10	Tokelau (N.Z.)	296.3

The skyline of Sydney, Australia's largest city. The Sydney Opera House, in the foreground, is perhaps the most photographed landmark in Sydney and all of Australia due to its unique sail-shaped roof design.

Aboriginal rock art depicting a kangaroo at Burrungui, Kakadu National Park, in the Northern Territory of Australia. The settlement date of Australia by Aboriginal people is still unclear as new archeological evidence is found. Some historians put the settlement period at roughly 45,000 years ago; others believe it may have been up to 80,000 years ago.

Aboriginal art is the oldest form of artistic expression found in the world. Although over 500 Aboriginal spoken languages are known to exist, Aboriginal peoples never developed a written language. Instead, their artwork served—and continues to serve—as a visual medium for storytelling, using a variety of techniques, symbols, and colors as forms of expression. Over 5,000 rock art sites are known to exist at Kakadu, with estimates as high as 100,000 total sites around Australia.

Mount Cook is the highest mountain in New Zealand at 12,218 feet (3,724 meters). Known as Aoraki by the indigenous Maori people of New Zealand, the mountain was first sighted by Europeans in 1642 and later named for Captain James Cook. The mountain is part of the Southern Alps, a mountain range on New Zealand's South Island.

Gross Domestic Product is a measure of the total goods and services generated by a country. Generally, manufacturing, high-tech services, and specialized agricultural products add more value than raw materials and basic food stuffs.

Australia derives its wealth and high standard of living from service industries, as well as mineral extraction and processing. New Zealand's economy is oriented towards the export of animal products. Papua New Guinea's subsistence economy generates little excess wealth.

Electricity Use, 2014

United States
12,997

Australia
10,071

New Zealand
9,013

*Nauru 2,424

*Samoa 502

kWh (kilowatt-hours) per person per year

Sources: World Bank, 2021
* 2016 estimate from the *World Factbook*, CIA, 2019

GDP of Island Nations

Fiji
Kiribati
Marshall Islands
Micronesia
Nauru
Palau

Samoa
Solomon Islands
Tonga
Tuvalu
Vanuatu

GDP of Island Territories

American Samoa (U.S.)
Cook Is. (N.Z.)
French Polynesia (Fr.)
Guam (U.S.)
New Caledonia (Fr.)
Niue (N.Z.)
Northern Mariana Is. (U.S.)
Tokelau (N.Z.)
Wallis & Futuna (Fr.)

Gross Domestic Product

GDP per capita

Over $30,000
$20,000 to $30,000
$10,000 to $19,999
$5,000 to $9,999
Less than $5,000
No data

Source: *World Factbook*, CIA, 2021

Land Use and Resources

Predominant land use

Commercial agriculture
Dairying
Livestock ranching
Primarily forestland
Limited agricultural activity

Major resources

Coal
Natural gas
Oil
Forest products
Au Gold
Ag Silver
Fe Iron ore
U   Uranium
Al Bauxite
Diamonds
Other minerals
Fishing
Major manufacturing and trade centers

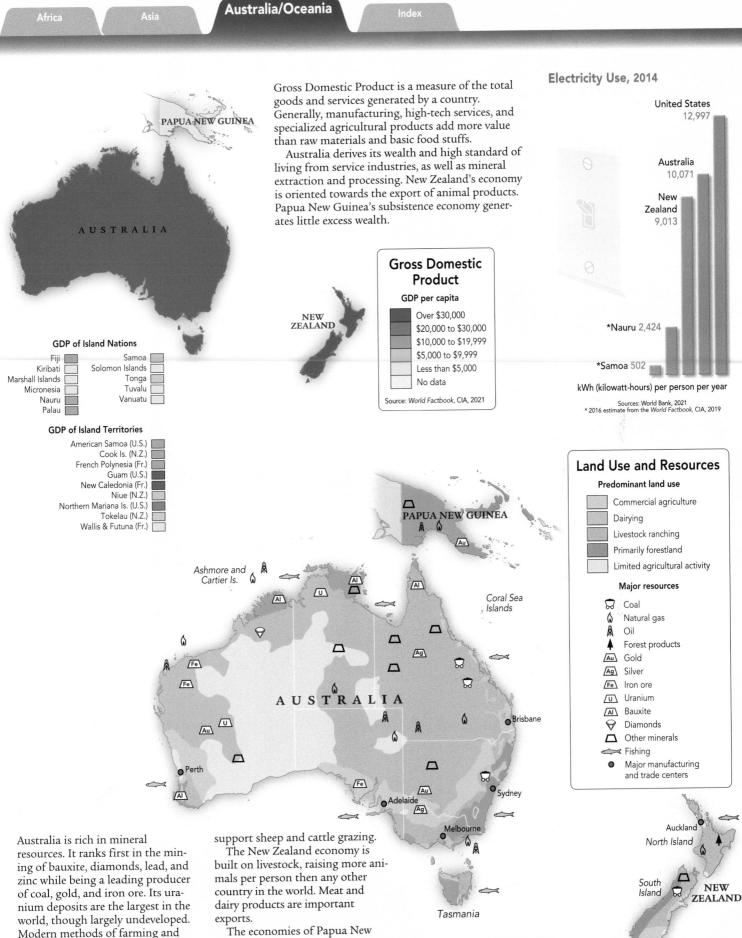

Australia is rich in mineral resources. It ranks first in the mining of bauxite, diamonds, lead, and zinc while being a leading producer of coal, gold, and iron ore. Its uranium deposits are the largest in the world, though largely undeveloped. Modern methods of farming and irrigation allow a very limited area of commercial agriculture to be highly productive. Despite arid conditions, vast areas of the interior support sheep and cattle grazing.

The New Zealand economy is built on livestock, raising more animals per person then any other country in the world. Meat and dairy products are important exports.

The economies of Papua New Guinea and the other island nations in the region rely primarily on subsistence agriculture and tourism.

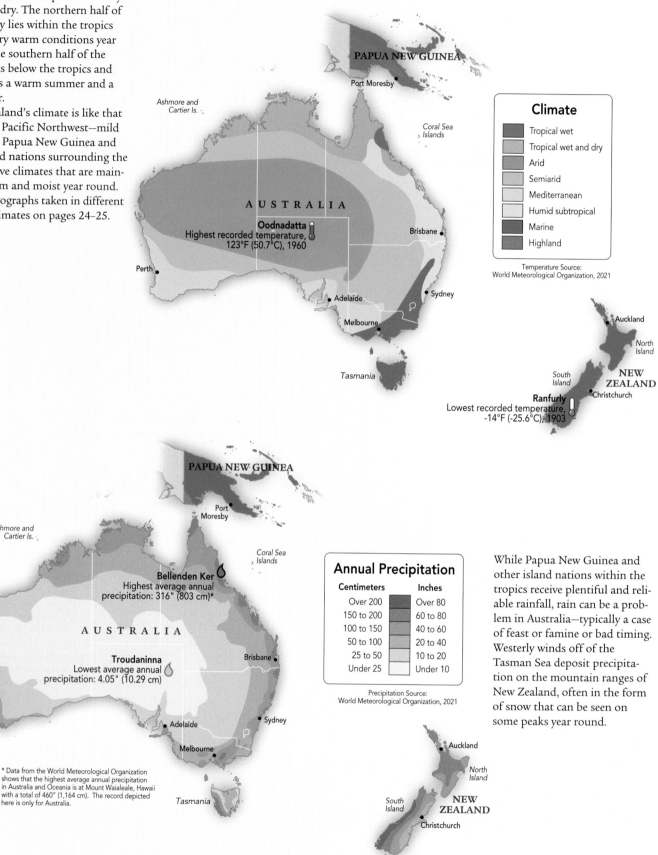

Australia's climate is predominately warm and dry. The northern half of the country lies within the tropics and has very warm conditions year round. The southern half of the country lies below the tropics and experiences a warm summer and a cool winter.

New Zealand's climate is like that of the U.S. Pacific Northwest—mild and moist. Papua New Guinea and other island nations surrounding the equator have climates that are mainly very warm and moist year round.

See photographs taken in different kinds of climates on pages 24–25.

PAPUA NEW GUINEA
Port Moresby

Ashmore and Cartier Is.

Coral Sea Islands

A U S T R A L I A

Oodnadatta
Highest recorded temperature, 123°F (50.7°C), 1960

Perth
Brisbane
Adelaide
Sydney
Melbourne

Tasmania

Climate

- Tropical wet
- Tropical wet and dry
- Arid
- Semiarid
- Mediterranean
- Humid subtropical
- Marine
- Highland

Temperature Source:
World Meteorological Organization, 2021

Auckland
North Island
South Island
NEW ZEALAND
Christchurch

Ranfurly
Lowest recorded temperature, -14°F (-25.6°C), 1903

PAPUA NEW GUINEA
Port Moresby

Ashmore and Cartier Is.

Coral Sea Islands

A U S T R A L I A

Bellenden Ker
Highest average annual precipitation: 316" (803 cm)*

Troudaninna
Lowest average annual precipitation: 4.05" (10.29 cm)

Perth
Brisbane
Adelaide
Sydney
Melbourne

Tasmania

Annual Precipitation

Centimeters	Inches
Over 200	Over 80
150 to 200	60 to 80
100 to 150	40 to 60
50 to 100	20 to 40
25 to 50	10 to 20
Under 25	Under 10

Precipitation Source:
World Meteorological Organization, 2021

* Data from the World Meteorological Organization shows that the highest average annual precipitation in Australia and Oceania is at Mount Waialeale, Hawaii with a total of 460" (1,164 cm). The record depicted here is only for Australia.

While Papua New Guinea and other island nations within the tropics receive plentiful and reliable rainfall, rain can be a problem in Australia—typically a case of feast or famine or bad timing. Westerly winds off of the Tasman Sea deposit precipitation on the mountain ranges of New Zealand, often in the form of snow that can be seen on some peaks year round.

Auckland
North Island
South Island
NEW ZEALAND
Christchurch

Climate Graphs

Average daily temperature range (in °F)
Average monthly precipitation (in inches)

100° — High
65°
32° — Low
0°

20"
10"
0"

BRISBANE, Australia

100°
65°
32°
0°
Jan Apr Jul Oct

20"
10"
0"

PERTH, Australia

100°
65°
32°
0°
Jan Apr Jul Oct

20"
10"
0"

AUCKLAND, New Zealand

100°
65°
32°
0°
Jan Apr Jul Oct

20"
10"
0"

PORT MORESBY, Papua New Guinea

100°
65°
32°
0°
Jan Apr Jul Oct

20"
10"
0"

ADELAIDE, Australia

100°
65°
32°
0°
Jan Apr Jul Oct

20"
10"
0"

MELBOURNE, Australia

100°
65°
32°
0°
Jan Apr Jul Oct

20"
10"
0"

SYDNEY, Australia

100°
65°
32°
0°
Jan Apr Jul Oct

20"
10"
0"

CHRISTCHURCH, New Zealand

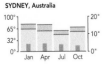

100°
65°
32°
0°
Jan Apr Jul Oct

20"
10"
0"

Abundant Australian forest-lands are limited to relatively narrow coastal regions where moisture, even if seasonal, is adequate. Most of the rest of the continent is covered by species of trees, bush, and grasses adapted to arid conditions. Eucalyptus are the most common trees in Australia.

Papua New Guinea has dense tropical rain forests, and New Zealand has mixed forests and grasslands arising from its temperate climate.

See photographs of different kinds of vegetation on pages 26–27.

Did You Know?

The "Outback" in Australia generally refers to any inland area removed from the population centers along the coast. "Bush" and "never-never" are Australian terms synonymous with "Outback"

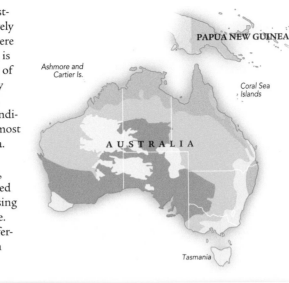

Vegetation

- Subtropical broadleaf evergreen forest
- Mixed forest
- Midlatitude scrubland
- Midlatitude grassland
- Desert
- Tropical seasonal and scrub
- Tropical rain forest
- Tropical savanna

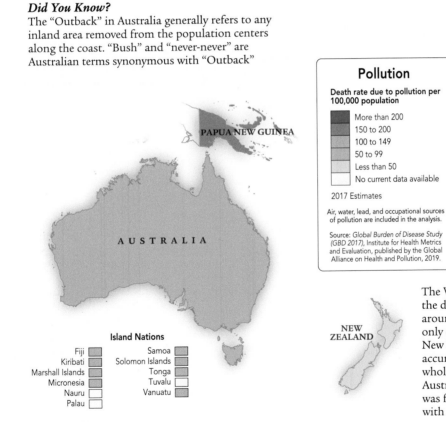

Pollution

Death rate due to pollution per 100,000 population

- More than 200
- 150 to 200
- 100 to 149
- 50 to 99
- Less than 50
- No current data available

2017 Estimates

Air, water, lead, and occupational sources of pollution are included in the analysis.

Source: *Global Burden of Disease Study (GBD 2017)*, Institute for Health Metrics and Evaluation, published by the Global Alliance on Health and Pollution, 2019.

Island Nations

Fiji
Kiribati
Marshall Islands
Micronesia
Nauru
Palau

Samoa
Solomon Islands
Tonga
Tuvalu
Vanuatu

The World Air Quality Index monitors the daily air quality in 380 major cities around the world. Their 2020 analysis only considered cities in Australia and New Zealand, which doesn't present an accurate representation of Oceania as a whole. Among the major cities in Australia and New Zealand, Canberra was found to have the worst air quality with a world ranking of 348th.

Countries in Oceania are at various stages of developing and enacting national and more localized strategies to combat air, water, and other forms of pollution—with Australia and New Zealand in the forefront. Papua New Guinea ranks six in the world in having the highest death rate from pollution in the world. At the other extreme, New Zealand has one of the lowest rates in the world.

Abbreviations

Abbr.	Full	Abbr.	Full	Abbr.	Full	Abbr.	Full	Abbr.	Full
Arch.	Archipelago	Den.	Denmark	Isth.	Isthmus	N. Mac.	North Macedonia	Sp.	Spain
Austl.	Australia	Dominican Rep.	Dominican Republic	It.	Italy	N.Z.	New Zealand	St., St-	Saint
Bos. & Her.	Bosnia & Herzegovina	fed. dist.	Federal District	Kos.	Kosovo	Pen.	Peninsula	Ste., Ste-	Sainte
C.	Cape	Fed. States of Micronesia	Federated States of Micronesia	L.	Lake	Plat.	Plateau	Str.	Strait
Can.	Canada	Fr.	France	Liecht.	Liechtenstein	Pt.	Point	Terr.	Territory
Cen. African Rep.	Central African Republic	Ft.	Fort	Mex.	Mexico	R.	River	U.K.	United Kingdom
Czech Rep.	Czech Republic	G.	Gulf	Mont.	Montenegro	Rep.	Republic	U.S.	United States
Dem. Rep. of Congo	Democratic Republic of the Congo	Gr.	Greece	Mor.	Morocco	Rep. of the Congo	Republic of the Congo	Val.	Valley
		I.	Island	Mt.	Mount	Res.	Reservoir		
		Is.	Islands	Mts.	Mountains	Russ.	Russia		
				N. Korea	North Korea	S. Africa	South Africa		
						S. Korea	South Korea		

For U.S. two-letter state abbreviations, see pages 52–53.

Afghanistan

Islamic republic, SW Asia

Area: 251,827 sq. mi. (652,230 sq. km.)
Population: 37,466,000
Language(s): Dari, Pashto

Monetary unit: afghani
Economy: bricks, textiles, soap, furniture, opium, wheat, fruit, nuts, natural gas

After the fall of the Taliban in 2001, the newly established Afghan Interim Authority restored, in a modified form, the national flag first introduced in 1928. Black represents the dark ages of the past; red, the blood shed in the struggle for independence; and green, for Islam.

Albania

Republic, S Europe

Area: 11,100 sq. mi. (28,748 sq. km.)
Population: 3,088,000
Language(s): Albanian

Monetary unit: lek
Economy: wheat, corn, potatoes, vegetables, footwear, apparel, clothing

On Nov. 28, 1443, the flag was first raised by Skanderbeg, the national hero. After independence from Turkish rule was proclaimed on Nov. 28, 1912, the flag was flown by various regimes, each of which identified itself by adding a symbol above the double-headed eagle. The current flag, which features only the eagle, was adopted on May 22, 1993.

Algeria

Republic, N Africa

Area: 919,595 sq. mi. (2,381,740 sq. km.)
Population: 43,577,000
Language(s): Arabic, French

Monetary unit: Algerian dinar
Economy: oil, natural gas, light industries, mining, wheat, barley, oats, grapes

In the early 19th century, during the French conquest of North Africa, Algerian resistance fighters led by Emir Abdelkader supposedly raised the current flag. Its colors and symbols are associated with Islam and the Arab dynasties of the region. The flag was raised over an independent Algeria on July 3, 1962.

Andorra

Principality, SW Europe

Area: 181 sq. mi. (468 sq. km.)
Population: 86,000
Language(s): Catalan, French

Monetary unit: euro
Economy: tourism, international banking, timber, furniture, rye, wheat, barley

The flag may date to 1866, but the first legal authority for it is unknown. The design was standardized in July 1993. Possible sources for its colors are the flags of neighboring Spain (red-yellow-red) and France (blue-white-red). The coat of arms incorporates both French and Spanish elements dating to the 13th century or earlier.

Angola

Republic, SW Africa

Area: 481,351 sq. mi. (1,246,700 sq. km.)
Population: 33,643,000
Language(s): Portuguese

Monetary unit: kwanza
Economy: bananas, sugarcane, coffee, sisal, iron ore, oil, diamonds, phosphates

After Portugal withdrew from Angola on Nov. 11, 1975, the flag of the leading rebel group gained recognition. Inspired by designs of the Viet Cong and the former Soviet Union, it includes a star for internationalism and progress, a cogwheel for industrial workers, and a machete for agricultural workers. The black stripe is for the African people.

Antigua and Barbuda

Islands republic, Caribbean

Area: 171 sq. mi. (443 sq. km.)
Population: 99,000
Language(s): English

Monetary unit: East Caribbean dollar
Economy: tourism, light manufacturing, cotton, fruits, vegetables, bananas

When "associated statehood" was granted by Great Britain on Feb. 27, 1967, the flag was introduced, and it remained after independence (Nov. 1, 1981). The sun represents the dawning of a new era, red for the dynamism of the people, black for the African heritage of most of the population, and the V-shape for victory. The bands of blue and white represent the sea and sand.

Argentina

Republic, South America

Area: 1,073,518 sq. mi.
(2,780,400 sq. km.)
Population: 45,865,000
Language(s): Spanish, Italian, English

Monetary unit: Argentine peso
Economy: food processing, motor vehicles, consumer durables, textiles, sunflower seeds, lemons, soybeans, grapes

The uniforms worn by Argentines when the British attacked Buenos Aires (1806) and the blue ribbons worn by patriots in 1810 may have been the origin of the light blue-white-light blue flag hoisted on Aug. 23, 1812. The flag's golden "sun of May" was added on Feb. 25, 1818, to commemorate the yielding of the Spanish viceroy in 1810.

Armenia

Republic, SW Asia

Area: 11,484 sq. mi. (29,743 sq. km.)
Population: 3,012,000
Language(s): Armenian, Kurdish

Monetary unit: dram
Economy: brandy, diamond-processing, machine tools, tires, mining, grapes

Armenia proclaimed independence in 1918, following the Russian Revolution. On Aug. 1, 1918, a flag was sanctioned with stripes of red (possibly symbolizing blood), blue (for homeland), and orange (for courage and work). The flag was replaced during Soviet rule, beginning in 1921. The flag was readopted on Aug. 24, 1990, when independence from the Soviet Union was announced.

Australia

Continent republic, SE of Asia

Area: 2,988,902 sq. mi.
(7,741,220 sq. km.)
Population: 25,810,000
Language(s): English

Monetary unit: Australian dollar
Economy: mining (gold, diamonds, uranium), gas, oil, food processing, wool, transport equipment, wheat, barley

After Australian confederation was achieved on Jan. 1, 1901, the flag was chosen in a competition. Like the blue flags of British colonies, it displays the Union Jack in the canton. Also shown are the Southern Cross and a "Commonwealth Star." The design became official on May 22, 1909, and it was recognized as the national flag on Feb. 14, 1954.

Austria

Republic, cen. Europe

Area: 32,383 sq. mi. (83,871 sq. km.)
Population: 8,885,000
Language(s): German, Croatian, Hungarian, and Slovene in parts of the country.

Monetary unit: euro
Economy: machinery, lumber, paper, motor vehicles, chemicals, mining (minerals, salt), iron, steel, tourism

The colors of the Austrian coat of arms date from the seal of Duke Frederick II in 1230. With the fall of the Austro-Hungarian Empire in 1918, the new Austrian republic adopted the red-white-red flag. The white is sometimes said to represent the Danube River. An imperial eagle, an Austrian symbol for centuries, is added to government flags.

Azerbaijan

Republic, SW Asia

Area: 33,436 sq. mi. (86,600 sq. km.)
Population: 10,282,000
Language(s): Azerbaijani, Lezghin, Russian

Monetary unit: Azerbaijani manat
Economy: oil, natural gas, oilfield equipment, steel, iron ore, fruit, grain, vegetables, rice

In the early 20th century anti-Russian nationalists exhorted the Azerbaijanis to "Turkify, Islamicize, and Europeanize," and the 1917 flag was associated with Turkey and Islam. In 1918 the crescent and star (also symbols of Turkic peoples) were introduced. Suppressed under Soviet rule, the flag was readopted on Feb. 5, 1991.

Bahamas

Islands republic, Caribbean

Area: 5,359 sq. mi. (13,880 sq. km.)
Population: 353,000
Language(s): English

Monetary unit: Bahamian dollar
Economy: tourism, banking, shellfish, pharmaceuticals, citrus, vegetables

The flag of The Bahamas was adopted on July 10, 1973, the date of independence from Britain. Several entries from a competition were combined to create the design. The two aquamarine stripes are for the surrounding waters, the gold stripe is for the sand and other rich land resources, and the black triangle is for the people and their strength.

Bahrain

Islamic kingdom, Persian Gulf

Area: 293 sq. mi. (760 sq. km.)
Population: 1,527,000
Language(s): Arabic

Monetary unit: Bahraini dinar
Economy: oil, petroleum refining, metal processing, banking, ship repairing

Red was the color of the Kharijite Muslims of Bahrain about 1820, and white was chosen to show amity with the British. The flag was recognized in 1933 but was used long before. The current flag law was adopted in 2002. The five white points represent the five pillars of Islam.

Bangladesh

Republic, S Asia

Area: 57,321 sq. mi. (148,460 sq. km.)
Population: 164,099,000
Language(s): Bengali

Monetary unit: taka
Economy: jute, cotton, garments, paper, leather, rice, tea, wheat, sugarcane

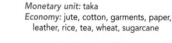

The flag is dark green to symbolize Islam, plant life, and the hope placed in Bengali youth. Its original design included a red disk and a silhouette of the country. On Jan. 13, 1972, the silhouette was removed and the disk shifted off-center. The disk is the "rising sun of a new country" colored by the blood of those who fought for independence.

Barbados

Island republic, Caribbean

Area: 166 sq. mi. (430 sq. km.)
Population: 302,000
Language(s): English

Monetary unit: Barbadian dollar
Economy: tourism, sugar, molasses, rum, light manufacturing, electrical components

The flag was designed by Grantley Prescod, a Barbadian art teacher. Its stripes of blue-yellow-blue are for sea, sand, and sky. The black trident head was inspired by the colonial flag of Barbados, which featured a trident-wielding Poseidon, or Neptune, figure. The flag was first hoisted on Nov. 30, 1966, the date of independence from Britain.

Belarus

Republic, E cen. Europe

Area: 80,155 sq. mi. (207,600 sq. km.)
Population: 9,442,000
Language(s): Belarusian, Russian

Monetary unit: Belarusian ruble
Economy: machine tools, motor vehicles, mineral products, textiles, grains, flax, sugar beets

In 1951 the former Soviet republic created a striped flag in red (for communism) and green (for fields and forests), with the hammer, sickle, and star of communism. In 1991–95 an older design was used, but the Soviet-era flag was then altered and readopted without communist symbols. The vertical stripe is typical of embroidery on peasant clothing.

Belgium

Constitutional monarchy, NW Europe

Area: 11,787 sq. mi. (30,528 sq. km.)
Population: 11,779,000
Language(s): Dutch, French, German

Monetary unit: euro
Economy: engineering, scientific instruments, transportation equipment, textiles, processed food

A gold shield and a black lion appeared in the seal of Count Philip of Flanders as early as 1162, and in 1787 cockades of black-yellow-red were used in a Brussels revolt against Austria. After a war for independence, the flag was recognized on Jan. 23, 1831. By 1838 the design, which was influenced by the French tricolor, became standard.

Belize

Republic, Central America

Area: 8,867 sq. mi. (22,966 sq. km.)
Population: 406,000
Language(s): Spanish, Creole, English

Monetary unit: Belizean dollar
Economy: tourism, textiles, fish, sugar, bananas, cacao, citrus fruits, timber

The flag of Belize (former British Honduras) was based on the flag of the nationalist People's United Party. Its coat of arms shows a mahogany tree, a shield, and a Creole and a Mestizo. The red stripes, symbolic of the United Democratic Party, were added on independence day (Sept. 21, 1981), when the flag was first officially hoisted.

Benin

Republic, W Africa

Area: 43,484 sq. mi. (112,622 sq. km.)
Population: 13,302,000
Language(s): French, Fon, Yoruba

Monetary unit: West African States franc
Economy: subsistence agriculture, textiles, food processing (palm products, cotton, cocoa)

Adopted on Nov. 16, 1959, the flag of the former French colony used the Pan-African colors. Yellow was for the savannas in the north and green was for the palm groves in the south. Red stood for the blood of patriots. In 1975 a Marxist-oriented government replaced the flag, but after the demise of communism it was restored on Aug. 1, 1990.

Bhutan

Constitutional monarchy, S Asia

Area: 14,824 sq. mi. (38,394 sq. km.)
Population: 857,000
Language(s): Dzongkha (Tibetan)

Monetary unit: ngultrum
Economy: cement, wood products, processed fruits, rice, corn, root crops

The flag of Bhutan ("Land of the Dragon") features a dragon grasping jewels; this represents natural wealth and perfection. The white color is for purity and loyalty, the gold is for regal power, and the orange-red is for Buddhist sects and religious commitment. The flag may have been introduced as recently as 1971.

Bolivia

Republic, South America

Area: 424,164 sq. mi. (1,098,581 sq. km.)
Population: 11,759,000
Language(s): Spanish, Aymara, Quechua, Guarani

Monetary unit: boliviano
Economy: mining, smelting, handicrafts, soybeans, quinoa, Brazil nuts

A version of the flag was first adopted on July 25, 1826, but on Nov. 5, 1851, the order of the stripes was changed to red-yellow-green. The colors were often used by the Aymara and Quechua peoples; in addition, red is for the valor of the army, yellow for mineral resources, and green for the land. The current flag law dates from July 14, 1888.

Bosnia and Herzegovina

Republic, SE Europe

Area: 19,767 sq. mi. (51,197 sq. km.)
Population: 3,825,000
Language(s): Bosnian, Croatian, Serbian

Monetary unit: marka
Economy: mining (iron ore, lead, zinc), vehicle assembly, textiles, wood products

The medium blue field is bisected by a yellow triangle (representing equality between the three peoples of the nation) with seven full and two half stars in white along the hypotenuse, intended to represent Europe. The half stars are intended to suggest the infinity of the star pattern.

Botswana

Republic, S Africa

Area: 224,607 sq. mi. (581,730 sq. km.)
Population: 2,351,000
Language(s): English, Setswana

Monetary unit: pula
Economy: mining (diamonds, copper), livestock, sorghum, maize, millet

Adopted in 1966, the flag was designed to contrast symbolically with that of neighboring South Africa, where apartheid was then in effect. The black and white stripes in Botswana's flag are for racial cooperation and equality. The background symbolizes water, a scarce resource in the expansive Kalahari Desert.

Brazil

Republic, South America

Area: 3,287,957 sq. mi. (8,515,770 sq. km.)
Population: 213,445,000
Language(s): Portuguese

Monetary unit: real
Economy: coffee, soybeans, wheat, rice, livestock, mining, aircraft, motor vehicles, textiles, shoes, chemicals

The original flag was introduced on Sept. 7, 1822, when Dom Pedro declared independence from Portugal. In 1889 the blue disk and the motto Ordem e Progresso ("Order and Progress") were added. The Brazilian states and territories are symbolized by the constellations of stars. Green is for the land, while yellow is for gold and other mineral wealth.

Brunei
Constitutional sultanate, SE Asia

Area: 2,226 sq. mi. (5,765 sq. km.)
Population: 471,000
Language(s): Malay, English

Monetary unit: Bruneian dollar
Economy: oil, natural gas production and refining, agriculture, forestry, fishing

Brunei became a British protectorate in 1888, and in 1906 diagonal stripes were added to its yellow flag. The yellow stood for the sultan, while white and black were for his two chief ministers. Introduced in September 1959, the coat of arms has a parasol as a symbol of royalty and a crescent and inscription for the state religion, Islam. The flag's design was retained after Brunei gained independence on Jan. 1, 1984.

Bulgaria
Republic, SE Europe

Area: 42,811 sq. mi. (110,879 sq. km.)
Population: 6,919,000
Language(s): Bulgarian

Monetary unit: lev
Economy: electricity, vegetables, fruits, tobacco, wine, wheat, barley

The flag was based on the Russian flag of 1699, but with green substituted for blue. Under communist rule, a red star and other symbols were added, but the old tricolor was reestablished on Nov. 27, 1990. The white is for peace, love, and freedom; green is for agriculture; and red is for the independence struggle and military courage.

Burkina Faso
Republic, W Africa

Area: 105,869 sq. mi. (274,200 sq. km.)
Population: 21,383,000
Language(s): French

Monetary unit: West African States franc
Economy: cotton, beverages, agricultural processing, peanuts, shea nuts, sesame

On Aug. 4, 1984, Upper Volta was renamed Burkina Faso by the revolutionary government of Thomas Sankara, and the current flag was adopted with Pan-African colors. The yellow star symbolizes leadership and revolutionary principles. The red stripe is said to stand for the revolutionary struggle, while the green stripe represents hope and abundance.

Burundi
Republic, E cen. Africa

Area: 10,745 sq. mi. (27,830 sq. km.)
Population: 12,241,000
Language(s): Kirundi, French, English

Monetary unit: Burundi franc
Economy: light consumer goods, assembly of imported components, coffee, cotton, tea, corn, beans, sorghum

The flag was adopted on June 28, 1967. Its white saltire (diagonal cross) and central disk symbolize peace. The red color is for the independence struggle, and green is for hope. The stars correspond to the national motto, "Unity, Work, Progress." They also recall the Tutsi, Hutu, and Twa peoples and the pledge to God, king, and country.

Cabo Verde
Islands republic, off W Africa

Area: 1,557 sq. mi. (4,033 sq. km.)
Population: 589,000
Language(s): Portuguese

Monetary unit: escudo
Economy: fish processing, shoes and garments, salt mining, bananas, corn, beans

After the elections of 1991, the flag was established with a blue field bearing a ring of 10 yellow stars to symbolize the 10 main islands of Cabo Verde. The stripes of white-red-white suggest peace and national resolve. Red, white, and blue also are a symbolic link to Portugal and the United States. The new flag became official on Sept. 25, 1992.

Cambodia
Constitutional monarchy, SE Asia

Area: 69,898 sq. mi. (181,035 sq. km.)
Population: 17,304,000
Language(s): Khmer

Monetary unit: riel
Economy: tourism, garments, rice milling, fishing, wood products, rice, rubber, corn

Artistic representations of the central ruined temple of Angkor Wat, a 12th-century temple complex, have appeared on Khmer flags since the 19th century. The current flag design dates to 1948. It was replaced in 1970 under the Khmer Republic and in 1976 under communist leadership, but it was again hoisted on June 30, 1993.

Cameroon
Republic, W cen. Africa

Area: 183,568 sq. mi. (475,440 sq. km.)
Population: 28,524,000
Language(s): French, English

Monetary unit: Central African States franc
Economy: petroleum products and refining, coffee, cocoa, cotton, rubber, bananas

The flag was officially hoisted on Oct. 29, 1957, prior to independence (Jan. 1, 1960). Green is for the vegetation of the south, yellow for the savannas of the north, and red for union and sovereignty. Two yellow stars were added (for the British Cameroons) in 1961, but these were replaced in 1975 by a single star symbolizing national unity.

Canada
Republic, North America

Area: 3,855,103 sq. mi. (9,984,670 sq. km.)
Population: 37,943,000
Language(s): English, French

Monetary unit: Canadian dollar
Economy: transportation equipment, chemicals, minerals, wood and paper products, food products, wheat, barley, oilseed

During Canada's first century of independence the Union Jack was still flown but with a Canadian coat of arms. The maple leaf design, with the national colors, became official on Feb. 15, 1965. Since 1868 the maple leaf has been a national symbol, and in 1921 a red leaf in the coat of arms stood for Canadian sacrifice during World War I.

Central African Republic
Republic, cen. Africa

Area: 240,535 sq. mi. (622,984 sq. km.)
Population: 5,358,000
Language(s): French, Sangho

Monetary unit: Central African States franc
Economy: mining (diamonds, gold), timber, brewing, sugar refining, cotton, coffee, tobacco, cassava, yams, millet

Barthélemy Boganda designed the flag in 1958. It combines French and Pan-African colors. The star is a guide for progress and an emblem of unity. The blue stripe is for liberty, grandeur, and the sky; the white is for purity, equality, and candor; the green and yellow are for forests and savannas; and the red is for the blood of humankind.

Chad
Republic, N cen. Africa

Area: 495,755 sq. mi. (1,284,000 sq. km.)
Population: 17,414,000
Language(s): Arabic, French

Monetary unit: Central African States franc
Economy: oil, cotton textiles, brewing, cotton, sorghum, millet, peanuts, sesame

In 1958 a tricolor of green-yellow-red (the Pan-African colors) was proposed, but that design was already used by the Mali-Senegal federation, another former French colony. Approved on Nov. 6, 1959, the current flag substitutes blue for the original green stripe. Blue is for hope and sky, yellow for the sun, and red for the unity of the nation.

Chile
Republic, South America

Area: 291,933 sq. mi. (756,102 sq. km.)
Population: 18,308,000
Language(s): Spanish

Monetary unit: Chilean peso
Economy: copper mining, foodstuffs, fish processing, grapes, apples, pears

On Oct. 18, 1817, the flag was established for the new republic. The blue is for the sky, and the star is "a guide on the path of progress and honor." The white is for the snow of the Andes Mountains while the red recalls the blood of patriots. In the 15th century the Araucanian Indians gave red-white-blue sashes to their warriors, although there is no established connection between the sashes and the flag.

China
Communist state, Asia

Area: 3,705,407 sq. mi. (9,596,960 sq. km.)
Population: 1,397,898,000
Language(s): Mandarin Chinese

Monetary unit: yuan
Economy: mining, steel, machine building, armaments, textiles and apparel, oil, cement, chemicals, rice, wheat, potatoes

The flag was hoisted on Oct. 1, 1949. The red is for communism and the Han Chinese. The large star was originally for the Communist Party, and the smaller stars were for the proletariat, the peasants, the petty bourgeoisie, and the "patriotic capitalists." The large star was later said to stand for China, the smaller stars for minorities.

Colombia
Republic, South America

Area: 439,736 sq. mi. (1,138,910 sq. km.)
Population: 50,356,000
Language(s): Spanish

Monetary unit: Colombian peso
Economy: textiles, food processing, oil, clothing and footwear, beverages, coffee, cut flowers, bananas, rice, tobacco, corn

In the early 19th century "the Liberator" Simon Bolivar created a yellow-blue-red flag for New Granada (which included Colombia, Venezuela, Panama, and Ecuador). The flag symbolized the yellow gold of the New World separated by the blue ocean from the red of "bloody Spain." The present Colombian flag was established on Dec. 10, 1861.

Comoros
Islands republic, off SE Africa

Area: 863 sq. mi. (2,235 sq. km.)
Population: 864,000
Language(s): Arabic, French, Shikomoro

Monetary unit: Comoran franc
Economy: fishing, perfume distillation, tourism, vanilla, cloves, ylang-ylang, coconuts, bananas, cassava

The Comoros flag, adopted in the 1990s, contains the green triangle and crescent that are traditional symbols of Islam. The four stars and four horizontal stripes represent the country's main islands of Mwali, Njazidja, Nzwani and Mayotte, this last a dependency of France, also claimed by Comoros. Upon adoption of a new constitution on Dec. 23, 2001, the flag became official.

Congo (Democratic Rep.)
Republic, Equatorial Africa

Area: 905,355 sq. mi. (2,344,858 sq. km.)
Population: 105,045,000
Language(s): French, Lingala

Monetary unit: Congolese franc
Economy: mining and processing (diamonds, copper, zinc), tobacco, palm oil, bananas, rubber

A new flag for the Democratic Republic of the Congo was unveiled on February 18, 2006, upon the adoption of a new constitution. This flag is similar in style to the one flown between 1963-1971, with a lighter blue color now used. The blue in the flag symbolizes peace; red the blood of the country's martyrs; yellow the country's wealth; and the star for the country's radiant future.

Congo (Republic)
Republic, Equatorial Africa

Area: 132,047 sq. mi. (342,000 sq. km.)
Population: 5,417,000
Language(s): French, Lingala

Monetary unit: Central African States franc
Economy: petroleum, diamonds, plywood, peanuts, bananas, sugarcane, coffee

First adopted on Sept. 15, 1959, the flag uses the Pan-African colors. Green was originally said to stand for Congo's agriculture and forests, and yellow for friendship and the nobility of the people, but the red was unexplained. Altered in 1969 by a Marxist government, the flag was restored to its initial form on June 10, 1991.

Costa Rica
Republic, Central America

Area: 19,730 sq. mi. (51,100 sq. km.)
Population: 5,151,000
Language(s): Spanish

Monetary unit: Costa Rican colón
Economy: tourism, textiles, plastics, electronic, medical equipment, coffee, bananas, sugar

The blue and white stripes originated in the flag colors of the United Provinces of Central America (1823–40). On Sept. 29, 1848, the red stripe was added to symbolize sunlight, civilization, and "true independence." The current design of the coat of arms, which is included on government flags, was established in 1964.

Côte d'Ivoire
Republic, W Africa

Area: 124,504 sq. mi. (322,463 sq. km.)
Population: 28,088,000
Language(s): French

Monetary unit: West African States franc
Economy: coffee, cocoa, palm oil, rubber, wood products, oil refining, diamonds, fishing

Adopted on Dec. 3, 1959, the flag of the former French colony has three stripes corresponding to the national motto (Unity, Discipline, Labor). The orange is for growth, the white is for peace emerging from purity and unity, and the green is for hope and the future. Unofficially the green is for forests and the orange is for savannas.

Croatia
Republic, SE Europe

Area: 21,851 sq. mi. (56,594 sq. km.)
Population: 4,209,000
Language(s): Croatian, Serbian

Monetary unit: kuna
Economy: chemicals and plastics, machine tools, fabricated metal, electronics, wheat, corn, barley, sugar beets

During the European uprisings of 1848, Croatians designed a flag based on that of Russia. In April 1941 the facist Ustaša used this flag, adding the checkered shield of Croatia. A communist star soon replaced the shield, but the current flag was adopted on Dec. 22, 1990. Atop the shield is a "crown" inlaid with historic coats of arms.

Cuba
Island communist state, Caribbean

Area: 42,803 sq. mi. (110,860 sq. km)
Population: 11,032,000
Language(s): Spanish

Monetary unit: Cuban peso
Economy: petroleum, nickel, cobalt, pharmaceuticals, sugar, tobacco, citrus

In the mid-19th century Cuban exiles designed the flag, which was later carried into battle against Spanish forces. It was adopted on May 20, 1902. The stripes were for the three military districts of Cuba and the purity of the patriotic cause. The red triangle was for strength, constancy, and equality, and the white star symbolized independence.

Cyprus
Island republic, E Mediterranean

The island of Cyprus is de facto divided between predominately Greek Republic of Cyprus (internationally recognized) and the predominantly Turkish northern third of the island (Turkish republic), recognized solely by Turkey and with the economy basically dependent on Turkey.

Area: (island) 3,572 sq. mi. (9,251 sq. km.)
Population: 1,282,000
Language(s): Greek, Turkish

Monetary unit: euro
Economy: tourism, food, beverage processing, cement, gypsum, ship repair, textiles, clay products

On Aug. 16, 1960, the Republic of Cyprus was proclaimed with a national flag of a neutral design. It bears the island in silhouette and a green olive wreath, for peace. In 1974 there was a Turkish invasion of the island. A puppet government, which adopted a flag based on the Turkish model, was set up on the northern third of Cyprus.

Czech Republic
Republic, cen. Europe

Area: 30,451 sq. mi. (78,867 sq. km.)
Population: 10,703,000
Language(s): Czech, Slovak

Monetary unit: Czech koruna
Economy: machinery, transport equipment, chemicals, coal, steel, wheat, sugar beets, fruit

When Czechs, Slovaks, and Ruthenians united to form Czechoslovakia in 1918, a simple white-red bicolor flag was chosen; in 1920 it incorporated a blue triangle at the hoist. Czechoslovakia divided into Slovakia and the Czech Republic in 1993, but the latter country readopted the Czechoslovak flag as its own.

Denmark
Constitutional monarchy, N Europe

Area: 16,639 sq. mi. (43,094 sq. km.)
Population: 5,895,000
Language(s): Danish

Monetary unit: Danish krone
Economy: metal processing, chemicals, machinery, electronics, furniture, dairy products, oil, gas

A traditional story claims that the Danish flag fell from heaven on June 15, 1219, but the previously existing war flag of the Holy Roman Empire was of a similar design, with its red field symbolizing battle and its white cross suggesting divine favor. In 1849 the state and military flag was altered and adopted as a symbol of the Danish people.

Djibouti
Republic, E Africa

Area: 8,958 sq. mi. (23,200 sq. km.)
Population: 938,000
Language(s): Arabic, French

Monetary unit: Djiboutian franc
Economy: agricultural processing, shipping, fruits, vegetables

First raised by anti-French separatists, the flag was officially hoisted on June 27, 1977. The color of the Afar people, green, stands for prosperity. The color of the Issa people, light blue, symbolizes sea and sky, and recalls the flag of Somalia. The white triangle is for equality and peace; the red star is for unity and independence.

Dominica

Island republic, Caribbean

Area: 290 sq. mi. (751 sq. km.)
Population: 75,000
Language(s): English

Monetary unit: East Caribbean dollar
Economy: bananas, cocoa, coconuts, coconut oil, copra, limes; soap

The flag was hoisted on Nov. 3, 1978, at independence from Britain. Its background symbolizes forests; its central disk is red for socialism and bears a sisserou (a rare local bird). The stars are for the parishes of the island. The cross of yellow, white, and black is for the Carib, Caucasian, and African peoples and for fruit, water, and soil.

Dominican Republic

Republic, Hispaniola, Caribbean

Area: 18,792 sq. mi. (48,670 sq. km.)
Population: 10,597,000
Language(s): Spanish

Monetary unit: Dominican peso
Economy: tourism, sugar processing, gold mining, textiles, cement, cocoa, tobacco, sugarcane, coffee, cotton, rice

On Feb. 28, 1844, Spanish-speaking Dominican revolutionaries added a white cross to the simple blue-red flag of eastern Hispaniola in order to emphasize their Christian heritage. On November 6 of that same year the new constitution established the flag but with the colors at the fly end reversed so that the blue and red would alternate.

Ecuador

Republic, South America

Area: 109,484 sq. mi. (283,561 sq. km.)
Population: 17,093,000
Language(s): Spanish, Quechua

Monetary unit: U.S. dollar
Economy: petroleum, textiles, wood products, chemicals, coffee, bananas, shrimp, cut flowers

Victorious against the Spanish on May 24, 1822, Antonio José de Sucre hoisted a yellow-blue-red flag. Other flags were later used, but on Sept. 26, 1860, the current flag design was adopted. The coat of arms is displayed on the flag when it is used abroad or for official purposes, to distinguish it from the flag of Colombia.

Egypt

Republic, NE Africa and Sinai Peninsula

Area: 386,662 sq. mi. (1,001,450 sq. km.)
Population: 106,437,000
Language(s): Arabic, English, French

Monetary unit: Egyptian pound
Economy: tourism, oil, mining, chemicals, salt, textiles, cotton, wheat, sugarcane

The 1952 revolt against British rule established the red-white-black flag with a central gold eagle. Two stars replaced the eagle in 1958, and in 1972 a federation with Syria and Libya was formed, adding instead the hawk of Quraysh (the tribe of Muhammad). On Oct. 9, 1984, the eagle of Saladin (a major 12th-century ruler) was substituted.

El Salvador

Republic, Central America

Area: 8,124 sq. mi. (21,041 sq. km.)
Population: 6,528,000
Language(s): Spanish

Monetary unit: U.S. dollar
Economy: food processing, beverages, petroleum, chemicals, fertilizer, textiles, coffee, sugar, corn, rice, beans

In the early 19th century, a blue-white-blue flag was designed for the short-lived United Provinces of Central America, of which El Salvador was a member. On Sept. 15, 1912, the flag was reintroduced in El Salvador. The coat of arms in the center resembles that used by the former federation and includes the national motto, "God, Union, Liberty."

Equatorial Guinea

Republic, W cen. Africa

Area: 10,831 sq. mi. (28,051 sq. km.)
Population: 857,000
Language(s): Spanish, French, Portuguese

Monetary unit: Central African States franc
Economy: oil, gas, timber, subsistence farming, cocoa, coffee, palm oil, fishing

The flag, lacking the coat of arms, was first hoisted at independence (Oct. 12, 1968). The coat of arms was added in 1979, showing a silk-cotton tree, or god tree, recalling early Spanish influence in the area. The sea, which links parts of the country, is reflected in the blue triangle. The green is for vegetation, white for peace, and red for the blood of martyrs in the liberation struggle.

Eritrea

Republic, E Africa

Area: 45,406 sq. mi. (117,600 sq. km.)
Population: 6,147,000
Language(s): Arabic, English, Tigrinya

Monetary unit: nakfa
Economy: food processing, beverages, clothing and textiles, light manufacturing, sorghum, lentils, vegetables, corn

Officially hoisted at the proclamation of independence on May 24, 1993, the national flag was based on that of the Eritrean People's Liberation Front. The red triangle is for the blood of patriots, the green is for agriculture, and the blue is for maritime resources. Around a central branch is a circle of olive branches with 30 leaves.

Estonia

Republic, N Europe

Area: 17,463 sq. mi. (45,228 sq. km.)
Population: 1,220,000
Language(s): Estonian, Russian

Monetary unit: euro
Economy: machinery, electronics, telecommunications, wood, paper, furniture, textiles, information technology

In the late 19th century an Estonian students' association adopted the blue-black-white flag. Blue was said to stand for the sky, black for the soil, and white for aspirations to freedom and homeland. The flag was officially recognized on July 4, 1920. It was replaced under Soviet rule, and readopted on Oct. 20, 1988.

Eswatini

Kingdom, SE Africa

Area: 6,704 sq. mi. (17,364 sq. km.)
Population: 1,113,000
Language(s): siSwati, English

Monetary unit: lilangeni
Economy: mining (coal, asbestos), wood pulp, sugar, soft drink concentrates, textiles

Eswatini was formerly known as Swaziland, and the flag dates to the creation of a military banner in 1941, when Swazi troops were preparing for the Allied invasion of Italy. On April 25, 1967, it was hoisted as the national flag. The crimson stripe stands for past battles, yellow for mineral wealth, and blue for peace. Featured are a Swazi war shield, two spears, and a "fighting stick."

Ethiopia

Republic, E Africa

Area: 426,373 sq. mi. (1,104,300 sq. km.)
Population: 110,871,000
Language(s): Oromo, Amharic

Monetary unit: birr
Economy: agriculture, food processing, hides, skins, gold, textiles, chemicals

The flag is red (for sacrifice), green (for labor, development, and fertility), and yellow (for hope, justice, and equality). Tricolor pennants were used prior to the official flag of Oct. 6, 1897, and a tricolor was flown by anti-government forces in 1991. On Feb. 6, 1996, the disk (for peace) and star (for unity and the future) were added.

Fiji

Islands republic, S Pacific

Area: 7,056 sq. mi. (18,274 sq. km.)
Population: 940,000
Language(s): English, Fijian, Hindustani

Monetary unit: Fijian dollar
Economy: subsistence farming, fishing, sugar, copra, fruit, gold, tourism

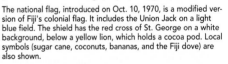

The national flag, introduced on Oct. 10, 1970, is a modified version of Fiji's colonial flag. It includes the Union Jack on a light blue field. The shield has the red cross of St. George on a white background, below a yellow lion, which holds a cocoa pod. Local symbols (sugar cane, coconuts, bananas, and the Fiji dove) are also shown.

Finland

Republic, N Europe

Area: 130,559 sq. mi. (338,145 sq. km.)
Population: 5,587,000
Language(s): Finnish, Swedish

Monetary unit: euro
Economy: timber, pulp, mining, electronics, scientific instruments, shipbuilding

In 1862, while Finland was under Russian control, a flag was proposed that would have a white background for the snows of Finland and blue for its lakes. The blue was in the form of a "Nordic cross" similar to those used by other Scandinavian countries. The flag was officially adopted by the newly independent country on May 29, 1918.

France
Republic, W Europe

Area: 248,573 sq. mi. (643,801 sq. km.)
Population: 62,814,000
Language(s): French

Monetary unit: euro
Economy: machinery, chemicals, automobiles, metallurgy, aircraft, electronics, wheat, cereals, sugar beets, wine grapes

From 1789, blue and red, the traditional colors of Paris, were included in flags with Bourbon royal white. The tricolor was made official in 1794. It embodied liberty, equality, fraternity, democracy, secularism, and modernization, but there is no symbolism attached to the individual colors. It has been the sole national flag since March 5, 1848.

Gabon
Republic, W cen. Africa

Area: 103,347 sq. mi. (267,667 sq. km.)
Population: 2,285,000
Language(s): French

Monetary unit: Central African States franc
Economy: oil, timber, mining (manganese, gold, uranium), cocoa, coffee, palm oil, ship repair

Shortly before proclaiming independence from France, Gabon adopted its national flag on Aug. 9, 1960. The central yellow stripe is for the Equator, which runs through the country. Green stands for the tropical forests that are one of Gabon's most important resources. Blue represents its extensive coast along the South Atlantic Ocean.

Gambia
Republic, W Africa

Area: 4,363 sq. mi. (11,300 sq. km.)
Population: 2,221,000
Language(s): English

Monetary unit: dalasi
Economy: peanuts, fish, hides, tourism, beverages, agricultural machine assembly, rice, millet, sorghum

The Gambia achieved independence from Britain on Feb. 18, 1965, under the current flag. The center stripe is blue to symbolize the Gambia River. The red stripe is for the sun and the equator. The green stripe is for agricultural produce, while the white stripes are said to stand for peace and unity.

Georgia
Republic, SW Asia

Area: 26,911 sq. mi. (69,700 sq. km.)
Population: 4,934,000
Language(s): Georgian, Russian

Monetary unit: lari
Economy: steel, machine tools, electric appliances, mining, chemicals, wood products, wine, citrus, grapes, tea

The five-cross design of the Georgian flag is believed to have been used in the Middle Ages. The central cross is the cross of St. George, the patron saint of Georgia. The red and white color is traditional, used in the flags of the independent kingdoms that eventually united to form Georgia. The current flag was adopted in 2004.

Germany
Republic, cen. Europe

Area: 137,847 sq. mi. (357,022 sq. km.)
Population: 79,903,000
Language(s): German

Monetary unit: euro
Economy: iron, steel, machine tools, electronics, wine and beer, chemicals, motor vehicles

In the early 19th century, German nationalists displayed black, gold, and red on their uniforms and tricolor flags. The current flag was used officially from 1848 to 1852 and readopted by West Germany on May 9, 1949. East Germany flew a similar flag but only the flag of West Germany was maintained upon reunification in 1990.

Ghana
Republic, W Africa

Area: 92,098 sq. mi. (238,533 sq. km.)
Population: 32,373,000
Language(s): English, local languages

Monetary unit: cedi
Economy: subsistence farming, mining (diamonds, gold), light manufacturing, cocoa, palm oil

On March 6, 1957, independence from Britain was granted and a flag, based on the red-white-green tricolor of a nationalist organization, was hoisted. A black "lodestar of African freedom" was added and the white stripe was changed to yellow, symbolizing wealth. Green is for forests and farms, red for the independence struggle.

Greece
Republic, S Europe

Area: 50,949 sq. mi. (131,957 sq. km.)
Population: 10,570,000
Language(s): Greek

Monetary unit: euro
Economy: tourism, food processing, mining, metal products, petroleum, textiles

In March 1822, during the revolt against Ottoman rule, the first Greek national flags were adopted; the most recent revision to the flag was made on Dec. 22, 1978. The colors symbolize Greek Orthodoxy while the cross stands for "the wisdom of God, freedom and country." The stripes are for the battle cry for independence: "Freedom or Death."

Grenada
Island republic, Caribbean

Area: 133 sq. mi. (344 sq. km.)
Population: 114,000
Language(s): English

Monetary unit: East Caribbean dollar
Economy: tourism, light assembly, banking, textiles, nutmeg, mace, bananas

Grenada's flag was officially hoisted at midnight on Feb. 7, 1974. Its background is green for vegetation and yellow for the sun, and its red border is symbolic of harmony and unity. The seven stars are for the original administrative subdivisions of Grenada. Nutmeg, a crop for which the "Isle of Spice" is internationally known, is represented as well.

Guatemala
Republic, Central America

Area: 42,042 sq. mi. (108,889 sq. km.)
Population: 17,423,000
Language(s): Spanish, Maya languages

Monetary unit: quetzal
Economy: coffee, bananas, sugar, timber, petroleum, chemicals, metals, rubber, textiles

The flag was introduced in 1871. It has blue and white stripes (colors of the former United Provinces of Central America) and a coat of arms with the quetzal (the national bird), a scroll, a wreath, and crossed rifles and sabers. Different artistic variations have been used but on Sept. 15, 1968, the present pattern was established.

Guinea
Republic, W Africa

Area: 94,926 sq. mi. (245,857 sq. km.)
Population: 12,878,000
Language(s): French

Monetary unit: Guinean franc
Economy: mining (bauxite, gold, diamonds), light manufacturing, bananas, coffee, pineapples

The flag was adopted on Nov. 10, 1958, following independence from France in October. Its simple design was influenced by the French tricolor. The red is said to be a symbol of sacrifice and labor, while the yellow is for mineral wealth, the tropical sun, and justice. Green symbolizes agricultural wealth and the solidarity of the people.

Guinea-Bissau
Republic, W Africa

Area: 13,948 sq. mi. (36,125 sq. km.)
Population: 1,976,000
Language(s): Crioulo, Portuguese

Monetary unit: West African States franc
Economy: cashews, peanuts, fish, seafood processing, timber, potential oil exports

The flag has been used since the declaration of independence from Portugal on Sept. 24, 1973. The black star on the red stripe was for African Party leadership, the people, and their will to live in dignity, freedom, and peace. Yellow was for the harvest and other rewards of work, and green was for the nation's vast jungles and agricultural lands.

Guyana
Republic, South America

Area: 83,000 sq. mi. (214,969 sq. km.)
Population: 788,000
Language(s): English

Monetary unit: Guyanese dollar
Economy: mining (bauxite, diamonds, gold), sugar, rum, shrimp, timber

Upon independence from Britain on May 26, 1966, the flag was first hoisted. The green stands for jungles and fields, white suggests the rivers which are the basis for the Indian word *guiana* ("land of waters"), red is for zeal and sacrifice in nation-building, and black is for perseverance. The flag is nicknamed "The Golden Arrowhead."

Haiti

Republic, Hispaniola, Caribbean

Area: 10,714 sq. mi. (27,750 sq. km.)
Population: 11,198,000
Language(s): Creole, French

Monetary unit: gourde
Economy: subsistence farming, sugar refining, flour milling, fruits, textiles, cement

After the French Revolution of 1789, Haiti underwent a slave revolt, but the French tricolor continued in use until 1803. The new blue-red flag represented the black and mulatto populations only. A black-red flag was used by various dictators, including François "Papa Doc" Duvalier and his son, but on Feb. 25, 1986, the old flag was reestablished.

Honduras

Republic, Central America

Area: 43,278 sq. mi. (112,090 sq. km.)
Population: 9,346,000
Language(s): Spanish

Monetary unit: lempira
Economy: coffee, bananas, sugar, tobacco, fishing, textiles, mining (zinc, silver)

Since Feb. 16, 1866, the Honduran flag has retained the blue-white-blue design of the flag of the former United Provinces of Central America, but with five central stars symbolizing the states of Honduras, El Salvador, Nicaragua, Costa Rica, and Guatemala. The flag design has often been associated with Central American reunification attempts.

Hungary

Republic, cen. Europe

Area: 35,918 sq. mi. (93,028 sq. km.)
Population: 9,728,000
Language(s): Hungarian

Monetary unit: forint
Economy: machinery, motor vehicles, pharmaceuticals, sugar beets, mining, textiles

The colors of the Hungarian flag were mentioned in a 1608 coronation ceremony, but they may have been used since the 13th century. The tricolor was adopted on Oct. 12, 1957, after the abortive revolution of 1956. The white is said to symbolize Hungary's rivers, the green its mountains, and the red the blood shed in its many battles.

Iceland

Island republic, off NW Europe

Area: 39,769 sq. mi. (103,000 sq. km.)
Population: 354,000
Language(s): Icelandic, English

Monetary unit: Icelandic krona
Economy: fishing and fish processing, aluminum, animal products, tourism, cement

Approval for an Icelandic flag was given by the king of Denmark on June 19, 1915; it became a national flag on Dec. 1, 1918, when the separate kingdom of Iceland was proclaimed. The flag was retained upon the creation of a republic on June 17, 1944, though with a darker blue color. The design has a typical "Scandinavian cross".

India

Republic, S Asia

Area: 1,269,219 sq. mi. (3,287,263 sq. km.)
Population: 1,339,331,000
Language(s): Hindi, English

Monetary unit: Indian rupee
Economy: agriculture, mining, coal, cut diamonds, crude oil, software services, textiles, machinery

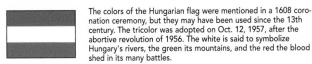

Earlier versions of the flag were used from the 1920s, but the current flag was hoisted officially on July 22, 1947. The orange was said to stand for courage and sacrifice, white for peace and truth, and green for faith and chivalry. The blue wheel is a chakra, associated with Emperor Ashoka's attempts to unite India in the 3rd century BC.

Indonesia

Republic, SE Asia

Area: 735,358 sq. mi. (1,904,569 sq. km.)
Population: 275,122,000
Language(s): Indonesian, English, Dutch, local languages

Monetary unit: Indonesian rupiah
Economy: oil, natural gas, timber, plywood, rubber; tourism, cacao, nutmeg, palm oil, tea

Indonesia's red and white flag was associated with the Majapahit empire which existed from the 13th to the 16th century. It was adopted on Aug. 17, 1945, and it remained after Indonesia won its independence from The Netherlands in 1949. Red is for courage and white for honesty. The flag is identical, except in dimensions, to the flag of Monaco.

Iran

Islamic republic, SW Asia

Area: 636,372 sq. mi. (1,648,195 sq. km.)
Population: 85,889,000
Language(s): Farsi (Persian)

Monetary unit: Iranian rial
Economy: oil, natural gas, mining, metals, vegetables oils, caviar, textiles, carpets

The tricolor flag was recognized in 1906 but altered after the revolution of 1979. Along the central stripe are the Arabic words Allahu akbar ("God is great"), repeated 22 times. The coat of arms can be read as a rendition of the word Allah, as a globe, or as two crescents. The green is for Islam, white is for peace, and red is for valor.

Iraq

Republic, SW Asia

Area: 169,235 sq. mi. (438,317 sq. km.)
Population: 39,650,000
Language(s): Arabic, Kurdish

Monetary unit: Iraqi dinar
Economy: oil, natural gas, agriculture, livestock, textiles

Adopted on July 31, 1963, the Iraqi flag is based on the liberation flag first flown in Egypt in 1952. Red is for the willingness to shed blood, green is for Arab lands, black is for past suffering, and white is for purity. On Jan. 14, 1991, the Arabic inscription "God is Great" was added, and in 2008 the script was restyled.

Ireland

Republic, off NW Europe

Area: 27,133 sq. mi. (70,273 sq. km.)
Population: 5,225,000
Language(s): English, Irish

Monetary unit: euro
Economy: engineering, machinery, tourism, brewing, distilling, mining, food products, textiles

In the 19th century various tricolor flags and ribbons became symbolic of Irish opposition to British rule. Many of them included the colors green (for the Catholics), orange (for the Protestants), and white (for the peace between the two groups). The tricolor in its modern form was recognized by the constitution on Dec. 29, 1937.

Israel

Republic, SW Asia

Area: 8,470 sq. mi. (21,937 sq. km.)
Population: 8,787,000
Language(s): Hebrew, Arabic, English

Monetary unit: Israeli shekel
Economy: high-technology, mining, textiles, chemicals, food processing, diamond cutting

Symbolic of the traditional tallit, or Jewish prayer shawl, and including the Star of David, the flag was used from the late 19th century. It was raised when Israel proclaimed independence on May 14, 1948, and the banner was legally recognized on Nov. 12, 1948. A dark blue was also substituted for the traditional lighter shade of blue.

Italy

Republic, S Europe

Area: 116,348 sq. mi. (301,340 sq. km.)
Population: 62,390,000
Language(s): Italian

Monetary unit: euro
Economy: iron, steel, ceramics, chemicals, fishing, textiles, automobiles, tourism, food processing

The first Italian national flag was adopted on Feb. 25, 1797, by the Cispadane Republic. Its stripes were vertically positioned on May 11, 1798, and thereafter it was honored by all Italian nationalists. The design was guaranteed by a decree (March 23, 1848) of King Charles Albert of Sardinia, ordering troops to carry the flag into battle.

Jamaica

Island republic, Caribbean

Area: 4,244 sq. mi. (10,991 sq. km.)
Population: 2,817,000
Language(s): English

Monetary unit: Jamaican dollar
Economy: bauxite, alumina, tourism, tropical fruits, rum, cement, gypsum, telecommunications

The flag was designed prior to independence from Britain (Aug. 6, 1962). The black color stood for hardships faced by the nation, green for agriculture and hope, and yellow for the natural wealth of Jamaica. This was summed up in the phrase, "Hardships there are, but the land is green and the sun shineth."

Japan

Islands constit. monarchy, W Pacific

Area: 145,914 sq. mi. (377,915 sq. km.)
Population: 124,687,000
Language(s): Japanese

Monetary unit: yen
Economy: motor vehicles, electronics, optical equipment, chemicals, fishing, mining, textiles

The flag features a red sun on a white background. Known as the Hinomaru, the flag was adopted for use on its ships in the early 1600s by the Tokugawa Shogunate. In 1870 the Meiji government designated the flag's use on merchant and naval vessels, designating the current design and proportions.

Jordan

Constitutional monarchy, SW Asia

Area: 34,495 sq. mi. (89,342 sq. km.)
Population: 10,910,000
Language(s): Arabic, English

Monetary unit: Jordanian dinar
Economy: phosphate mining, cement, chemicals, pharmaceuticals, wheat, fruits, olives, tourism

In 1917 Hussein ibn Ali raised the Arab Revolt flag. With the addition of a white seven-pointed star, this flag was adopted by Transjordan on April 16, 1928, and retained upon Jordan's independence on March 22, 1946. White is for purity, black for struggle and suffering, red for bloodshed, and green for Arab lands.

Kazakhstan

Republic, W cen. Asia

Area: 1,052,090 sq. mi. (2,724,900 sq. km.)
Population: 19,246,000
Language(s): Kazakh, Russian

Monetary unit: tenge
Economy: oil, mining (manganese, titanium, gold), chemicals, agriculture, livestock, textiles

The flag was adopted in June 1992. Light blue is a traditional color of the nomads of Central Asia; it symbolizes peace and well-being. The golden sun and eagle represent freedom and the high ideals of the Kazakhs. Along the edge is a band of traditional Kazakh ornamentation; the band was originally in red but is now in golden yellow.

Kenya

Republic, E cen. Africa

Area: 224,081 sq. mi. (580,367 sq. km.)
Population: 54,685,000
Language(s): Kiswahili, English

Monetary unit: Kenyan shilling
Economy: coffee, cotton, tea, rice, mining (gold, salt), consumer goods, oil refining, tourism

Upon independence from Britain (Dec. 12, 1963), the Kenyan flag became official. It was based on the flag of the Kenya African National Union. Black is for the people, red for humanity and the struggle for freedom, green for the fertile land, and white for unity and peace. The shield and spears are traditional weapons of the Masai people.

Kiribati

Islands republic, W Pacific

Area: 313 sq. mi. (811 sq. km.)
Population: 113,000
Language(s): English, I-Kiribati

Great Britain acquired the Gilbert and Ellice Islands in the 19th century. In 1976 the Gilbert Islands separated from the Ellice Islands to form Kiribati, and a new flag was adopted based on the coat of arms granted to the islands in 1937. It has waves of white and blue, for the Pacific Ocean, as well as a yellow sun and a local frigate bird.

Monetary unit: Australian dollar
Economy: fishing, handicrafts, breadfruit, copra

Korea, North

Communist state, E Asia

Area: 46,540 sq. mi. (120,538 sq. km.)
Population: 25,831,000
Language(s): Korean

Monetary unit: North Korean won
Economy: military products, mining (magnesite, precious metals), machinery, textiles

The traditional Korean T'aeguk flag (still used by South Korea) was official in North Korea until July 10, 1948, when the current flag was introduced. Its red stripe and star are for the country's commitment to communism, while blue is said to stand for a commitment to peace. The white stripes stand for purity, strength, and dignity.

Korea, South

Republic, E Asia

Area: 38,502 sq. mi. (99,720 sq. km.)
Population: 51,715,000
Language(s): Korean, English

Monetary unit: South Korean won
Economy: electronics, motor vehicles, shipbuilding, chemicals, agriculture, mining, fishing

The flag was adopted in August 1882. Its white background is for peace, while the central emblem represents yin-yang (Korean: um-yang), the duality of the universe. The black bars recall sun, moon, earth, heaven and other Confucian principles. Outlawed under Japanese rule, the flag was revived in 1948 and slightly modified in 1950 and 1984.

Kosovo

Republic, SE Europe

Area: 4,203 sq. mi. (10,887 sq. km.)
Population: 1,935,000
Language(s): Albanian, Serbian, Bosnian

Monetary unit: euro
Economy: mining (lignite, lead, zinc, nickel, chrome, aluminum, magnesium), building materials

The flag of Kosovo, adopted at independence in February 2008, shows the shape of Kosovo in yellow on a medium blue field. Six white stars representing the country's major ethnic groups form an arc above the Kosovo silhouette. This design was chosen after a competition having nearly 1000 entries.

Kuwait

Constitutional monarchy, W Asia

Area: 6,880 sq. mi. (17,818 sq. km.)
Population: 3,032,000
Language(s): Arabic, English

Monetary unit: Kuwaiti dinar
Economy: oil, fishing, construction materials, industrial chemicals

The red flag of Kuwait, in use since World War I, was replaced by the current flag on Oct. 24, 1961, shortly after independence from Britain. The symbolism is from a poem written over six centuries ago. The green stands for Arab lands, black is for battles, white is for the purity of the fighters, and red is for the blood on their swords.

Kyrgyzstan

Republic, W cen. Asia

Area: 77,202 sq. mi. (199,951 sq. km.)
Population: 6,019,000
Language(s): Kyrgyz, Russian, Uzbek

Monetary unit: som
Economy: cotton, wheat, tobacco, wool, mining (gold, mercury, uranium, coal), machinery

The Kyrgyz flag replaced a Soviet-era design on March 3, 1992. The red recalls the flag of the national hero Mansas the Noble. The central yellow sun has 40 rays, corresponding to the followers of Mansas and the tribes he united. On the sun is the stylized view of the roof of a yurt, a traditional nomadic home that is now seldom used.

Laos

Communist state, SE Asia

Area: 91,429 sq. mi. (236,800 sq. km.)
Population: 7,574,000
Language(s): Lao, French, English

Monetary unit: kip
Economy: rice, corn, tobacco, fishing, timber, mining (tin, gypsum), opium

The Lao flag was first used by anti-colonialist forces from the mid-20th century. The white disk honored the Japanese who had supported the Lao independence movement, but it also symbolized a bright future. Red was said to stand for the blood of patriots, and blue was for the promise of future prosperity. The flag was adopted on Dec. 2, 1975.

Latvia

Republic, N Europe

Area: 24,938 sq. mi. (64,589 sq. km.)
Population: 1,863,000
Language(s): Latvian, Russian

Monetary unit: euro
Economy: wood, wood products, synthetic fibers, chemicals, machinery, electronics, processed foods

The basic flag design was used by a militia unit in 1279, according to a 14th-century source. Popularized in the 19th century among anti-Russian nationalists, the flag flew in 1918 and was legally adopted on Jan. 20, 1923. Under Soviet control the flag was suppressed, but it was again legalized in 1988 and flown officially from Feb. 27, 1990.

Lebanon

Republic, SW Asia

Area: 4,015 sq. mi. (10,400 sq. km.)
Population: 5,261,000
Language(s): Arabic, French, English

Monetary unit: Lebanese pound
Economy: banking, tourism, food processing, wine, jewelry, cement, textiles, citrus, grapes, tomatoes, apples, vegetables

On Sept. 1, 1920, French-administered Lebanon adopted a flag based on the French tricolor. The current red-white flag was established by the constitution of 1943, which divided power among the Muslim and Christian sects. On the central stripe is a cedar tree, which is a biblical symbol for holiness, peace, and eternity.

Lesotho

Constitutional monarchy, S Africa

Area: 11,720 sq. mi. (30,355 sq. km.);
Population: 2,178,000
Language(s): Sesotho, English, Zulu

Monetary unit: loti
Economy: food, beverages, textiles, apparel assembly, handicrafts, tourism, corn, wheat, sorghum

This flag was unfurled for the first time on October 4, 2006, to mark the occasion of Lesotho's 40th anniversary of independence from Britain. Lesotho states that the new flag shows it "at peace with itself and its neighbors". Blue signifies rain, white stands for peace, and green indicates prosperity. The black Basotho hat represents the country's indigenous people.

Liberia

Republic, W Africa

Area: 43,000 sq. mi. (111,369 sq. km.)
Population: 5,214,000
Language(s): English, local languages

Monetary unit: Liberian dollar
Economy: rubber processing, rice, palm oil, coffee, cocoa, timber, iron ore, diamonds

In the 19th century land was purchased on the African coast by the American Colonization Society in order to return freed slaves to Africa. On April 9, 1827, a flag based on that of the United States was adopted, featuring a white cross. On Aug. 24, 1847, after independence, the cross was replaced by a star and the number of stripes was reduced.

Libya

Transitional state, N Africa

Area: 679,362 sq. mi. (1,759,540 sq. km.)
Population: 7,017,000
Language(s): Arabic, Italian, English

Monetary unit: Libyan dinar
Economy: oil, natural gas, iron, steel, textiles, barley, wheat, dates, olives, fruits

In 1947 three regions united to become the United Kingdom of Libya. A flag consisting of red, black, and green stripes with a centered white crescent and star became official in 1949. In 1969 the monarchy was overthrown by Muammar al-Qaddafi, who changed the flag to solid green in 1977. Following the overthrow of Qaddafi in 2011, the 1949 flag was reinstated.

Liechtenstein

Constitutional monarchy, cen. Europe

Area: 62 sq. mi. (160 sq. km.)
Population: 39,000
Language(s): German

Monetary unit: Swiss franc
Economy: electronics, metal manufacturing, dental products, ceramics, pharmaceuticals, precision instruments, tourism

The blue-red flag was given official status in October 1921. At the 1936 Olympics it was learned that this same flag was used by Haiti; thus, in 1937 a yellow crown was added, which symbolizes the unity of the people and their prince. Blue stands for the sky, red for the evening fires in homes. The flag was last modified on Sept. 18, 1982.

Lithuania

Republic, N Europe

Area: 25,212 sq. mi. (65,300 sq. km.)
Population: 2,712,000
Language(s): Lithuanian, Russian, Polish

Monetary unit: euro
Economy: dairy, livestock, food products, textiles, paper, machinery

The tricolor flag of Lithuania was adopted on Aug. 1, 1922. It was long suppressed under Soviet rule until its reestablishment on March 20, 1989. The yellow color suggests ripening wheat and freedom from want. Green is for hope and the forests of the nation, while red stands for love of country, sovereignty, and valor in defense of liberty.

Luxembourg

Constitutional monarchy, W Europe

Area: 998 sq. mi. (2,586 sq. km.)
Population: 640,000
Language(s): German, French, Luxembourgish

Monetary unit: euro
Economy: banking and financial services, construction, real estate services, grapes

In the 19th century the national colors, from the coat of arms of the dukes of Luxembourg, came to be used in a tricolor of red-white-blue, coincidentally the same as the flag of its neighbor, The Netherlands, though with a lighter shade of blue and at different proportions. It was recognized by law on Aug. 16, 1972.

Madagascar

Island republic, off SE Africa

Area: 226,658 sq. mi. (587,041 sq. km.)
Population: 27,534,000
Language(s): Malagasy, French

Monetary unit: Malagasy ariary
Economy: tobacco, coffee, sugar, cloves, vanilla, sisal, livestock, graphite, soap

The Madagascar flag was adopted in late October 1958, shortly after the newly proclaimed Malagasy Republic became autonomous on October 14, 1958. The flag combines the traditional Malagasy colors of white and red with a stripe of green. The white and red are said to stand for purity and sovereignty, while the green represents the coastal regions and symbolizes hope.

Malawi

Republic, SE Africa

Area: 45,747 sq. mi. (118,484 sq. km.)
Population: 20,309,000
Language(s): English, Chichewa, Chinyanja

Monetary unit: Malawian kwacha
Economy: tea, tobacco, peanuts, sorghum, sugar, fishing, textiles, cement

In 1964, independent Malawi adopted a flag that was striped black for the African people, red for the blood of the martyrs, and green for the vegetation and climate. A red setting sun was on the black stripe. A new flag in 2010 reordered the stripes to red-black-green and replaced the half sun with a full sun. The old flag was restored in 2012.

Malaysia

Constitutional monarchy, SE Asia

Area: 127,355 sq. mi. (329,847 sq. km.)
Population: 33,519,000
Language(s): Malay, English, Chinese

Monetary unit: ringgit
Economy: rubber, palm oil, cocoa, pineapples, natural gas, tin, electronics

The flag hoisted on May 26, 1950 had 11 stripes, a crescent, and an 11-pointed star. The number of stripes and star points was increased to 14 on Sept. 16, 1963. Yellow is a royal color in Malaysia while red, white, and blue indicate connections with the Commonwealth. The crescent is a reminder that the population is mainly Muslim.

Maldives

Islands republic, Indian Ocean

Area: 115 sq. mi. (298 sq. km.)
Population: 391,000
Language(s): Dhivehi, English

Monetary unit: rufiyaa
Economy: coconuts, shipping, boat building, fishing, tourism

Maldivian ships long used a plain red ensign like those flown by Arabian and African nations. While a British protectorate in the early 20th century, the Maldives adopted a flag which was only slightly altered upon independence (July 26, 1965). The green panel and white crescent are symbolic of Islam, progress, prosperity, and peace.

Mali

Republic, W cen. Africa

Area: 478,841 sq. mi. (1,240,192 sq. km.)
Population: 20,138,000
Language(s): French; local languages

Monetary unit: West African States franc
Economy: food processing (sorghum, rice, millet), mining (phosphate, gold), livestock, leather goods

Designed for the Mali-Senegal union of 1959, the flag originally included a human figure, the Kanaga, in its center. In 1960 Senegal and Mali divided. Muslims in Mali objected to the Kanaga, and on March 1, 1961, the figure was dropped. Green, yellow, and red are the Pan-African colors and are used by many former French territories.

Malta

Island republic, Mediterranean

Area: 122 sq. mi. (316 sq. km.)
Population: 461,000
Language(s): Maltese, English

Monetary unit: euro
Economy: tourism, electronics, ship building and repair, potatoes, tomatoes, citrus fruit

The Maltese flag was supposedly based on an 11th-century coat of arms, and a red flag with a white cross was used by the Knights of Malta from the Middle Ages. The current flag dates from independence within the Commonwealth (Sept. 21, 1964). The George Cross was granted by the British for the heroic defense of the island in World War II.

Marshall Islands

Islands republic, W Pacific

Area: 70 sq. mi. (181 sq. km.)
Population: 79,000
Language(s): Marshallese, English

Monetary unit: U.S. dollar
Economy: copra, tuna processing, tourism, coconuts, tomatoes, melons, taro, fruits, breadfruit

The island nation hoisted its flag on May 1, 1979. The blue stands for the ocean. The white is for brightness while the orange is for bravery and wealth. The two stripes joined symbolize the Equator, and they increase in width to show growth and vitality. The rays of the star are for the municipalities; its four long rays recall a Christian cross.

Mauritania

Republic, W Africa

Area: 397,955 sq. mi. (1,030,700 sq. km.)
Population: 4,079,000
Language(s): Arabic, local languages

Monetary unit: ouguiya
Economy: mining (iron ore, copper), millet, rice, dates, livestock, fish processing

Mauritania gained its independence from France in 1960. Mauritania's flag, used from 1959 to 2017, contained the yellow crescent moon and gold star on a green background. The red stripes at the top and bottom of the field were added in 2017 to represent the blood of its citizens in their struggle against France. The green background of the flag and its star and crescent are traditional Muslim symbols that have been in use for centuries.

Mauritius

Island republic, Indian Ocean

Area: 788 sq. mi. (2,040 sq. km.)
Population: 1,386,000
Language(s): Creole, French, Bhojpuri, English

Monetary unit: Mauritian rupee
Economy: sugarcane, molasses, tea, tobacco, textiles, tourism

The current Mauritius flag began use in 1959, before the island nation gained independence from the United Kingdom in 1968. Red is symbolic of the country's struggle for independence; yellow, the light of freedom shining over the nation; green, the fertile land of the island, and blue, the Indian Ocean.

Mexico

Republic, North America

Area: 758,449 sq. mi. (1,964,375 sq. km.)
Population: 130,207,000
Language(s): Spanish

Monetary unit: Mexican peso
Economy: mining (silver, gold, copper), oil, chemicals, motor vehicles, consumer goods, tourism

The green-white-red tricolor was officially established in 1821. Green is for independence, white for Roman Catholicism, and red for union. The emblem depicts the scene supposedly witnessed by the Aztecs in 1325: an eagle with a snake in its beak standing upon a cactus growing out of rocks in the water. The flag was modified on Sept. 17, 1968.

Micronesia

Islands federation, W Pacific

Area: 271 sq. mi. (702 sq km)
Population: 102,000
Language(s): English, local languages

Monetary unit: U.S. dollar
Economy: tourism, construction, fish processing, handicrafts (wood, pearls), bananas, black pepper

On Nov. 30, 1978, the flag of the former United Nations trust territory was approved by an interim congress. Based on the symbolism of the territory, the flag has stars for the four states of Micronesia. The blue background color symbolizes the Pacific Ocean.

Moldova

Republic, E Europe

Area: 13,070 sq. mi. (33,851 sq. km.)
Population: 3,324,000
Language(s): Moldovan/Romanian, Russian

Monetary unit: Moldovan leu
Economy: food processing, cereals, fruits and vegetables, wine, sugar, machinery

By 1989, Moldovans protested against communist rule, and the traditional tricolor of blue-yellow-red, which had flown briefly in 1917–18, became a popular symbol. It replaced the communist flag in May 1990 and remained after independence in 1991. The shield has an eagle on whose breast are the head of an aurochs, a crescent, a star, and a flower.

Monaco

Constitutional monarchy, S Europe

Area: 0.77 sq. mi. (2.00 sq. km.)
Population: 31,000
Language(s): French, English, Italian

Monetary unit: euro
Economy: banking, insurance, tourism, construction

The flag of the Principality of Monaco, officially adopted in 1881, contains the heraldic colors of the ruling Grimaldi family. Those colors date to the 14th century and appear on the Grimaldi coat of arms as a series of red lozenges on a white background.

Mongolia

Republic, cen. Asia

Area: 603,909 sq. mi. (1,564,116 sq. km.)
Population: 3,199,000
Language(s): Khalkha Mongol

Monetary unit: tugrik
Economy: livestock, agriculture, animal products, cashmere, mining (coal, oil, copper, gold)

In 1945, the flag symbolizing communism (red) and Mongol nationalism (blue) was established. Near the hoist is a soyombo, a grouping of philosophical symbols (flame, sun, moon, yin-yang, triangles, and bars). Yellow traditionally stood for the "Yellow Hat Sect" of Tibetan Buddhism. On Feb. 12, 1992, a five-pointed star (for communism) was removed from the flag.

Montenegro

Republic, SE Europe

Area: 5,333 sq. mi. (13,812 sq. km.)
Population: 607,000
Language(s): Montenegrin, Serbian

Monetary unit: euro
Economy: steelmaking, aluminum, agricultural processing, tourism

The flag of Montenegro was adopted on July 13, 2004. The flag is red with a gold coat of arms in the center. The coat of arms, based on that of the Njegoš dynasty, consists of a double-headed golden eagle with a crown above its head, holding a scepter in one claw, an orb in the other, with a shield containing a golden lion passant over green grass with blue sky above.

Morocco

Constitutional monarchy, NW Africa

Area: 172,414 sq. mi. (446,550 sq. km.)
Population: 34,314,000
Language(s): Arabic, French

Monetary unit: Moroccan dirham
Economy: food processing, wine, leather goods, fishing, mining (phosphates, copper, silver), tourism

After Morocco was subjected to the rule of France and Spain in the 20th century, the plain red flag, which had been displayed on its ships, was modified on Nov. 17, 1915. To its center was added the ancient pentagram known as the "Seal of Solomon." The flag continued in use even after the French granted independence in 1956.

Mozambique

Republic, SE Africa

Area: 308,642 sq. mi. (799,380 sq. km.)
Population: 30,888,000
Language(s): Portuguese, local languages

Monetary unit: metical
Economy: subsistence agriculture, cashew nuts, sugar, tea, coal, bauxite, aluminum, shrimp

In the early 1960s, anti-Portuguese groups adopted flags of green (for forests), black (for the majority population), white (for rivers and the ocean), gold (for peace and mineral wealth), and red (for the blood of liberation). The current flag was readopted in 1983; on its star are a book, a hoe, and an assault rifle.

Myanmar
Republic, SE Asia

Area: 261,228 sq. mi. (676,578 sq. km.)
Population: 57,069,000
Language(s): Burmese

Monetary unit: kyat
Economy: wood and wood products, construction materials, mining (copper, tin, tungsten), rice, beans, sesame

The design of the flag of Myanmar consists of three equal horizontal stripes of yellow (top), green, and red; centered on the green band is a large white five-pointed star that partially overlaps onto the adjacent colored stripes. The design revives the triband colors used by Burma from 1943-45, during the Japanese occupation.

Namibia
Republic, SW Africa

Area: 318,261 sq. mi. (824,292 sq. km.)
Population: 2,678,000
Language(s): English, Afrikaans

Monetary unit: Namibian dollar
Economy: diamonds, copper, zinc, lead, salt, sheep, fishing, food processing

The flag was adopted on Feb. 2, 1990, and hoisted on independence from South Africa, March 21, 1990. Its colors are those of the South West Africa People's Organization: blue (for sky and ocean), red (for heroism and determination), and green (for agriculture). The gold sun represents life and energy while the white stripes are for water resources.

Nepal
Republic, S Asia

Area: 56,827 sq. mi. (147,181 sq. km.)
Population: 30,425,000
Language(s): Nepali, local languages

Monetary unit: Nepalese rupee
Economy: tourism, carpets, textiles, jute, sugar, rice, corn, wheat, sugarcane

Established on Dec. 16, 1962, Nepal's flag consists of two united pennant shapes; it is the only non-rectangular national flag in the world. In the upper segment is a moon with a crescent attached below; in the bottom segment appears a stylized sun. The symbols are for different dynasties and express a hope for the immortality of the nation. The crimson and blue colors are common in Nepali art.

Netherlands
Constitutional monarchy, NW Europe

Area: 16,040 sq. mi. (41,543 sq. km.)
Population: 17,337,000
Language(s): Dutch

Monetary unit: euro
Economy: farming, food processing, horticulture, natural gas, chemicals, microelectronics

The history of the Dutch flag dates to the use of orange, white, and blue as the livery colors of William I, Prince of Orange, and the use of the tricolor at sea in 1577. By 1660 the color red was substituted for orange. The flag was legalized by pro-French "patriots" on Feb. 14, 1796, and reaffirmed by royal decree on Feb. 19, 1937.

New Zealand
Islands republic, SW Pacific

Area: 103,799 sq. mi. (268,838 sq. km.)
Population: 4,991,000
Language(s): English, Maori

Monetary unit: New Zealand dollar
Economy: food processing, mining (coal, gold), natural gas, manufacturing, banking, insurance, tourism

The Maori of New Zealand accepted British control in 1840, and a colonial flag was adopted on Jan. 15, 1867. It included the Union Jack in the canton and the letters "NZ" at the fly end. Later versions used the Southern Cross. Dominion status was granted on Sept. 26, 1907, and independence on Nov. 25, 1947, but the flag was unchanged.

Nicaragua
Republic, Central America

Area: 50,336 sq. mi. (130,370 sq. km.)
Population: 6,244,000
Language(s): Spanish

Monetary unit: córdoba
Economy: coffee, sugar, shrimp, lobster, gold, machinery, chemicals, textiles

On Aug. 21, 1823, a blue-white-blue flag was adopted by the five member states of the United Provinces of Central America, which included Nicaragua. From the mid-19th century various flag designs were used in Nicaragua, but the old flag was readopted in 1908, with a modified coat of arms, and reaffirmed by law on Aug. 27, 1971.

Niger
Republic, W cen. Africa

Area: 489,191 sq. mi. (1,267,000 sq. km.)
Population: 23,607,000
Language(s): French, Hausa

Monetary unit: West African States franc
Economy: uranium mining, petroleum, cement, bricks, soap, textiles, cowpeas, cotton, peanuts, millet, sorghum

The flag of Niger was chosen on Nov. 23, 1959. The white color is for purity, innocence, and civic spirit. The orange is for the Sahara Desert and the heroic efforts of citizens to live within it, while the orange central disk represents the sun. The green color stands for agriculture and hope; it is suggestive of the Niger River valley.

Nigeria
Republic, W cen. Africa

Area: 356,669 sq. mi. (923,768 sq. km.)
Population: 219,464,000
Language(s): English, Hausa

Monetary unit: naira
Economy: crude oil, mining (tin, coal), rubber products, cocoa, peanuts, cotton, palm oil, corn, rice, sorghum, rubber

The Nigerian flag became official upon independence from Britain on Oct. 1, 1960. The flag design is purposefully simple in order not to favor the symbolism of any particular ethnic or religious group. Agriculture is represented by the green stripes while unity and peace are symbolized by the white stripe.

North Macedonia
Republic, SE Europe

Area: 9,928 sq. mi. (25,713 sq. km.)
Population: 2,128,000
Language(s): Macedonian, Albanian

Monetary unit: North Macedonian denar
Economy: wheat, corn, tobacco, iron, steel, chromium, lead, zinc

Used since 1995, the North Macedonian flag features a "golden sun". The gold and red colors originated in an early coat of arms of the region. Greece had long opposed the country's use of the name "Macedonia" until a bilateral agreement was put into effect in Feb. 2019, when Greece recognized North Macedonia as the country's official name.

Norway
Constitutional monarchy, N Europe

Area: 125,021 sq. mi. (323,802 sq. km.)
Population: 5,510,000
Language(s): Norwegian

Monetary unit: Norwegian krone
Economy: gas, oil, food processing, fishing, timber, mining, chemicals, high-tech products, tourism

The first distinctive Norwegian flag was created in 1814 while the country was under Swedish rule. It was based on the red Danish flag with its white cross. In 1821 the Norwegian parliament developed the current flag design. From 1844 to 1899, the official flag included a symbol of Swedish-Norwegian union. It was removed in 1899, six years before independence in 1905.

Oman
Sultanate, SE Arabian Peninsula

Area: 119,499 sq. mi. (309,500 sq. km.)
Population: 3,695,000
Language(s): Arabic, English, Urdu

Monetary unit: Omani rial
Economy: oil, natural gas, dates, limes, bananas, alfalfa, fishing

The flag dates to Dec. 17, 1970, and it was altered on Nov. 18, 1995. The white is for peace and prosperity, red is for battles, and green is for the fertility of the land. Unofficially, white recalls the imamate, red the sultanate, and green Al-Jabal Al-Akhdar ("The Green Mountain"). The coat of arms has two swords, a dagger, and a belt.

Pakistan
Republic, S Asia

Area: 307,374 sq. mi. (796,095 sq. km.)
Population: 238,181,000
Language(s): Punjabi, Pashto, Urdu, English

Monetary unit: Pakistani rupee
Economy: textiles, food processing, pharmaceuticals, coal, gypsum, natural gas, fertilizer, chemicals

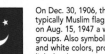

On Dec. 30, 1906, the All India Muslim League approved this typically Muslim flag, with its star and crescent. At independence on Aug. 15, 1947 a white stripe was added for minority religious groups. Also symbolized are prosperity and peace by the green and white colors, progress by the crescent, and knowledge and light by the star.

Palau
Islands republic, W Pacific

Area: 177 sq. mi. (459 sq. km.)
Population: 22,000
Language(s): Palauan, English, Filipino

Monetary unit: U.S. dollar
Economy: tourism, fishing, subsistence agriculture, coconuts, cassava

Approved on Oct. 22, 1980, and hoisted on Jan. 1, 1981, the Palauan flag was left unaltered at independence in 1994. The golden disk represents the full moon, which is said on Palau to be propitious for fishing, planting, and other activities and gives the people "a feeling of warmth, tranquility, peace, love, and domestic unity."

Panama
Republic, Central America

Area: 29,120 sq. mi. (75,420 sq. km.)
Population: 3,929,000
Language(s): Spanish

Monetary unit: balboa
Economy: construction, brewing, sugar milling, copper, mahogany forests, bananas, rice, corn, coffee, sugarcane

The Panamanian flag became official on July 4, 1904, after independence from Colombia was won through the intervention of the United States, which was determined to construct the Panama Canal. The flag was influenced by the United States, and its quartered design was said to symbolize the power sharing of Panama's two main political parties.

Papua New Guinea
Islands republic, W Pacific

Area: 178,704 sq. mi. (462,840 sq. km.)
Population: 7,400,000
Language(s): Tok Pisin, English, Hiri Motu

Monetary unit: kina
Economy: subsistence farming, palm oil, plywood, copper, oil, silver, coffee, tea

The formerly German-, British-, and Australian-controlled territory officially recognized its flag on March 11, 1971, and flag usage was extended to ships at independence (Sept. 16, 1975). The colors red and black are shown extensively in local art and clothing. Featured emblems are a bird of paradise and the Southern Cross constellation.

Paraguay
Republic, South America

Area: 157,048 sq. mi. (406,752 sq. km.)
Population: 7,273,000
Language(s): Spanish, Guarani

Monetary unit: guarani
Economy: food processing (meat, sugar, vegetable oils), wood products, tobacco, cotton, cement, textiles

Under the dictator José Gaspar Rodríguez de Francia (1814–40) the French colors were adopted for the flag. The coat of arms (a golden star surrounded by a wreath, and "Republic of Paraguay") is on the obverse side, but the seal of the treasury (a lion, staff, and liberty cap, with the motto "Peace and Justice") is on the reverse; the flag is unique in this respect.

Peru
Republic, South America

Area: 496,225 sq. mi. (1,285,216 sq. km.)
Population: 32,201,000
Language(s): Spanish, Quechua, Aymara

Monetary unit: sol
Economy: mining (gold, copper, silver), oil, petroleum products, fishing, cotton, sugar, coffee, cocoa

Partisans in the early 19th century adopted a red-white-red flag resembling that of Spain, but they soon made its stripes vertical. In 1825, the current design was established. The shield includes figures symbolic of national wealth—the vicuña (a relative of the alpaca), a cinchona tree, and a cornucopia with gold and silver coins.

Philippines
Archipelago republic, W Pacific

Area: 115,831 sq. mi. (300,000 sq. km.)
Population: 110,818,000
Language(s): Filipino, English

Monetary unit: Philippine peso
Economy: copra, fruit, sugar, timber, mining (iron ore, gold, nickel), textiles, electronics assembly

In 1898, during the Spanish-American War, Filipinos established the basic flag in use today; it was officially adopted in 1936. The white triangle is for liberty. The golden sun and stars are for the three main areas of the Philippines: Luzon, the Visayan Islands, and Mindanao. The red color is for courage and the blue color is for sacrifice.

Poland
Republic, cen. Europe

Area: 120,728 sq. mi. (312,685 sq. km.)
Population: 38,186,000
Language(s): Polish

Monetary unit: zloty
Economy: machine building, iron and steel, coal mining, chemicals, shipbuilding, food processing

The colors of the Polish flag originated in its coat of arms, a white eagle on a red shield, dating from 1295. The precise symbolism of the colors is not known, however. Poland's simple flag of white-red horizontal stripes was adopted on Aug. 1, 1919. The flag was left unaltered under the Soviet-allied communist regime (1944 to 1990).

Portugal
Republic, W Europe

Area: 35,556 sq. mi. (92,090 sq. km.)
Population: 10,264,000
Language(s): Portuguese, Mirandese

Monetary unit: euro
Economy: fishing, cork, oil refining, chemicals, communications equipment, shipbuilding, wine, tourism

The central shield includes five smaller shields, for a victory over the Moors in 1139, and a red border with gold castles. Behind the shield is an armillary sphere (an astronomical device) recalling world explorations and the kingdom of Brazil. Red and green were used in many early Portuguese flags. The current flag dates to June 30, 1911.

Qatar
Emirate, E Arabian Peninsula

Area: 4,473 sq. mi. (11,586 sq. km.)
Population: 2,480,000
Language(s): Arabic, English

Monetary unit: Qatari riyal
Economy: oil, natural gas, fishing, ammonia, fertilizers, cement, commercial ship repair

The 1868 treaty between Great Britain and Qatar may have inspired the creation of the flag. Qataris chose mauve or maroon instead of red (a more typical color among Arab countries) perhaps to distinguish it from the flag used in Bahrain. The country name, in Arabic script, has sometimes been added to the flag.

Romania
Republic, E Europe

Area: 92,043 sq. mi. (238,391 sq. km.)
Population: 21,230,000
Language(s): Romanian, Hungarian

Monetary unit: Romanian leu
Economy: oil, natural gas, light machinery, motor vehicles, mining, timber, metallurgy, chemicals

In 1834, Walachia, an ancient region of Romania, chose a naval ensign with stripes of red, blue, and yellow. A horizontal Romanian tricolor was flown between 1848 to 1867. The vertical stripes returned from 1867 to 1948. During the communist era, the coat of arms of the people's republic was added; and then removed with the fall of the regime on Dec. 27, 1989.

Russia
Federation, E Europe and N Asia

Area: 6,601,668 sq. mi. (17,098,242 sq. km.)
Population: 142,321,000
Language(s): Russian

Monetary unit: Russian ruble
Economy: oil, natural gas, transportation, medical, electronic equipment, chemicals, agriculture

Tsar Peter the Great visited the Netherlands in order to modernize the Russian navy, and in 1699, he chose a Dutch-influenced flag for Russian ships. The flag soon became popular on land as well. After the Russian Revolution, it was replaced by the communist red banner, but the tricolor again became official on Aug. 21, 1991.

Rwanda
Republic, E cen. Africa

Area: 10,169 sq. mi. (26,338 sq. km.)
Population: 12,943,000
Language(s): Kinyarwanda, French, English

Monetary unit: Rwandan franc
Economy: cement, agricultural products, plastic goods, cigarettes, agriculture, minerals

In 2001, Rwanda adopted a new flag, to promote national unity after the genocide of the early 1990s. The large blue stripe represents happiness and peace, and the smaller yellow and green stripes are for economic development and for prosperity. The sun with its 24 rays stands for unity, transparency, and enlightenment.

Saint Kitts and Nevis — *Islands republic, Caribbean*

Area: 101 sq. mi. (261 sq. km.)
Population: 54,000
Language(s): English

Monetary unit: East Caribbean dollar
Economy: tourism, cotton, salt, copra, clothing, footwear, beverages, sugarcane, rice, yams, fish

On Sept. 19, 1983, at the time of its independence from Great Britain, St. Kitts and Nevis hoisted the current flag. It has green (for fertility), red (for the struggle against slavery and colonialism), and black (for African heritage). The yellow flanking stripes are for sunshine, and the two stars, one for each island, are for hope and liberty.

Saint Lucia — *Island republic, Caribbean*

Area: 238 sq. mi. (616 sq. km.)
Population: 167,000
Language(s): English, French patois

Monetary unit: East Caribbean dollar
Economy: tourism, clothing, electronic component assembly, beverages, bananas, coconuts, vegetables

The flag was hoisted on March 1, 1967, when the former colony assumed a status of association with the United Kingdom; it was slightly altered in 1979. The blue represents Atlantic and Caribbean waters. The white and black colors are for racial harmony, while the black triangle also represents volcanoes. The yellow triangle is for sunshine.

Saint Vincent and the Grenadines

Archipelago republic, Caribbean

Area: 150 sq. mi. (389 sq. km.)
Population: 101,000
Language(s): English, French patois

Monetary unit: East Caribbean dollar
Economy: tourism, food processing, cement, bananas, coconuts

At independence from Britain in 1979, a national flag was designed, but it was replaced by the current flag on Oct. 22, 1985. The three green diamonds are arranged in the form of a V. Green is for the rich vegetation and the vitality of the people, yellow is for sand and personal warmth, and blue is for sea and sky.

Samoa — *Islands republic, SW Pacific*

Area: 1,093 sq. mi. (2,831 sq. km.)
Population: 205,000
Language(s): Samoan, English

Monetary unit: tala
Economy: fishing, coconut oil and cream, copra, pineapples, automotive parts, textiles, beer

The first national flag of Samoa may date to 1873. Under British administration, a version of the current flag was introduced on May 26, 1948. On Feb. 24, 1949, a fifth star, as can be seen in the sky, was added to the Southern Cross. White in the flag is said to stand for purity, blue for freedom, and red for courage. The flag was left unaltered upon independence in 1962.

San Marino — *Republic, enclave in Italy*

Area: 24 sq. mi. (61 sq. km.)
Population: 34,000
Language(s): Italian

Monetary unit: euro
Economy: tourism, banking, textiles, electronics, ceramics, wheat, grapes

The colors of the flag, blue and white, were first used in the national cockade in 1797. The coat of arms in its present form was adopted on April 6, 1862, when the crown was added as a symbol of national sovereignty. Also in the coat of arms are three towers (Guaita, Cesta, and Montale) from the fortifications on Mount Titano.

São Tomé and Príncipe — *Islands republic, off W Africa*

Area: 372 sq. mi. (964 sq. km.)
Population: 214,000
Language(s): Portuguese

Monetary unit: dobra
Economy: light construction, textiles, soap, cocoa, coconuts, palm kernels

The national flag was adopted upon independence from Portugal on July 12, 1975. Its colors are associated with Pan-African independence. The red triangle stands for equality and the nationalist movement. The stars are for the African population living on the nation's two main islands. Green is for vegetation and yellow is for the tropical sun.

Saudi Arabia — *Islamic kingdom, Arabian Peninsula*

Area: 830,000 sq. mi. (2,149,690 sq. km.)
Population: 34,784,000
Language(s): Arabic

Monetary unit: Saudi riyal
Economy: crude oil production, petroleum refining, petrochemicals, ammonia, industrial gases, wheat, barley, tomatoes

The Saudi flag, made official in 1932, but altered in 1973, originated in the military campaigns of Muhammad. The color green is associated with Fatimah, the Prophet's daughter, and the Arabic inscription is translated as "There is no God but Allah and Muhammad is the Prophet of Allah." The saber symbolizes the militancy of the faith.

Senegal — *Republic, W Africa*

Area: 75,955 sq. mi. (196,722 sq. km.)
Population: 16,082,000
Language(s): French, local languages

Monetary unit: West African States franc
Economy: agriculture and fish processing, phosphate mining, peanuts, millet, corn

In a federation with French Sudan (now Mali) on April 4, 1959, Senegal used a flag with a human figure in the center. After the federation broke up in August 1960, Senegal substituted a green star for the central figure. Green is for hope and religion, yellow is for natural riches and labor, and red is for independence, life, and socialism.

Serbia — *Republic, SE Europe*

Area: 29,913 sq. mi. (77,474 sq. km.)
Population: 6,974,000
Language(s): Serbian, Hungarian

Monetary unit: Serbian dinar
Economy: machinery, electronics, chemicals, pharmaceuticals, electrical equipment, mining, agriculture

In 1882 Serbia established a state flag consisting of the red-white-blue tricolour with the royal Serbian coat of arms. The coat of arms, centered vertically and shifted left of center, was added following the independence of Montenegro in 2004.

Seychelles — *Islands republic, Indian Ocean*

Area: 176 sq. mi. (455 sq. km.)
Population: 96,000
Language(s): Seychellois Creole, English, French

Monetary unit: Seychelles rupee
Economy: fishing, tourism, beverages, coconuts, cinnamon, vanilla, cassava, sweet potatoes, copra

The former British colony underwent a revolution in 1977. The government was democratized in 1993, and on Jan. 8, 1996, a new flag was designed. The blue color is for sky and sea, yellow is for the sun, red is for the people and their work for unity and love, white is for social justice and harmony, and green is for the land and natural environment.

Sierra Leone — *Republic, W Africa*

Area: 27,699 sq. mi. (71,740 sq. km.)
Population: 6,807,000
Language(s): English, Mende, Temne

Monetary unit: leone
Economy: diamond mining, iron ore, rutile and bauxite mining, small-scale manufacturing, rice, coffee, cocoa, palm kernels

Under British colonial control, Sierra Leone was founded as a home for freed slaves. With independence on April 27, 1961, the flag was hoisted. Its stripes stand for agriculture and the mountains (green); unity and justice (white); and the aspiration to contribute to world peace, especially through the use of the natural harbor at Freetown (blue).

Singapore — *Island republic, SE Asia*

Area: 278 sq. mi. (719 sq. km.)
Population: 5,866,000
Language(s): Mandarin Chinese, Malay, English, Tamil

Monetary unit: Singapore dollar
Economy: electonics, chemicals, financial services, oil drilling equipment, petroleum refining, biomedical products

On Dec. 3, 1959, the flag was acquired, and it was retained after separation from Malaysia on Aug. 9, 1965. The red and white stripes stand for universal brotherhood, equality, purity, and virtue. The crescent symbolizes the growth of a young country, while the five stars are for democracy, peace, progress, justice, and equality.

Slovakia
Republic, cen. Europe

Area: 18,933 sq. mi. (49,035 sq. km.)
Population: 5,436,000
Language(s): Slovak, Hungarian, Roma

Monetary unit: euro
Economy: automobiles, metal products, electricity, gas, oil, nuclear fuel, chemicals, grains, potatoes, sugar beets

In 1189, the kingdom of Hungary (including Slovakia) introduced a double-barred cross in its coat of arms; this symbol was altered in 1848–49 by Slovak nationalists. After a period of communist rule, the tricolor was made official in 1989. On Sept. 3, 1992, the shield was added to the white-blue-red flag to differentiate it from the flag of Russia.

Slovenia
Republic, S cen. Europe

Area: 7,827 sq. mi. (20,273 sq. km.)
Population: 2,102,000
Language(s): Slovenian, Serbo-Croatian

Monetary unit: euro
Economy: metal products, lead and zinc smelting, electronics, wood products, textiles, chemicals, hops, wheat

Under the current flag, Slovenia proclaimed independence on June 25, 1991, but it was opposed for a time by the Yugoslav army. The flag is the same as that of Russia and Slovakia except for the coat of arms. It depicts the peaks of Triglav (the nation's highest mountain), the waves of the Adriatic coast, and three stars on a blue background.

Solomon Islands
Archipelago republic, SW Pacific

Area: 11,157 sq. mi. (28,896 sq. km.);
Population: 691,000
Language(s): Melanesian dialect, English

Monetary unit: Solomon Islands dollar
Economy: fishing, timber, copra, rice, palm oil, cocoa

The flag was introduced on Nov. 18, 1977, eight months before independence from Britain. The yellow stripe stands for the sun. The green triangle is for the trees and crops of the fertile land, while the blue triangle symbolizes rivers, rain, and the ocean. The five stars represented the original five districts of the island.

Somalia
Republic, E Africa

Area: 246,201 sq. mi. (637,657 sq. km.)
Population: 12,095,000
Language(s): Somali, Arabic

Monetary unit: Somali shilling
Economy: sugar refining, textiles, wireless communication, bananas, sorghum, corn, coconuts, rice, sugarcane, mangoes

From the mid-19th century, areas in the Horn of Africa with Somali populations were divided between Ethiopia, France, Britain, and Italy. On Oct. 12, 1954, with the partial unification of these areas, the flag was adopted with a white star, each point referring to a Somali homeland. The colors were influenced by the colors of the United Nations.

South Africa
Republic, S Africa

Area: 470,693 sq. mi. (1,219,090 sq. km.)
Population: 56,979,000
Language(s): Afrikaans, English, isiZulu, isiXhosa, and other local languages

Monetary unit: rand
Economy: mining (platinum, gold, chromium), auto assembly, metalworking, machinery, corn, wheat, sugarcane, fruits

With the decline of apartheid, the flag was hoisted on April 27, 1994, and confirmed in 1996. Its six colors collectively represent Zulus, English or Afrikaners, Muslims, supporters of the African National Congress, and other groups. The Y-symbol stands for "merging history and present political realities" into a united and prosperous future.

South Sudan
Republic, E cen. Africa

Area: 248,777 sq. mi. (644,329 sq. km.)
Population: 10,984,000
Language(s): Arabic, English

Monetary unit: South Sudan pound
Economy: sorghum, maize, rice, millet, wheat, gum arabic, sugarcane

The flag of the Sudan People's Liberation Movement was adopted following the 2005 end of the second civil war. The colors of the horizontal bars resemble those of the Kenya flag. Black represents the people, red is for blood shed to achieve liberation, green represents agriculture, and white is in hope of peace. The blue of the triangle represents the Nile and the star represents unity in South Sudan.

Spain
Constitutional monarchy, SW Europe

Area: 195,124 sq. mi. (505,370 sq. km.)
Population: 47,261,000
Language(s): Castilian Spanish, Catalan, Galician, Basque

Monetary unit: euro
Economy: textiles, metal products, chemicals, shipbuilding, automobiles, tourism, pharmaceuticals, medical equipment

The colors of the flag have no official symbolic meaning. Introduced in 1785, by King Charles III, the flag was changed only under the Spanish Republic (1931–39). Under different regimes, however, the coat of arms has been altered. The current design dates from Dec. 18, 1981, with the death of Francisco Franco and the resurgence of democracy.

Sri Lanka
Island republic, off SE India

Area: 25,332 sq. mi. (65,610 sq. km.)
Population: 23,044,000
Language(s): Sinhala, Tamil, English

Monetary unit: Sri Lankan rupee
Economy: rubber processing, tea, telecommunications, insurance, banking, gemstones, textiles, tourism

From the 5th century BC, the Lion flag was a symbol of the Sinhalese people. The flag was replaced by the Union Jack in 1815, but readopted upon independence in 1948. The stripes of green (for Muslims) and orange (for Hindus) were added in 1951. In 1972, four leaves of the Bo tree were added as a symbol of Buddhism; the leaves were altered in 1978.

Sudan
Republic, E cen. Africa

Area: 718,723 sq. mi. (1,861,484 sq. km.)
Population: 46,751,000
Language(s): Arabic, English

Monetary unit: Sudanese pound
Economy: oil, cotton processing, textiles, cotton, groundnuts, sorghum, millet

The flag was first hoisted on May 20, 1970. It uses Pan-Arab colors. Black is for al-Mahdi (a leader in the 1800s) and the name of the country (sudan in Arabic means black); white recalls the revolutionary flag of 1924 and suggests peace and optimism; red is for patriotic martyrs, socialism, and progress; and green is for prosperity and Islam.

Suriname
Republic, South America

Area: 63,251 sq. mi. (163,820 sq. km.)
Population: 615,000
Language(s): Dutch, English, Surinamese

Monetary unit: Suriname dollar
Economy: gold mining, oil, lumber, food processing, fishing, rice, bananas, shrimp, vegetables

Adopted on Nov. 25, 1975, four days before independence from the Dutch, the flag of Suriname features green stripes for jungles and agriculture, white for justice and freedom, and red for the progressive spirit of a young nation. The yellow star is symbolic of the unity of the country, its golden future, and the people's spirit of sacrifice.

Sweden
Constitutional monarchy, N Europe

Area: 173,860 sq. mi. (450,295 sq. km.)
Population: 10,262,000
Language(s): Swedish

Monetary unit: Swedish krona
Economy: iron and steel, precision equipment, wood pulp and paper products, motor vehicles, barley, wheat, sugar beets

From the 14th century, the coat of arms of Sweden had a blue field with three golden crowns, and the earlier Folkung dynasty used a shield of blue and white wavy stripes with a gold lion. The off-center "Scandinavian cross" was influenced by the flag of the rival kingdom of Denmark. The current flag law was adopted on June 22, 1906.

Switzerland
Republic, cen. Europe

Area: 15,937 sq. mi. (41,277 sq. km.)
Population: 8,454,000
Language(s): French, German, Italian, Romansh

Monetary unit: Swiss franc
Economy: machinery, chemicals, watches, textiles, precision instruments, tourism, banking, insurance, grains, fruits

The Swiss flag is ultimately based on the war flag of the Holy Roman Empire. Schwyz, one of the original three cantons of the Swiss Confederation, placed a narrow white cross in the corner of its flag in 1240. This was also used in 1339 at the Battle of Laupen. Following the 1848 constitution, the flag was recognized by the army, and it was established as the national flag on land on Dec. 12, 1889.

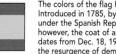

Zimbabwe

Republic, S cen. Africa

Area: 150,872 sq. mi. (390,757 sq. km.)
Population: 14,030,000
Language(s): English, Shona, Ndebele and other local languages

Monetary unit: multiple currencies (including U.S. dollar and South African rand)
Economy: mining (coal, gold, platinum), wood products, cement, chemicals, fertilizer, textiles, tobacco, corn, cotton

On April 18, 1980, elections brought the Black majority to power under the current flag. The black color is for the ethnic majority, while red is for blood, green for agriculture, yellow for mineral wealth, and white for peace and progress. At the hoist is a red star (for socialism) and the ancient "Zimbabwe Bird" from the Great Zimbabwe ruins.

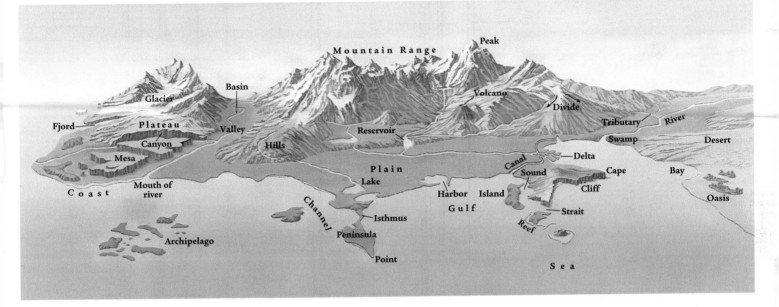

Glossary

This glossary provides brief definitions of some of the geographical terms and foreign terms used in this atlas. It does not include names of peoples, languages, religions, and geologic eras. For definitions of those terms, please refer to a standard dictionary such as *Merriam-Webster's Intermediate Dictionary* or *Merriam-Webster's Collegiate® Dictionary*.

In addition, this glossary includes information about a small set of place-names that are used in the atlas but whose meaning may not be immediately self-explanatory from the maps, graphs, or text in which they appear. More detailed information on place-names can be found in *Merriam-Webster's Geographical Dictionary*.

acid rain : rain having increased acidity caused by atmospheric pollutants

agglomeration : a cluster containing a large city and the populated areas surrounding it

alpine : of or relating to mountains

Altiplano : the region comprising a series of high plains in western Bolivia and extending into southeastern Peru

amphitheater : a flat or gently sloping area surrounded by abrupt slopes

Anatolia : the part of Turkey comprising the peninsula forming the western extremity of Asia

An Nafud : a desert in northern Saudi Arabia

aqueduct
1 : a conduit for carrying a large quantity of flowing water
2 : a structure for conveying a canal over a river or hollow

archipelago : a group of islands

arid : having insufficient rainfall to support agriculture

Arnhem Land : a coastal region of northern Australia containing a large aboriginal reservation

atoll : a coral island consisting of a reef surrounding a lagoon

bab — an Arabic word meaning "strait"

bank
1 : an undersea elevation rising especially from the continental shelf
2 : the rising ground bordering a lake, river, or sea
3 — see SANDBANK

basin
1 a : a large or small depression in the surface of the land or in the ocean floor
b : the entire tract of country drained by a river and its tributaries
c : a great depression in the surface of Earth occupied by an ocean
2 : a broad area of Earth beneath which the strata dip usually from the sides toward the center

bay — see INLET

bight : a bay formed by a bend in a coast

biodiversity : biological diversity in an environment as indicated by numbers of different species of plants and animals

Bosporus : the strait connecting the Sea of Marmara with the Black Sea

Brittany : a historical region in northwestern France

broadleaf : composed of plants having leaves that are not needles

canal : an artificial waterway for navigation or for draining or irrigating land

canyon : a deep narrow valley with steep sides and often with a stream flowing through it

cap — a French word meaning "cape"

cape : a point or extension of land jutting out into water as a peninsula or as a projecting point

cascade : one of a series of steep usually small falls of water

cataract : steep rapids in a river

causeway : a raised way across wet ground or water

cay : a low island or reef of sand or coral

Central America : the narrow southern portion of North America made up of Guatemala, El Salvador, Honduras, Nicaragua, Costa Rica, Panama, and Belize

channel : a strait or narrow sea between two close land areas

city : an inhabited place usually of greater size or importance than a town

cliff : a very steep, vertical, or overhanging face of rock, earth, or ice

coast : the land near a shore

collectivity — see TERRITORIAL COLLECTIVITY

colony : a distant territory belonging to or under the control of a nation

coniferous : composed of plants having needle-shaped leaves

continent : one of the six or seven great divisions of land on Earth

continental shelf : a shallow submarine plain of varying width forming a border to a continent and typically ending in a comparatively steep slope to the deep ocean floor

country
1 : an indefinite usually extended expanse of land
2 : a state or nation or its territory

crown land : land belonging to a monarchy and yielding revenues that the reigning sovereign is entitled to

crust : the outer part of Earth composed essentially of crystalline rocks

current : a part of the ocean moving continuously in a certain direction

Cyrenaica : the easternmost part of Libya settled by ancient Greeks

Dalmatia : a region on the Adriatic coast

Damaraland : the plateau region of central Namibia

Dardanelles : the strait connecting the Sea of Marmara with the Aegean Sea

dasht — a Persian word meaning "desert"

deciduous : composed of plants having leaves that fall off seasonally or at a certain stage of development in the life cycle

defile : a narrow passage or gorge

deforestation : the action or process of clearing of forests

delta : the triangular or fan-shaped piece of land made by deposits of mud and sand at the mouth of a river

density : the average number of individuals per unit of space

dependency : a territorial unit under the jurisdiction of a nation but not formally annexed by it

depression : an area of land in which the central part lies lower than the margin

desert : arid land with usually little vegetation that is incapable of supporting a considerable population without an artificial water supply

diaspora : the movement, migration, or scattering of a people away from an established or ancestral homeland

division : a portion of a territorial unit marked off for a particular purpose (as administrative or judicial functions)

duchy : the territory of a duke or duchess

elevation
1 : the height above sea level
2 : a place that rises above its surroundings

eminence : a natural elevation

emirate : the state or jurisdiction of an emir (a ruler in an Islamic country)

enclave : a foreign territorial unit enclosed within a larger territory [The difference between an *enclave* and an *exclave* is one of perspective. An enclosed territorial unit is an enclave with respect to the territory that surrounds it, but it is an exclave of the country to which it belongs.]

endangered species : a species threatened with extinction

Equator : the great circle of Earth that is everywhere equally distant from the North Pole and the South Pole and divides the surface into Northern Hemisphere and Southern Hemisphere

erg : a desert region of shifting sand

escarpment : a long cliff or steep slope separating two comparatively level or more gently sloping surfaces and resulting from erosion or faulting

estuary : an arm of the sea at the lower end of a river

Eurasian : of Europe and Asia

European Union : an economic, scientific, and political organization consisting of Austria, Belgium, Bulgaria, Croatia, Cyprus, Czech Republic, Denmark, Estonia, Finland, France, Germany, Greece, Hungary, Ireland, Italy, Latvia, Lithuania, Luxembourg, Malta, Netherlands, Poland, Portugal, Romania, Slovakia, Slovenia, Spain, and Sweden

evergreen : composed of plants having foliage that remains green and functional through more than one growing season

exclave : a portion of a country separated from the main part and surrounded by foreign territory — compare ENCLAVE

fjord : a narrow inlet of the sea between cliffs or steep slopes

free association : a relationship affording sovereignty with independent control of internal affairs and foreign policy except defense

geothermal : produced by the heat of the Earth's interior

geyser : a spring that throws forth intermittent jets of heated water and steam

glacier : a large body of ice moving slowly down a slope or valley or spreading outward on a land surface

Gobi : the desert in a plateau region in southern Mongolia and extending into China

Gondwana : the hypothetical land area believed to have once connected the Indian Subcontinent and the landmasses of the Southern Hemisphere

gorge : a narrow steep-walled canyon or part of a canyon

Gran Chaco : the thinly populated swampy region of South America divided between Argentina, Bolivia, and Paraguay

great circle : a circle on the surface of the Earth a portion of which is the shortest distance between any two points

grid : a network of uniformly spaced horizontal and perpendicular lines (as for locating points on a map)

gulf — see INLET

habitat : a place or environment where a plant or animal naturally or normally lives and grows

harbor : a protected part of a body of water that is deep enough to furnish anchorage; *esp* : one with port facilities

headland : a point of usually high land jutting out into a body of water

headstream : a stream that is the source of a river

hemisphere : the northern or southern half of the Earth as divided by the Equator or the eastern or western half as divided by a meridian

highland : elevated or mountainous land

hill — see MOUNTAIN

Horn of Africa : the easternmost projection of land in Africa

humid : characterized by perceptible moisture

hydroelectric : relating to electricity produced by waterpower

ice cap : an area having a cover of perennial ice and snow

ice field : a glacier flowing outward from the center of an extensive area of relatively level land

ice shelf : an extensive ice cap originating on land but continuing out to sea beyond the depths at which it rests on the sea bottom

indigenous : having originated in a particular region or environment

Indochina : the peninsula comprising Myanmar, Thailand, Laos, Cambodia, Vietnam, and the western part of Malaysia

inlet
1 : a recess in the shore of a larger body of water [In this sense, *inlet* is a general term for *bay* or *gulf*. The chief difference between a bay and a gulf is one of size. A bay is usually smaller than a gulf.]
2 : a narrow water passage between peninsulas or through a barrier island leading to a bay or lagoon

intermittent lake : a lake that is sometimes dry

intermittent stream : a stream that is sometimes dry

intermontane : situated between mountains

International Date Line : the line coinciding approximately with the meridian 180 degrees from the Prime Meridian fixed by international agreement as the place where each calendar day first begins

island : an area of land surrounded by water and smaller than a continent

islet : a little island

isthmus : a narrow strip of land connecting two larger land areas

jebel — an Arabic word meaning "mountain"

key : any of the coral islets off the southern coast of Florida

kill : a channel — used chiefly in place-names in Delaware, Pennsylvania, and New York

kingdom : a major territorial unit headed by a king or queen

kum — a Turkic word meaning "desert"

Labrador : a peninsula divided between the Canadian provinces of Quebec and Newfoundland and Labrador

lac — a French word meaning "lake"

lagoon : a shallow sound, channel, or pond near or connected with a larger body of water

laguna — a Spanish word meaning "lagoon" or "lake"

lake : a considerable inland body of standing water

landform : a natural feature of a land surface

landmass : a large area of land

Lapland : the region north of the Arctic Circle divided between Norway, Sweden, Finland, and Russia

legend : an explanatory list of the symbols on a map or chart

Llano Estacado : the plateau region of eastern and southeastern New Mexico and western Texas

Llanos : the region of vast plains in northern South America that is drained by the Orinoco River and its tributaries

locality : a specific location

loch : a lake in Scotland

lough : a lake in Ireland

lowland : low or level country

magnetic pole : either of two small regions which are located respectively in the polar areas of the Northern Hemisphere and the Southern Hemisphere and toward which a compass needle points from any direction throughout adjacent regions

marine : influenced or determined by proximity to the sea

marsh : a tract of soft wet land

massif : a principal mountain mass

Melanesia : the islands in the southwestern Pacific northeast of Australia and south of the Equator

mesa : an isolated relatively flat-topped natural elevation usually less extensive than a plateau

Mesopotamia : the historical region between the Tigris and Euphrates rivers

metropolitan : constituting the chief or capital city and sometimes including its suburbs

Micronesia : the widely scattered islands of the western Pacific east of the Philippines

midlatitude : of the area approximately between 30 to 60 degrees north or south of the Equator

mineral : a naturally occurring crystalline element or compound that has a definite chemical composition and results from processes other than those of plants and animals

monarchy : a nation or state having a government headed by a hereditary chief of state with life tenure

mountain
1 : an elevated mass of land that projects above its surroundings [Among the many types of natural land elevations, a distinction needs to be made between *hill, mountain,* and *peak.* A hill is likely to be lower than a mountain or peak and typically has a rounded summit. A mountain is larger and projects more conspicuously than a hill, while a peak is usually a prominent type of mountain having a well-defined summit.]
2 : an elongated ridge

mouth : the place where a stream enters a larger body of water

municipality : a primarily urban political unit

narrows : a strait connecting two bodies of water

national park : an area of special scenic, historical, or scientific importance set aside and maintained by a national government

notch : a deep close pass

novaya — a Russian word meaning "new"

oasis : a fertile or green area in an arid region

occidental — a Spanish or French word meaning "western"

ocean : any of the large bodies of water into which the whole body of salt water that covers much of Earth is divided

Oceania : the lands of the central and southern Pacific

Okavango : a large marsh in northern Botswana

oriental — a Spanish or French word meaning "eastern"

Pampas : the extensive generally grass-covered plains region of South America lying east of the Andes Mountains

Pangaea : the hypothetical land area believed to have once connected the landmasses of the Southern Hemisphere with those of the Northern Hemisphere

pass : a low place in a mountain range

passage : a place through which it is possible to pass

Patagonia : a barren tableland mostly in Argentina

peak — see MOUNTAIN

peninsula : a portion of land nearly surrounded by water

per capita : per unit of population

pico — a Spanish or Portuguese word meaning "peak"

piedmont : the area lying or formed at the base of mountain

plain
1 : an extensive area of level or rolling treeless country
2 : a broad unbroken expanse

plate : any of the large movable segments into which Earth's crust is divided

plateau : a usually extensive land area having a relatively level surface raised sharply above adjacent land on at least one side
[Sometimes the word is used synonymously with *tableland.*]

point : a place having a precisely indicated position

polar : of or relating to the region around the North Pole or the South Pole

polder : a tract of lowland reclaimed from a body of water

pole : either extremity of Earth's axis

Polynesia : the islands of the central Pacific

pool
1 : a small and rather deep body of water
2 : a quiet place in a stream
3 : a body of water forming above a dam

Prime Meridian : the meridian of 0 degrees longitude which runs through the original site of the Royal Greenwich Observatory at Greenwich, England and from which other longitudes are reckoned

princely state : a state governed by a prince in pre-independent India

principality : the territory of a prince

profile : a drawing showing comparative elevations of land surface along a given strip

projection : an estimate of a future possibility based on current trends

promontory
1 : a high point of land or rock projecting into a body of water
2 : a prominent mass of land overlooking or projecting into a lowland

protectorate : a political unit dependent on the authority of another

punta — a Spanish or Italian word meaning "point"

race : a narrow channel through which a strong or rapid current of water flows

rain forest
1 : a tropical woodland with an annual rainfall of at least 100 inches (254 centimeters) and marked by lofty trees forming a continuous canopy
2 : woodland of a usually rather mild climatic area that receives heavy rainfall and that usually includes numerous kinds of trees with one or two types that dominate

range : a series of mountains

reef : a chain of rocks or coral or a ridge of sand at or near the surface of water

region
1 : a primary administrative subdivision of a country
2 : an indefinite area of Earth
3 : a broad geographical area distinguished by similar features

republic
1 : a political unit having a form of government headed by a chief of state who is not a monarch

2 : a political unit having a form of government in which supreme power resides in a body of citizens entitled to vote and is exercised by elected officers and representatives responsible to them and governing according to law
3 : a constituent political and territorial unit of a country

reservation : a tract of public land set aside for a special use

reservoir : an artificial lake where water is collected and kept in quantity for use

ridge
1 : a range of hills or mountains
2 : an elongate elevation on an ocean bottom

rift valley : an elongated valley formed by the depression of a block of the Earth's crust between two faults or groups of faults of approximately parallel orientation

río — a Spanish word meaning "river"

river : a natural stream of water of usually considerable volume

roadstead : a place less enclosed than a harbor where ships may ride at anchor

Rub' al-Khali : the vast desert region of the southern Arabian Peninsula

rural : of or relating to the country

Sahel : the semidesert southern fringe of the Sahara that stretches from Mauritania to Chad

san — a Spanish word meaning "saint"

sandbank : a large deposit of sand forming a shoal

santa; santo — Spanish words meaning "saint"

são — a Portuguese word meaning "saint"

savanna : a tropical or subtropical grassland containing scattered trees

scale : an indication of the relationship between the distances on a map and the corresponding actual distances

Scandinavia
1 : the peninsula occupied by Norway and Sweden
2 : the region of northern Europe comprising Denmark, Norway, and Sweden and often including Finland and Iceland

scrubland : land covered with vegetation chiefly consisting of stunted trees or shrubs

sea
1 : a more or less landlocked body of salt water
2 : an ocean
3 : an inland body of water

semiarid : having from about 10 to 20 inches (25 to 51 centimeters) of annual precipitation

semidesert : an arid area that has some of the characteristics of a desert but has greater annual precipitation

serra — a Portuguese word meaning "mountain range"

shan — a Chinese word meaning "mountain range"

shield : the ancient mass of hard rock that forms the core of a continent

shoal : a ridge or large deposit of sand that makes the water shallow

shore : the land bordering a usually large body of water

Siberia : a vast region mostly in Russia extending from the Pacific Ocean to the Ural Mountains

sierra — a Spanish word meaning "mountain range"

site : the location of some particular thing

sound
1 : a long broad inlet of the ocean generally parallel to the coast
2 : a long passage of water connecting two larger bodies of water or separating a mainland and an island

source : the point of origin of a stream of water

spa : a town or resort with mineral springs

spring : a source of water issuing from the ground

state
1 : a sovereign politically organized body of people usually occupying a definite territory
2 : one of the constituent units of a nation having a federal government

steppe
1 : one of the vast usually level and treeless tracts in southeastern Europe or Asia
2 : arid land found usually in regions of extreme temperature range

strait : a comparatively narrow passageway connecting two large bodies of water

strata : layers having parallel layers of other kinds above or below or both above and below

subarctic : characteristic of regions bordering the Arctic Circle

subcontinent : a major subdivision of a continent

subduction zone : an area in which the edge of one of Earth's plates descends below the edge of another

subsistence agriculture : a system of farming that provides all or almost all the goods required by the farm family usually without any significant surplus for sale

subtropical : characteristic of regions bordering on the tropics

Sudd : the lowland swamp region of South Sudan

sultanate : a state or nation governed by a sultan

supercontinent : a former large continent from which other continents are believed to have broken off and drifted away

swamp : a tract of wetland often partially or intermittently covered with water

tableland : a broad level elevated area [Sometimes the word is used synonymously with *plateau*.]

territorial collectivity : a French overseas territorial unit enjoying some degree of local authority and having a status lesser than an overseas department but greater than an overseas territory

territory
1 a : a geographical area belonging to or under the jurisdiction of a governmental authority
  b : an administrative subdivision of a country
  c : a part of the U.S. not included within any state but organized with a separate legislature
  d : a geographical area dependent on an external government but having some degree of autonomy
2 : an indeterminate geographical area

tidewater : low-lying coastal land

Tierra del Fuego : an archipelago divided between Argentina and Chile

time zone : a geographic region within which the same standard time is used

tract : a stretch of land

Transcaucasia : the region in southeastern Europe south of the Caucasus Mountains and between the Black and Caspian seas

trench : a long, narrow, and usually steep-sided depression in the ocean floor

tributary : a stream feeding a larger stream or a lake

Tripolitania : an historical region of northern Africa originally a Phoenician colony

tropic : either of the regions lying between the two parallels of the Earth's latitude that are approximately 23 $\frac{1}{2}$ degrees north of the Equator (Tropic of Cancer) and approximately 23 $\frac{1}{2}$ degrees south of the Equator (Tropic of Capricorn)

tundra : a treeless plain having permanently frozen subsoil and vegetation consisting chiefly of mosses, lichens, herbs, and very small shrubs

union territory : a centrally administered subdivision of India consisting of an island group, the area surrounding a city, or an area containing a linguistic minority

upland : high land especially at some distance from the sea

urban : of or relating to the city

valley
1 : an elongated depression of Earth's surface usually between ranges of hills or mountains
2 : an area drained by a river and its tributaries

volcán — a Spanish word meaning "volcano"

volcano : a mountain composed wholly or in part of material ejected from a vent in the Earth's crust

Walachia : an historical region in Romania

waterway : a navigable body or course of water

wilderness : a region uncultivated and uninhabited by human beings and more or less in its natural state

woodland : land covered with woody vegetation